Flying Witch

Chihiro Ishizuka

6

Contents

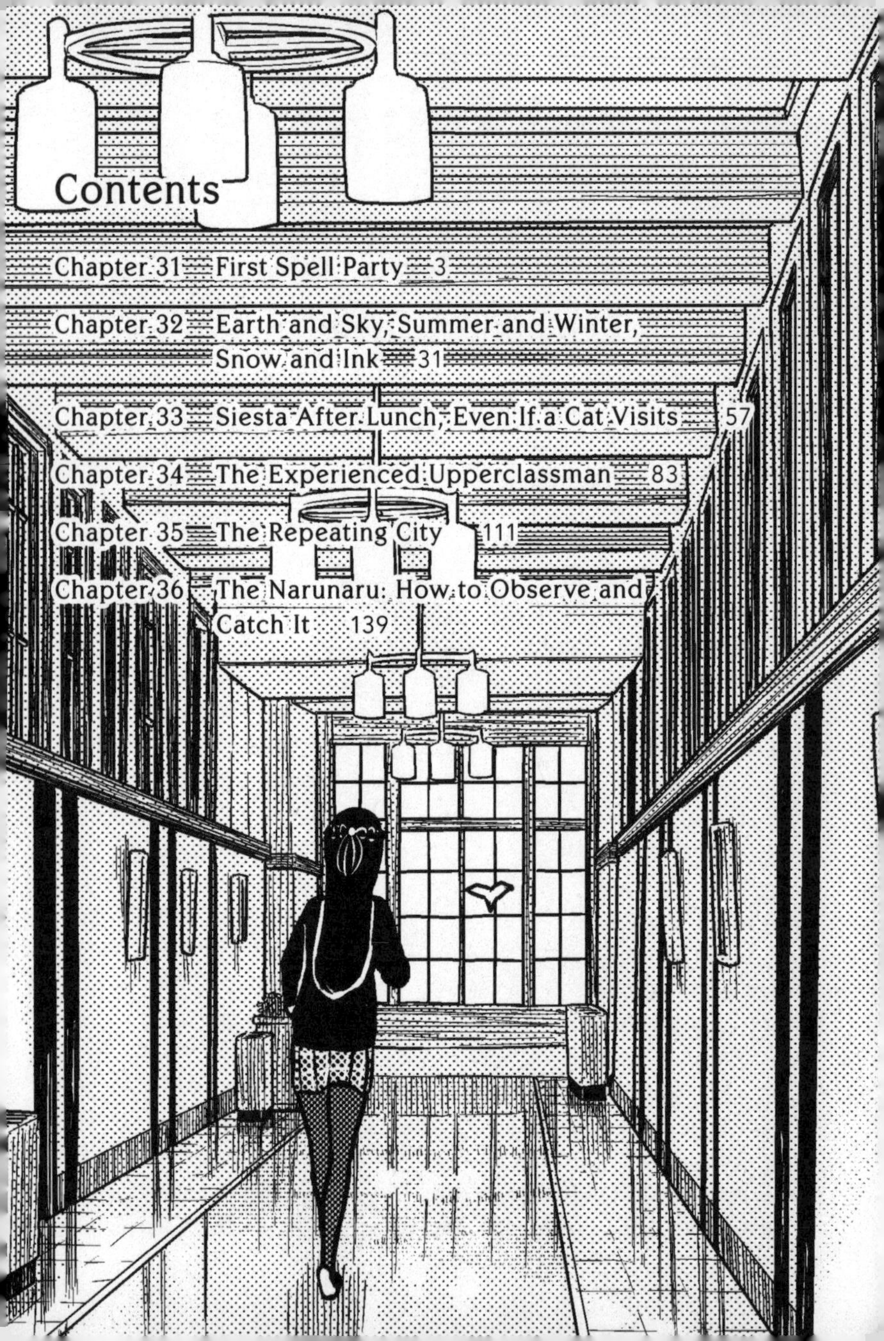

Chapter 31
First Spell Party

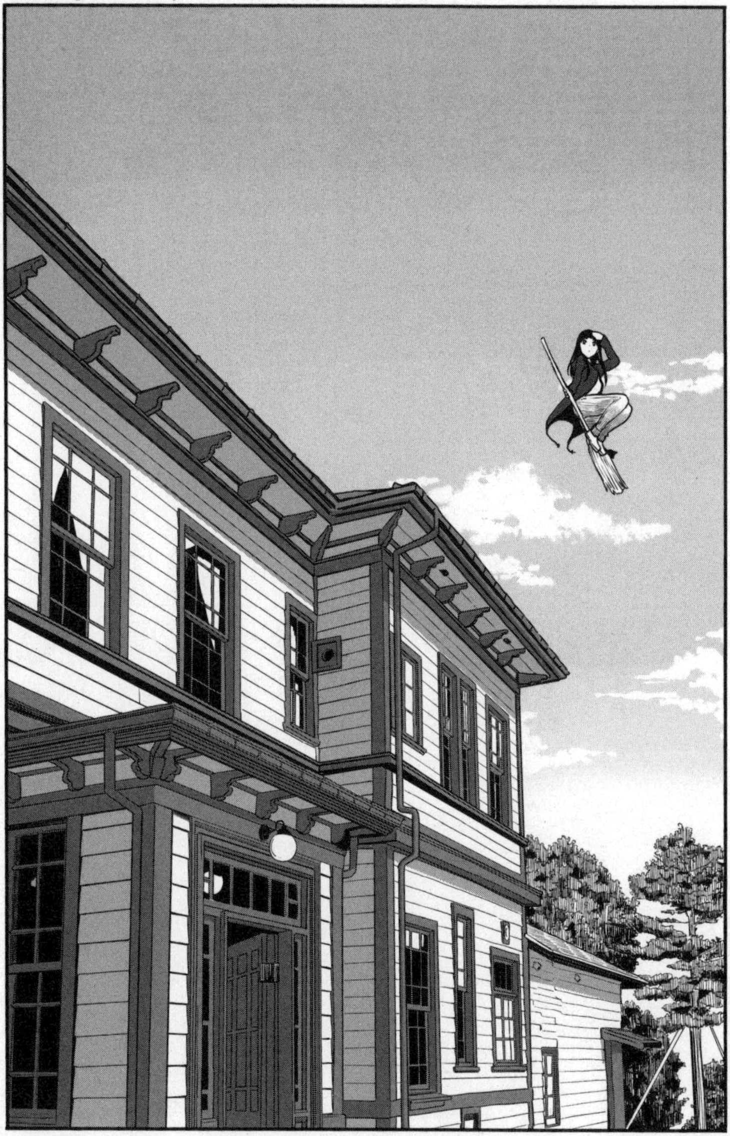

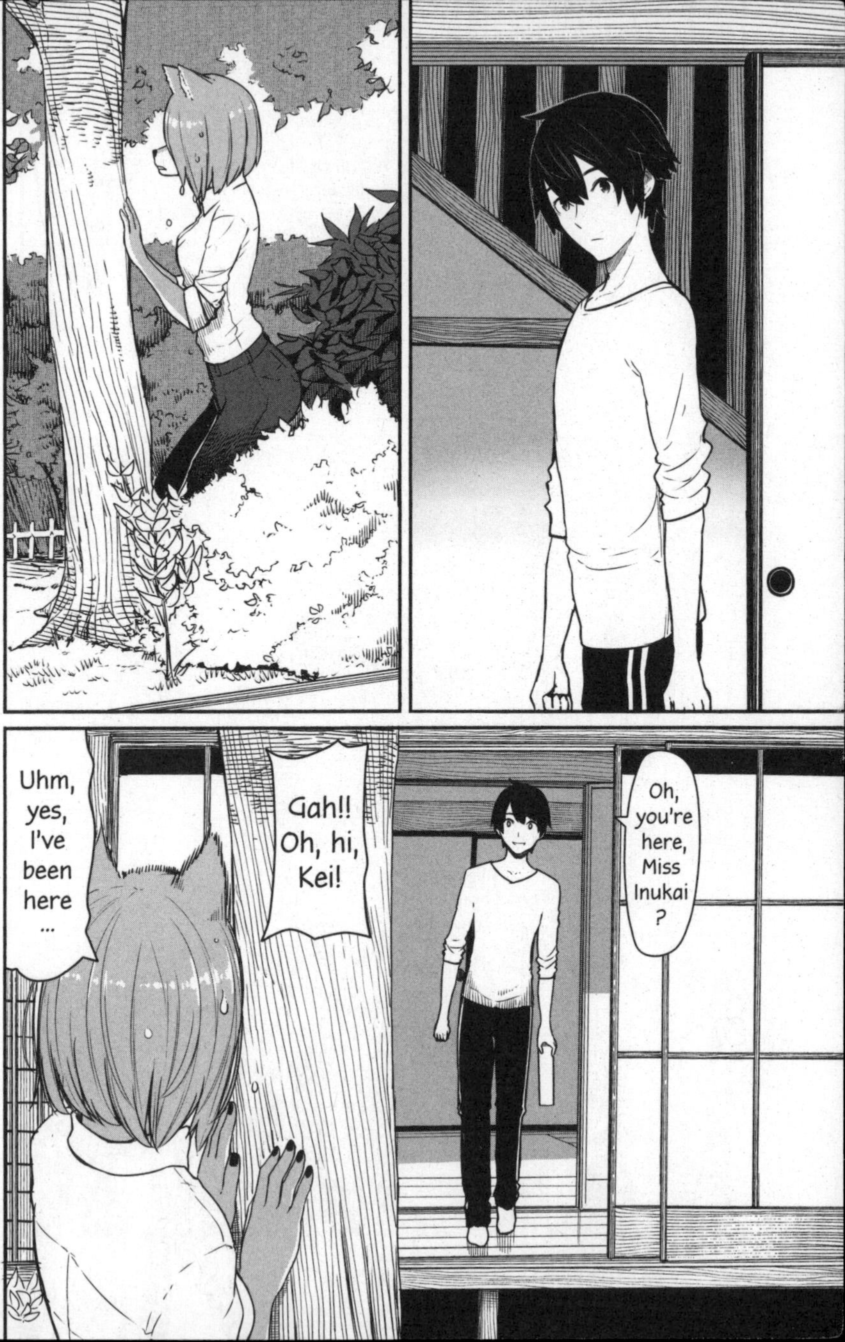
Oh, you're here, Miss Inukai?
Gah!! Oh, hi, Kei!
Uhm, yes, I've been here ...

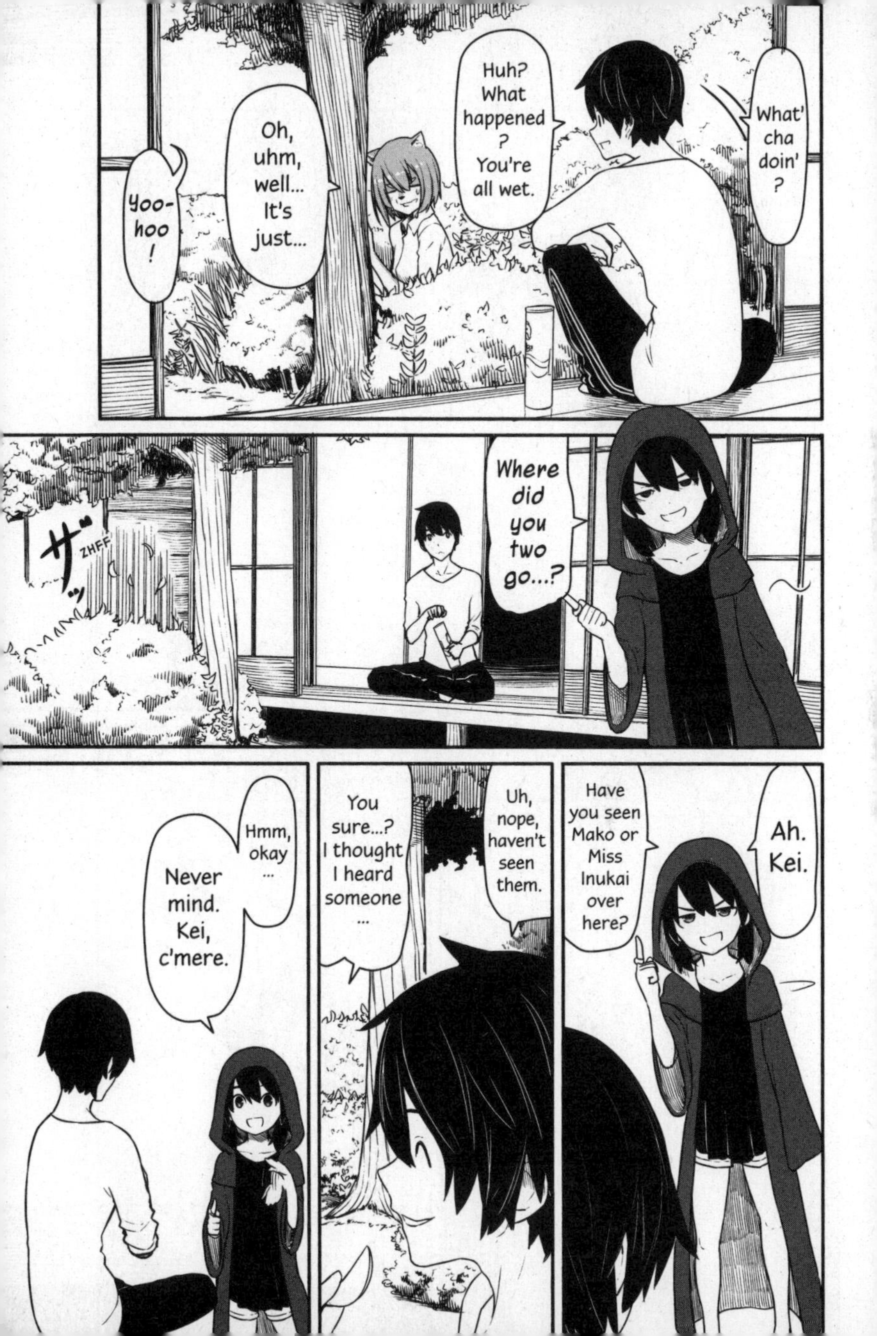
What'cha doin'?
Huh? What happened? You're all wet.
Oh, uhm, well... It's just...
Yoo-hoo!
Where did you two go...?
ZHFF
Ah. Kei.
Have you seen Mako or Miss Inukai over here?
Uh, nope, haven't seen them.
You sure...? I thought I heard someone ...
Hmm, okay ...
Never mind. Kei, c'mere.

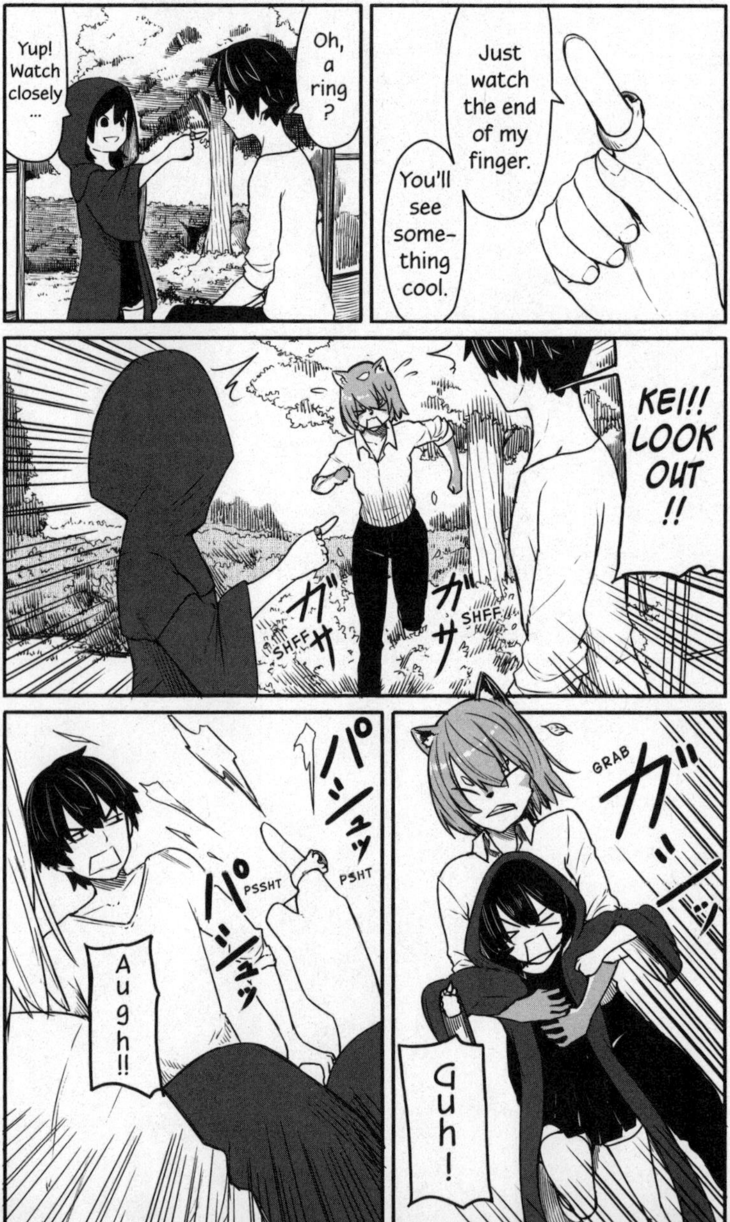
Just watch the end of my finger.
You'll see some-thing cool.
Oh, a ring?
Yup! Watch closely ...
KEI!! LOOK OUT!!
ガサ
SHFF
ガサ
SHFF
GRAB
ガッ
Guh!
パシュッ
PSHT
パシュッ
PSSHT
Augh!!

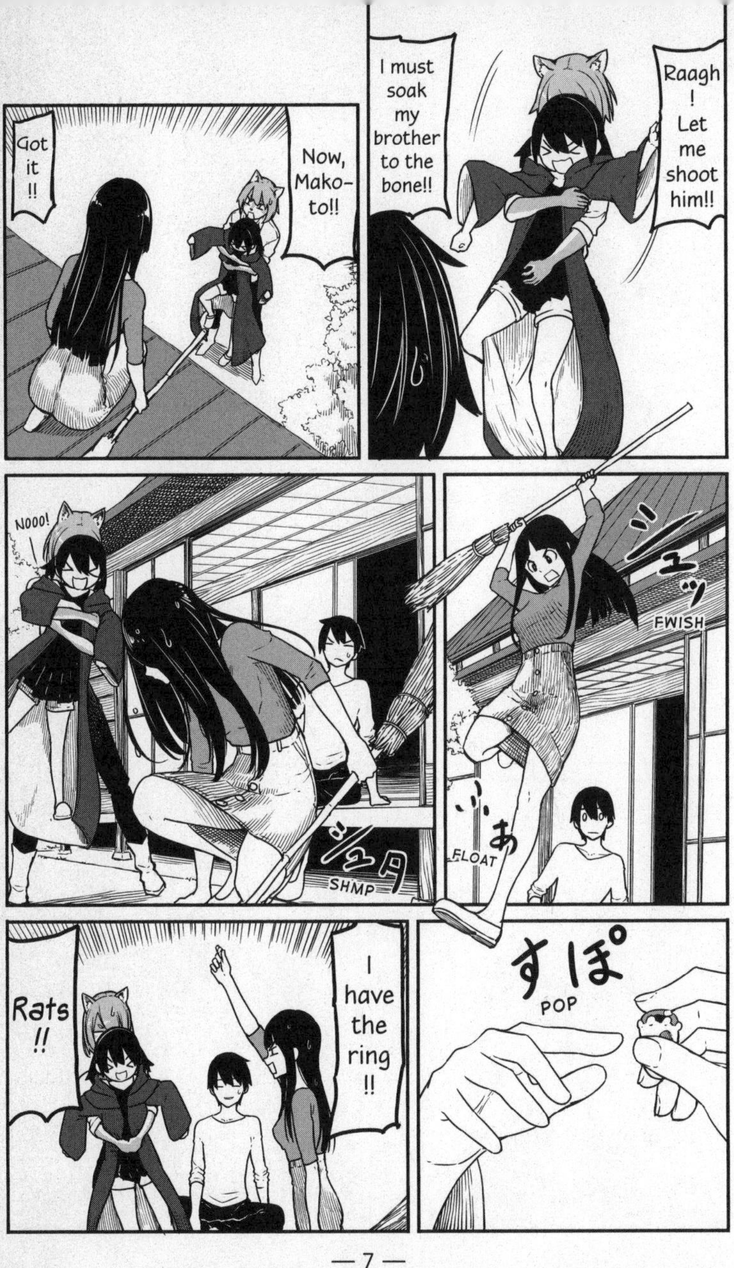
Raagh! Let me shoot him!!
I must soak my brother to the bone!!
Now, Mako-to!!
Got it!!
シュッ
FWISH
ふぁ
FLOAT
NOOO!
SHMP
すぽ
POP
I have the ring!!
Rats!!

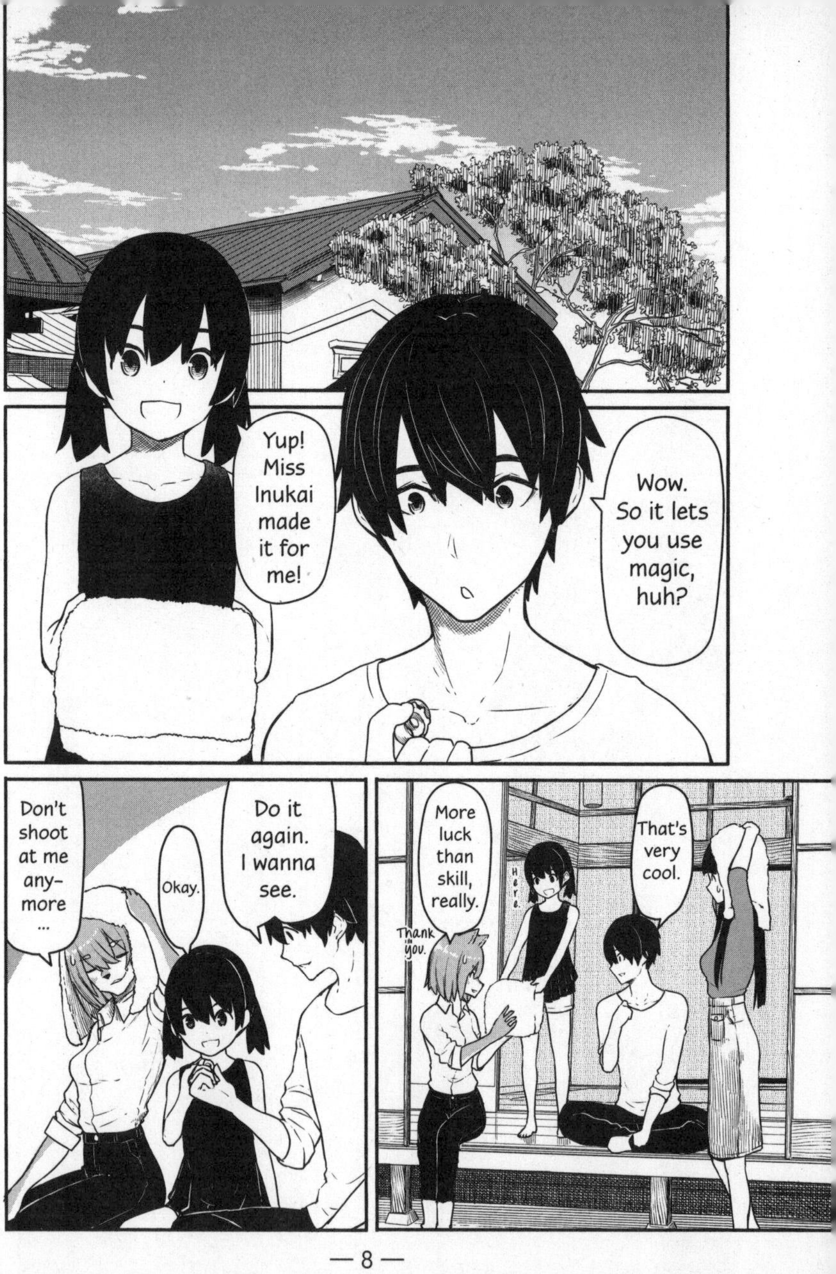
Wow. So it lets you use magic, huh?
Yup! Miss Inukai made it for me!
That's very cool.
More luck than skill, really.
Here.
Thank you.
Do it again. I wanna see.
Okay.
Don't shoot at me any-more ...

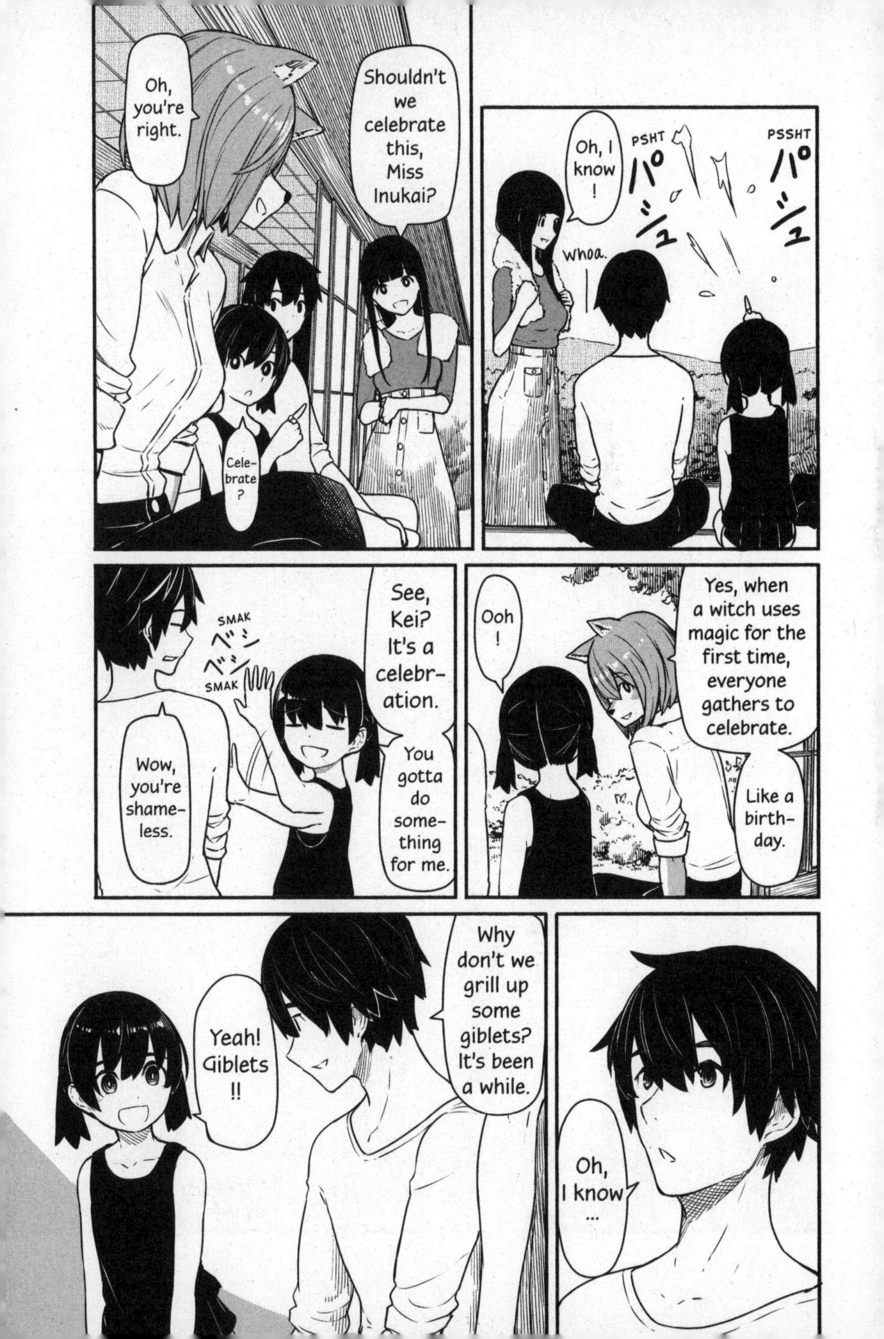
PSSHT
PSHT
Oh, I know!
Whoa.
Shouldn't we celebrate this, Miss Inukai?
Oh, you're right.
Celebrate?
Yes, when a witch uses magic for the first time, everyone gathers to celebrate.
Ooh!
Like a birthday.
See, Kei? It's a celebration.
You gotta do something for me.
SMAK
SMAK
Wow, you're shameless.
Oh, I know...
Why don't we grill up some giblets? It's been a while.
Yeah! Giblets!!

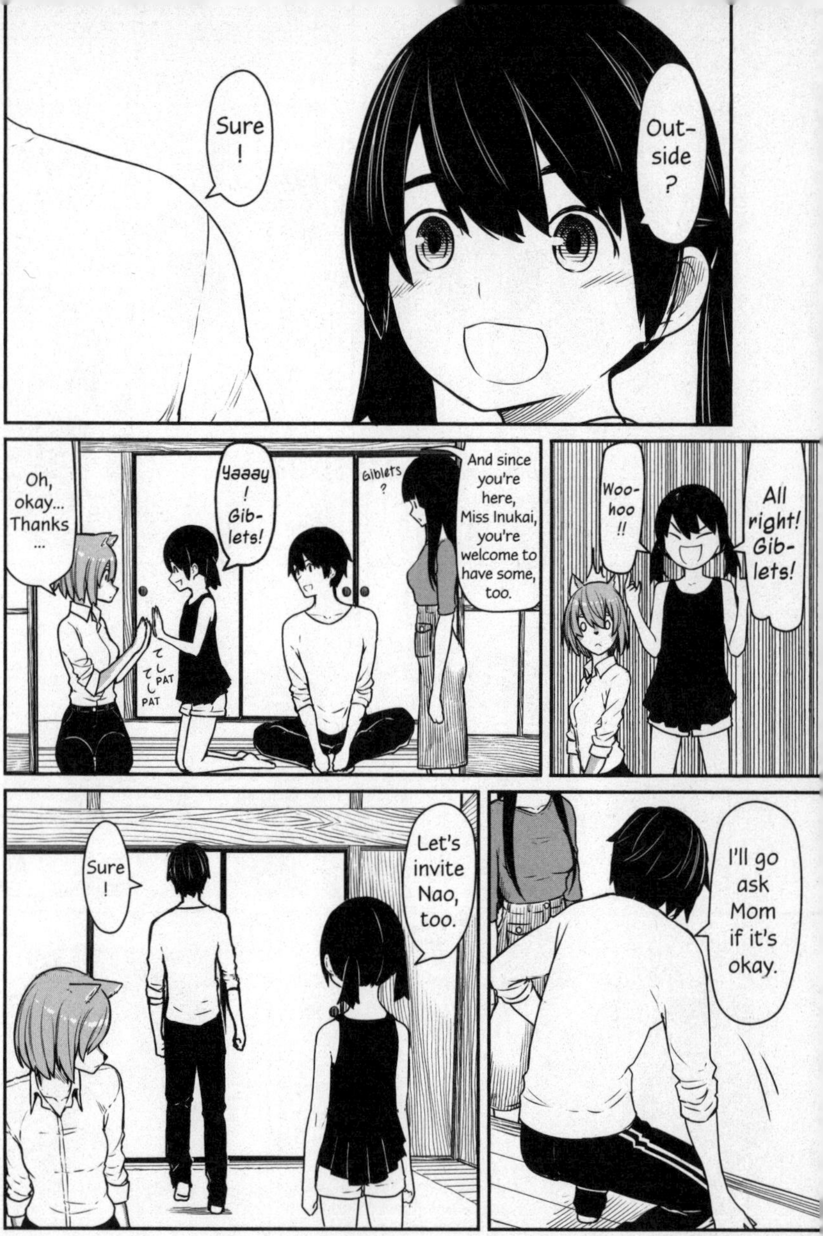
Out-side?
Sure!
All right! Gib-lets!
Woo-hoo!!
And since you're here, Miss Inukai, you're welcome to have some, too.
Giblets?
Yaaay! Gib-lets!
Oh, okay... Thanks...
てしてし PAT PAT
I'll go ask Mom if it's okay.
Let's invite Nao, too.
Sure!

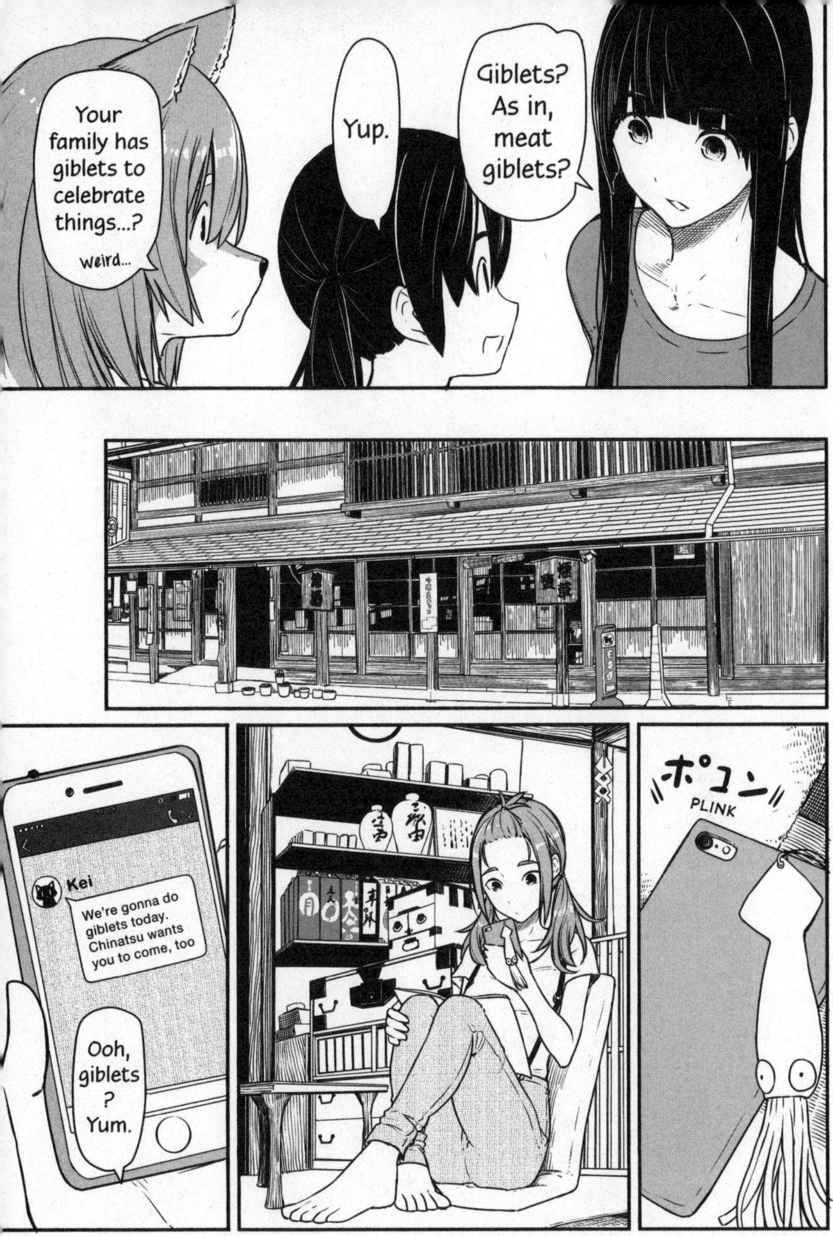
Giblets? As in, meat giblets?
Yup.
Your family has giblets to celebrate things...?
weird...
ポコン
PLINK
Kei
We're gonna do giblets today. Chinatsu wants you to come, too
Ooh, giblets? Yum.

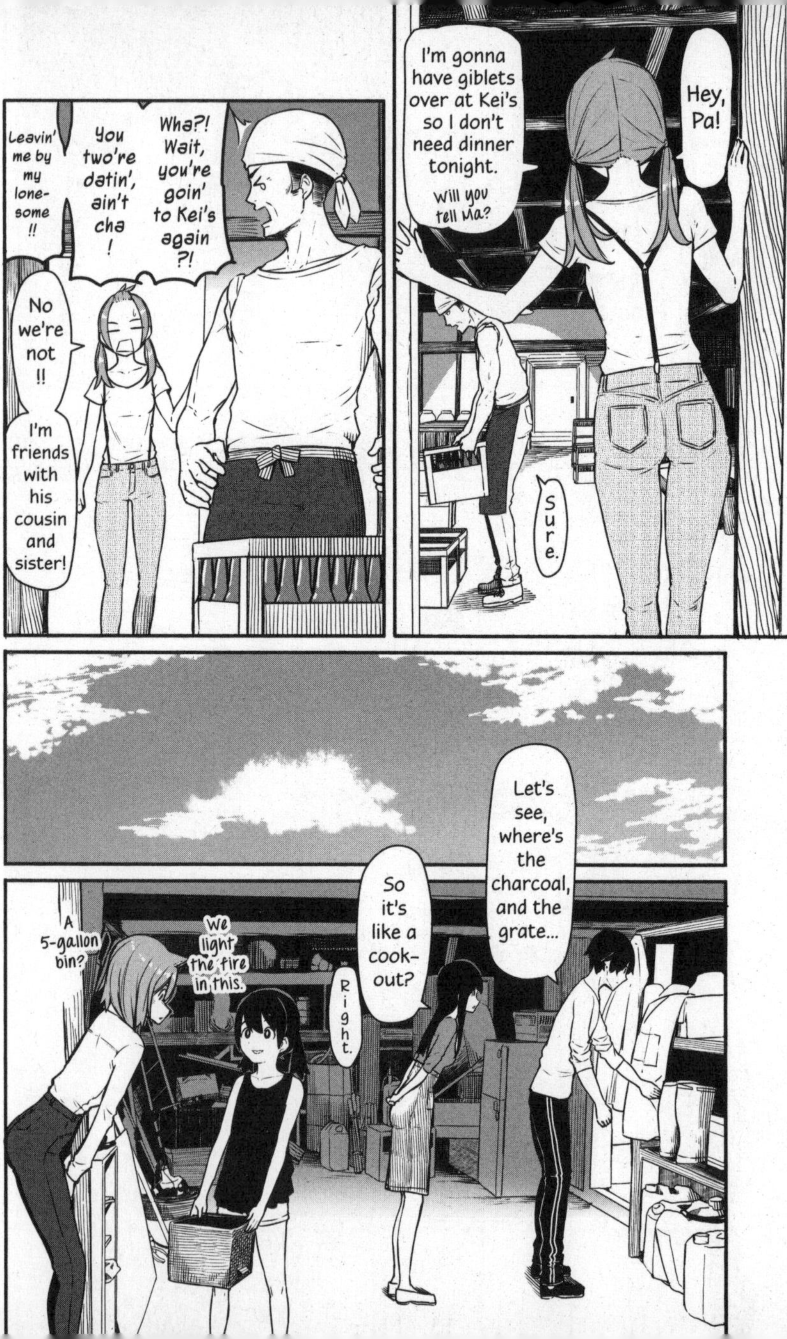
Hey, Pa!
I'm gonna have giblets over at Kei's so I don't need dinner tonight.
Will you tell Ma?
Sure.
Wha?! Wait, you're goin' to Kei's again ?!
You two're datin', ain't cha !
Leavin' me by my lone-some !!
No we're not !!
I'm friends with his cousin and sister!
Let's see, where's the charcoal, and the grate...
So it's like a cook-out?
Right.
We light the fire in this.
A 5-gallon bin?

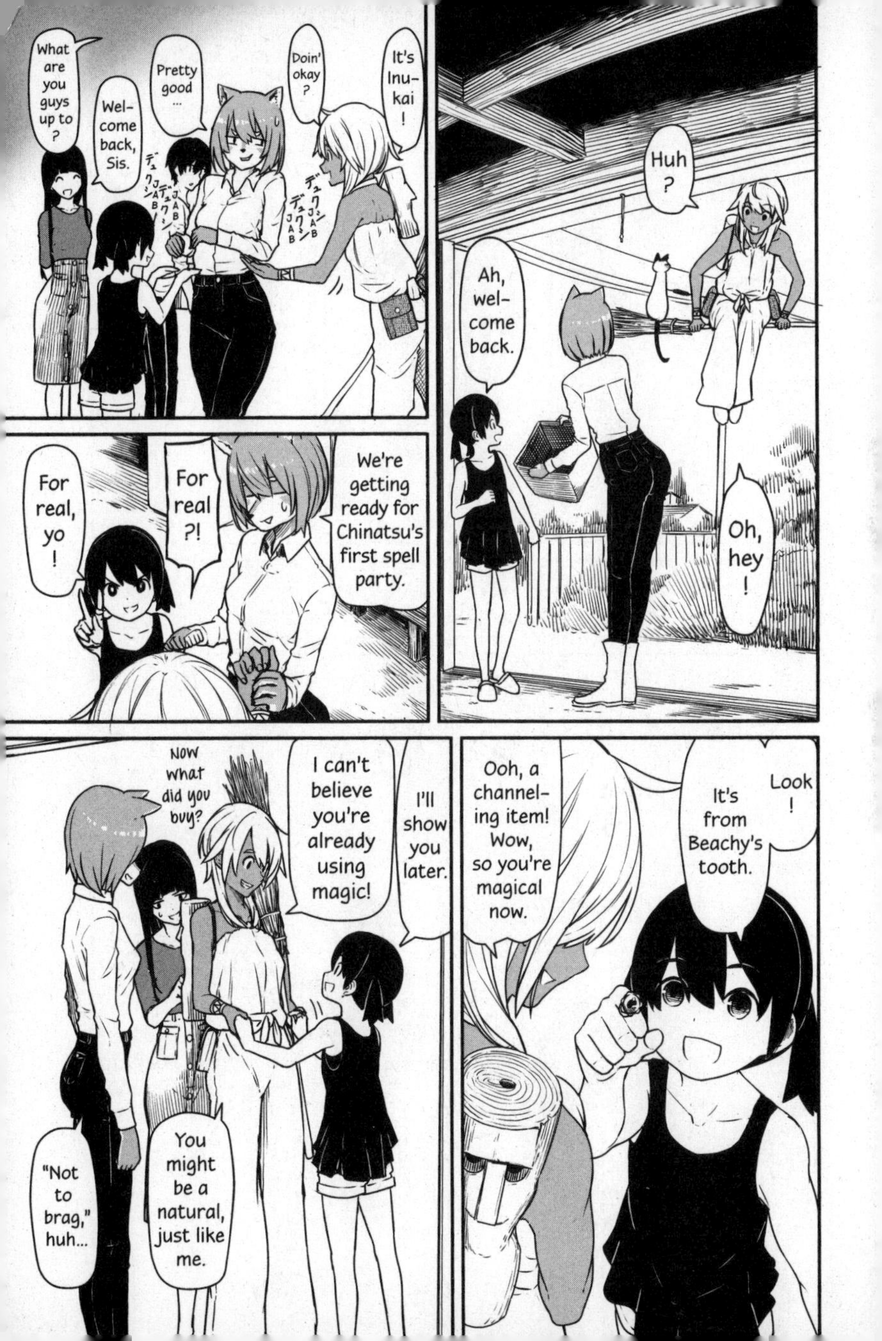
Huh?
Ah, welcome back.
Oh, hey!
It's Inukai!
Doin' okay?
デュクシ JAB デュクシ JAB
Pretty good...
Welcome back, Sis.
デュクシ JAB デュクシ JAB
What are you guys up to?
We're getting ready for Chinatsu's first spell party.
For real?!
For real, yo!
Look!
It's from Beachy's tooth.
Ooh, a channeling item! Wow, so you're magical now.
I'll show you later.
I can't believe you're already using magic!
Now what did you buy?
You might be a natural, just like me.
"Not to brag," huh...

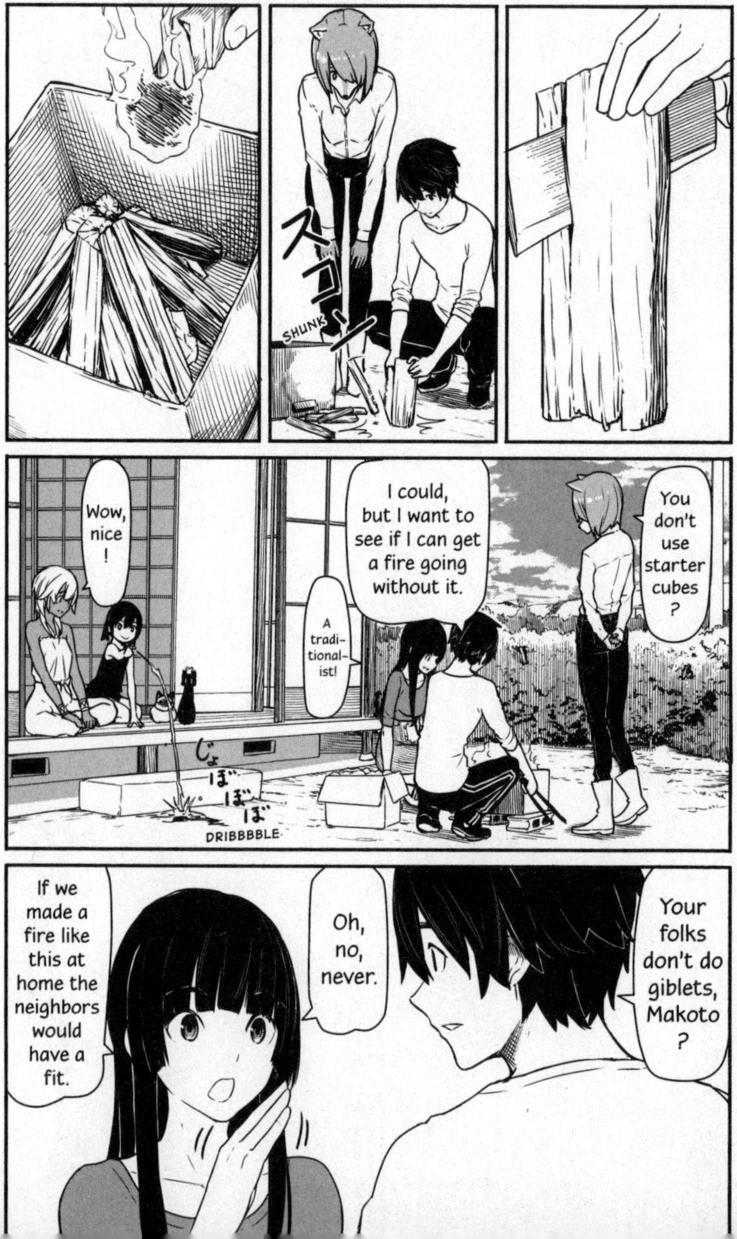
SHUNK
You don't use starter cubes?
I could, but I want to see if I can get a fire going without it.
A tradi-tionalist!
Wow, nice!
じょぼぼぼ
DRIBBBBLE
Your folks don't do giblets, Makoto?
Oh, no, never.
If we made a fire like this at home the neighbors would have a fit.

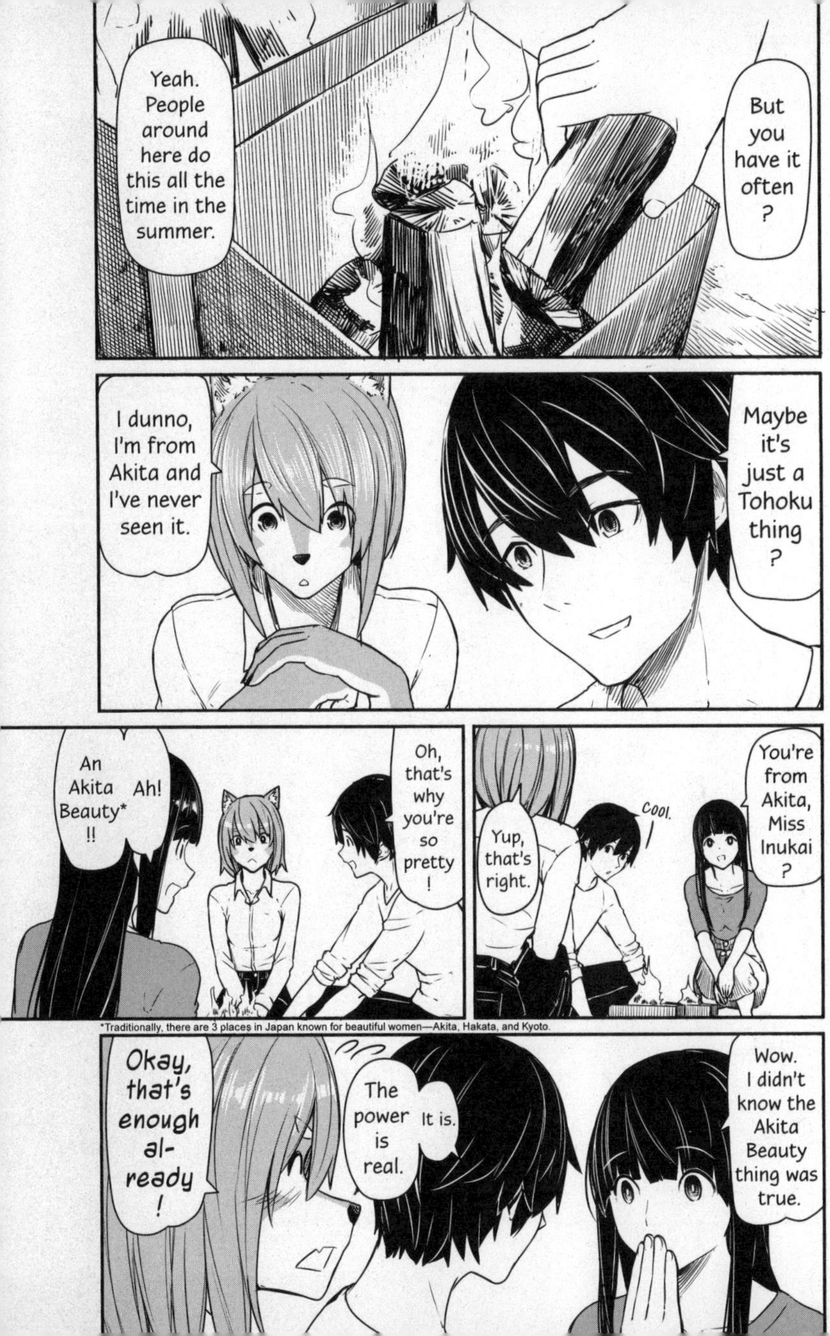
But you have it often?
Yeah. People around here do this all the time in the summer.
Maybe it's just a Tohoku thing?
I dunno, I'm from Akita and I've never seen it.
You're from Akita, Miss Inukai?
COOL.
Yup, that's right.
Oh, that's why you're so pretty!
Ah!
An Akita Beauty* !!
Wow. I didn't know the Akita Beauty thing was true.
It is.
The power is real.
Okay, that's enough al-ready!
*Traditionally, there are 3 places in Japan known for beautiful women—Akita, Hakata, and Kyoto.

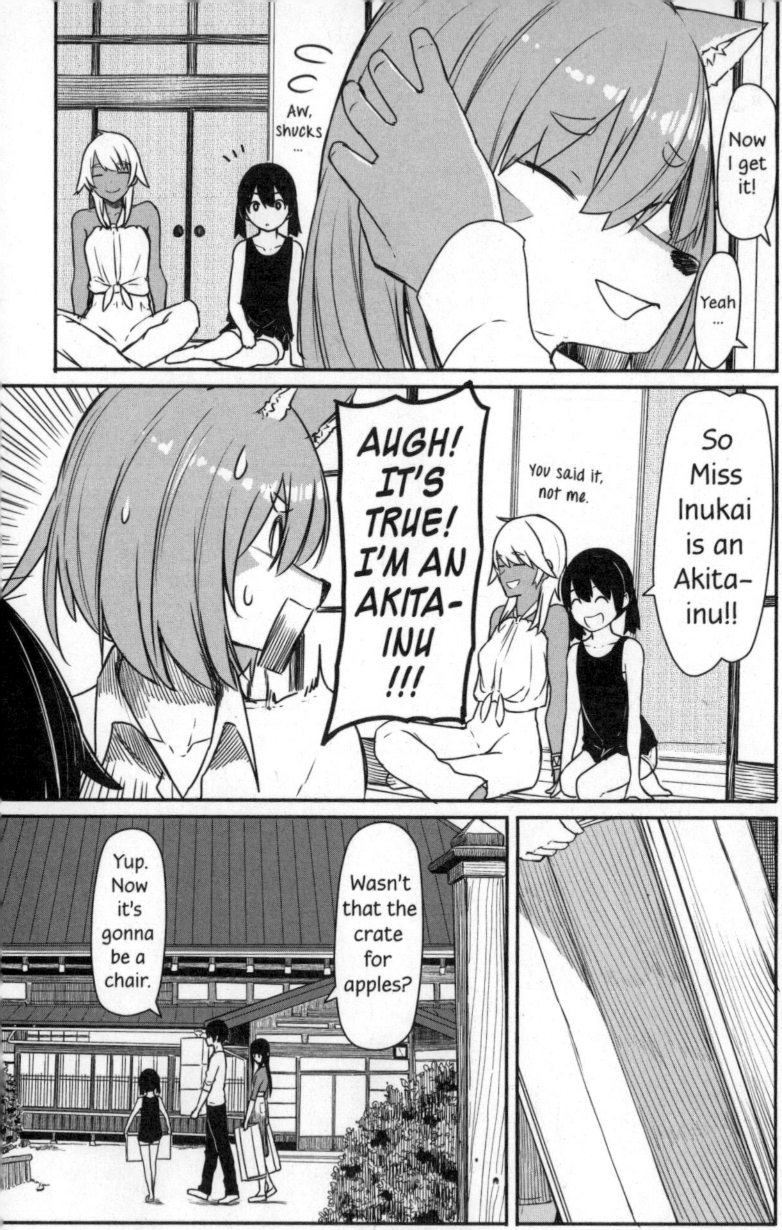
Now I get it!
Yeah ...
AW, shucks ...
So Miss Inukai is an Akita-inu!!
You said it, not me.
AUGH! IT'S TRUE! I'M AN AKITA-INU !!!
Wasn't that the crate for apples?
Yup. Now it's gonna be a chair.

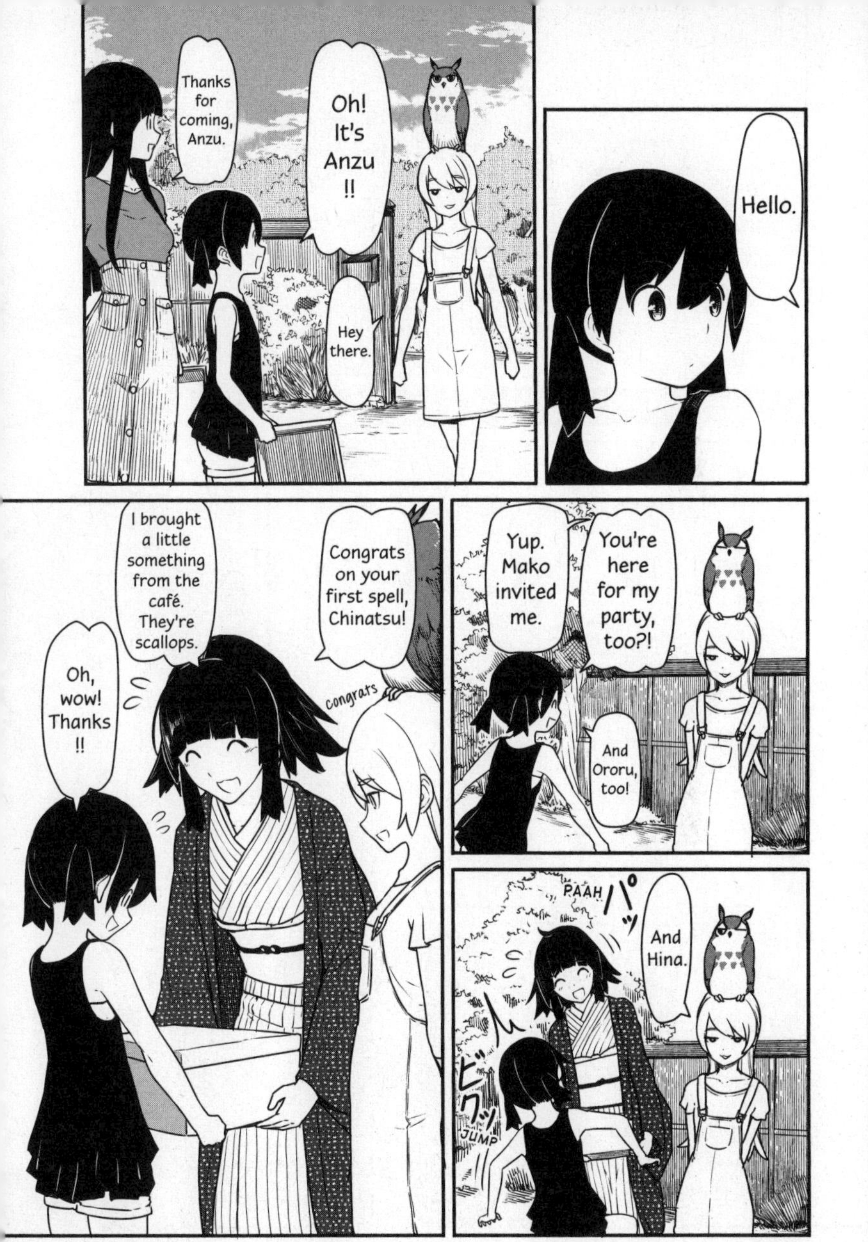
Hello.
Oh! It's Anzu !!
Hey there.
Thanks for coming, Anzu.
You're here for my party, too?!
Yup. Mako invited me.
And Ororu, too!
And Hina.
PAAH パッ
ビクッ JUMP
Congrats on your first spell, Chinatsu!
congrats
I brought a little something from the café. They're scallops.
Oh, wow! Thanks !!

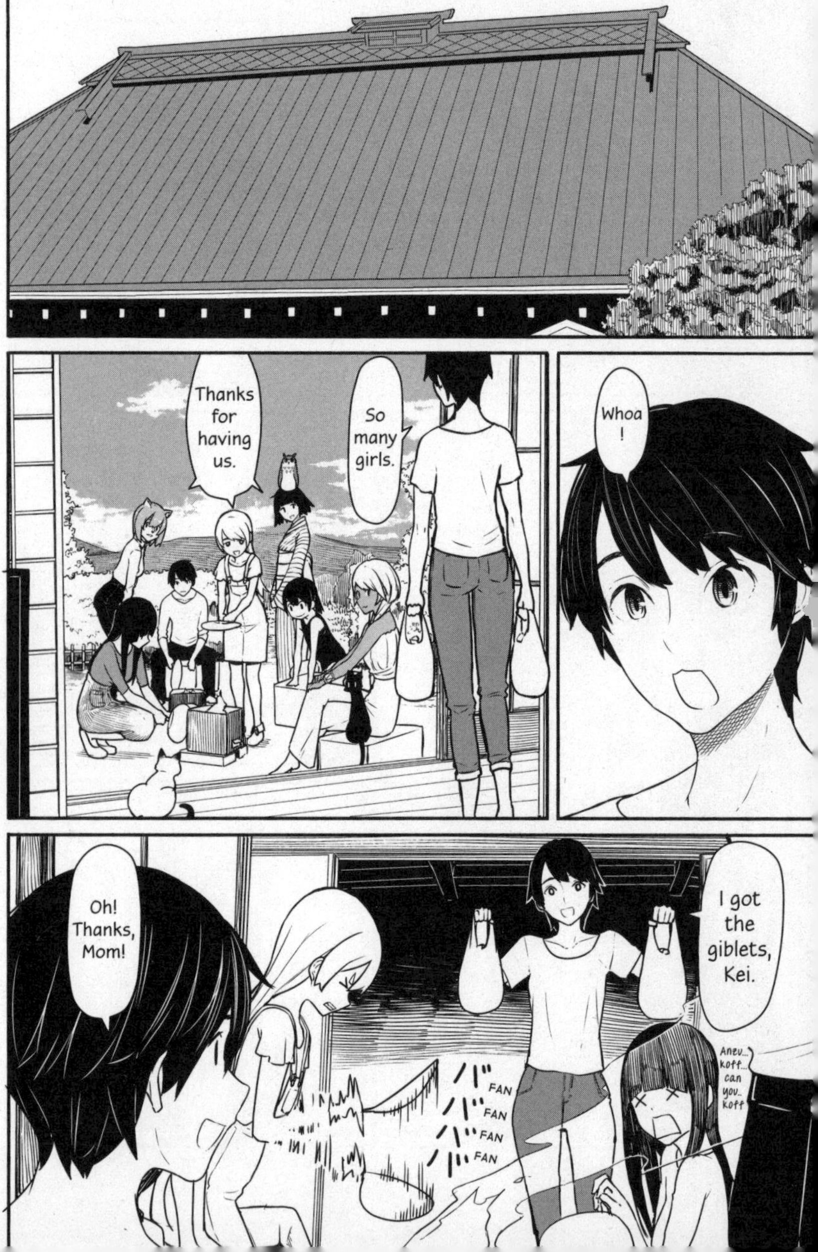
Whoa!
So many girls.
Thanks for having us.
I got the giblets, Kei.
Anzu... koff... can you.. koff
バ FAN
バ FAN
バ FAN
バ FAN
Oh! Thanks, Mom!

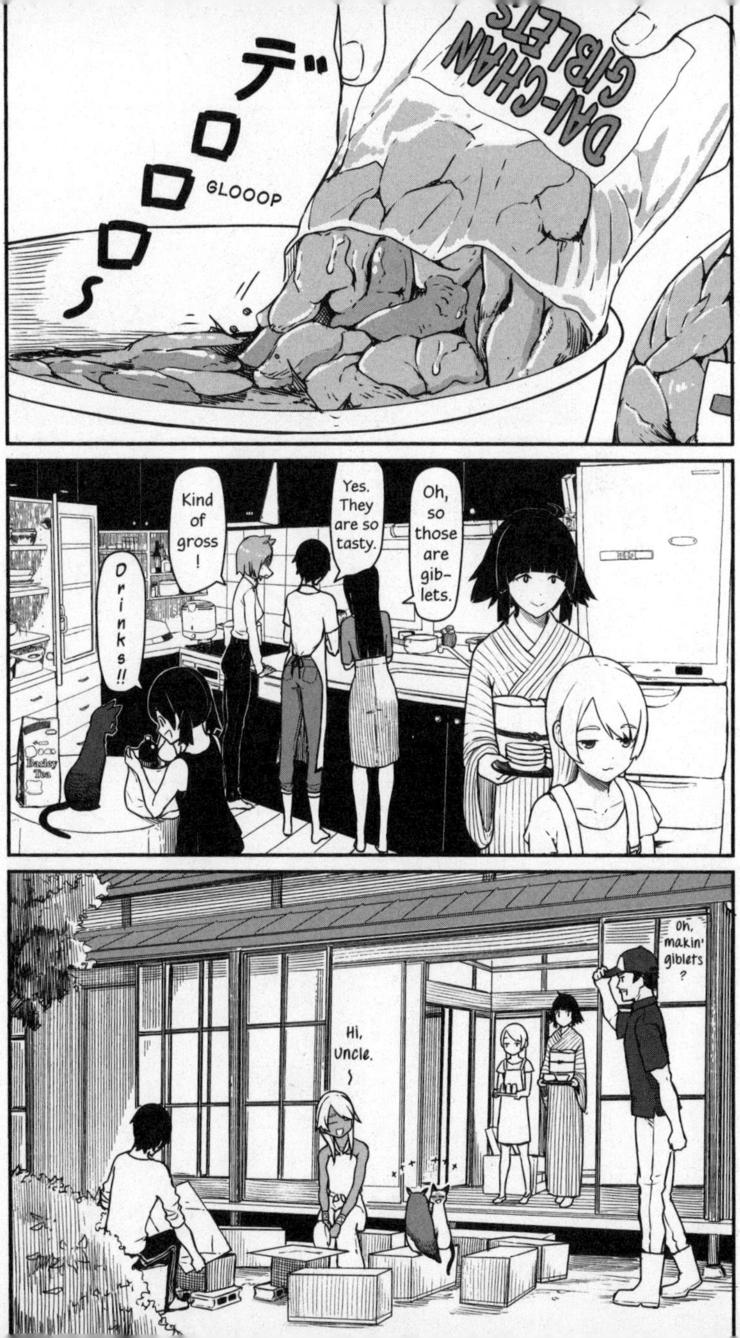
DAI-CHAN GIBLETS
デロロロ~
GLOOOP
Oh, so those are gib-lets.
Yes. They are so tasty.
Kind of gross!
Barley Tea
Drinks!!
Oh, makin' giblets?
Hi, Uncle.

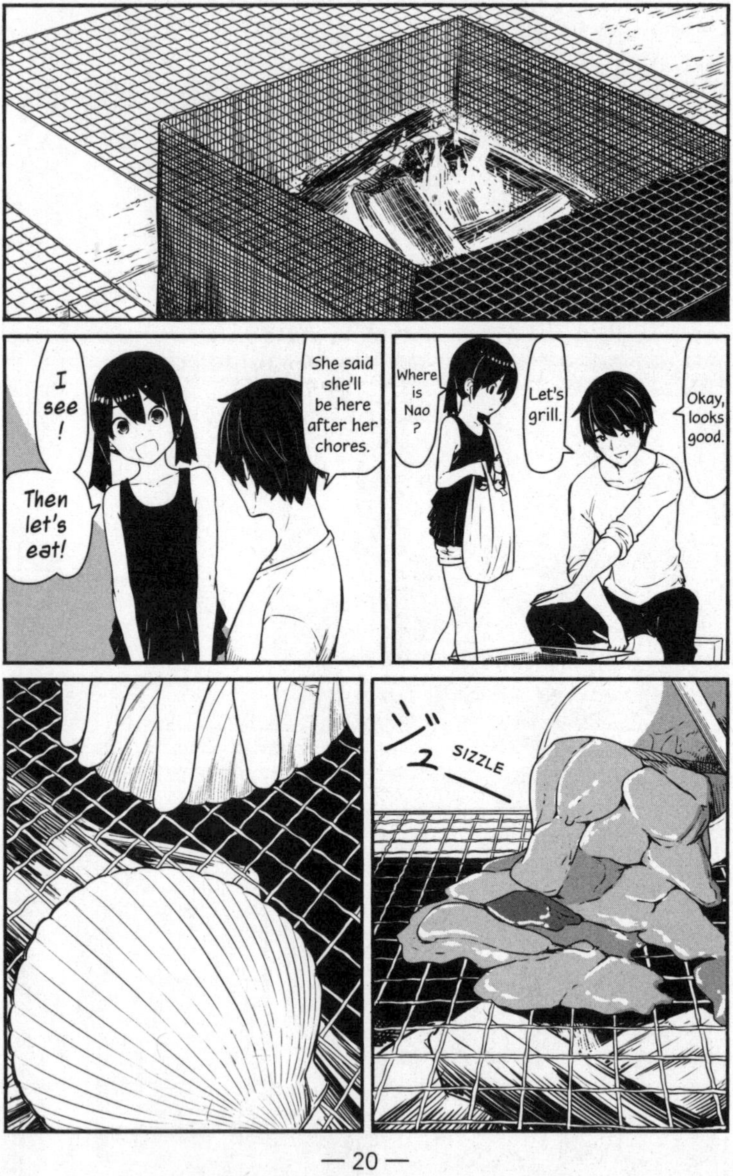
Okay, looks good.
Let's grill.
Where is Nao?
She said she'll be here after her chores.
I see!
Then let's eat!
ジュ
SIZZLE

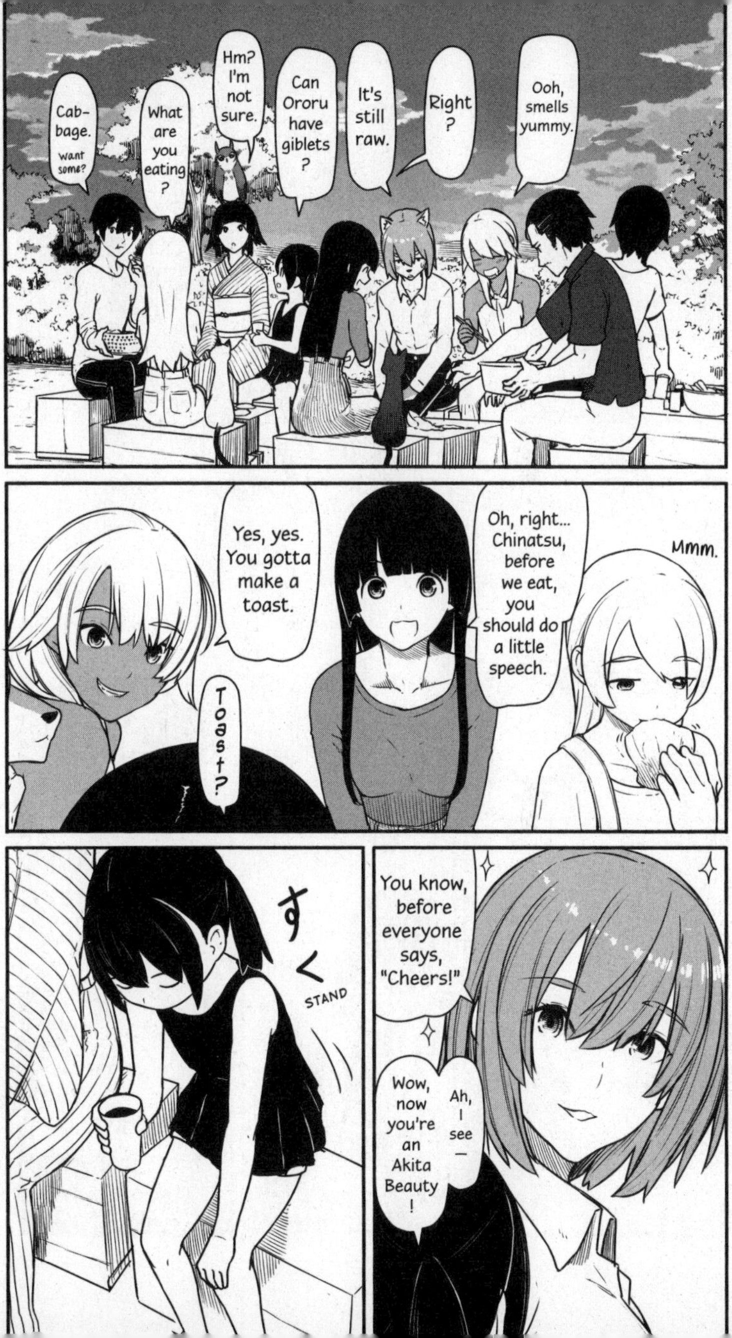
Ooh, smells yummy.
Right?
It's still raw.
Can Ororu have giblets?
Hm? I'm not sure.
What are you eating?
Cab-bage.
Want some?
Mmm.
Oh, right... Chinatsu, before we eat, you should do a little speech.
Yes, yes. You gotta make a toast.
Toast?
You know, before everyone says, "Cheers!"
Ah, I see —
Wow, now you're an Akita Beauty!
すく
STAND

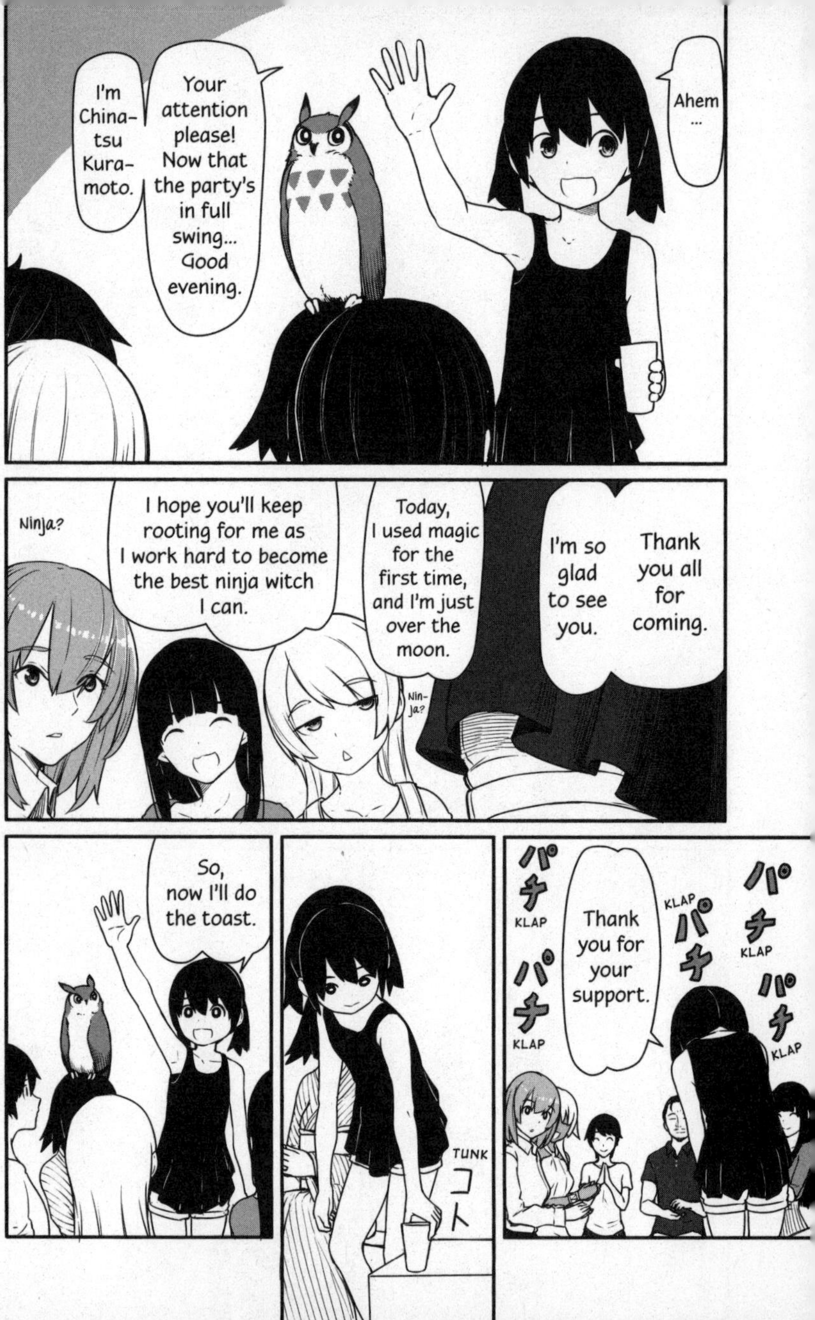
Ahem...
Your attention please! Now that the party's in full swing... Good evening.
I'm Chinatsu Kuramoto.
Thank you all for coming.
I'm so glad to see you.
Today, I used magic for the first time, and I'm just over the moon.
I hope you'll keep rooting for me as I work hard to become the best ninja witch I can.
Ninja?
Ninja?
パチ KLAP
パチ KLAP
パチ KLAP
パチ KLAP
Thank you for your support.
コト TUNK
So, now I'll do the toast.

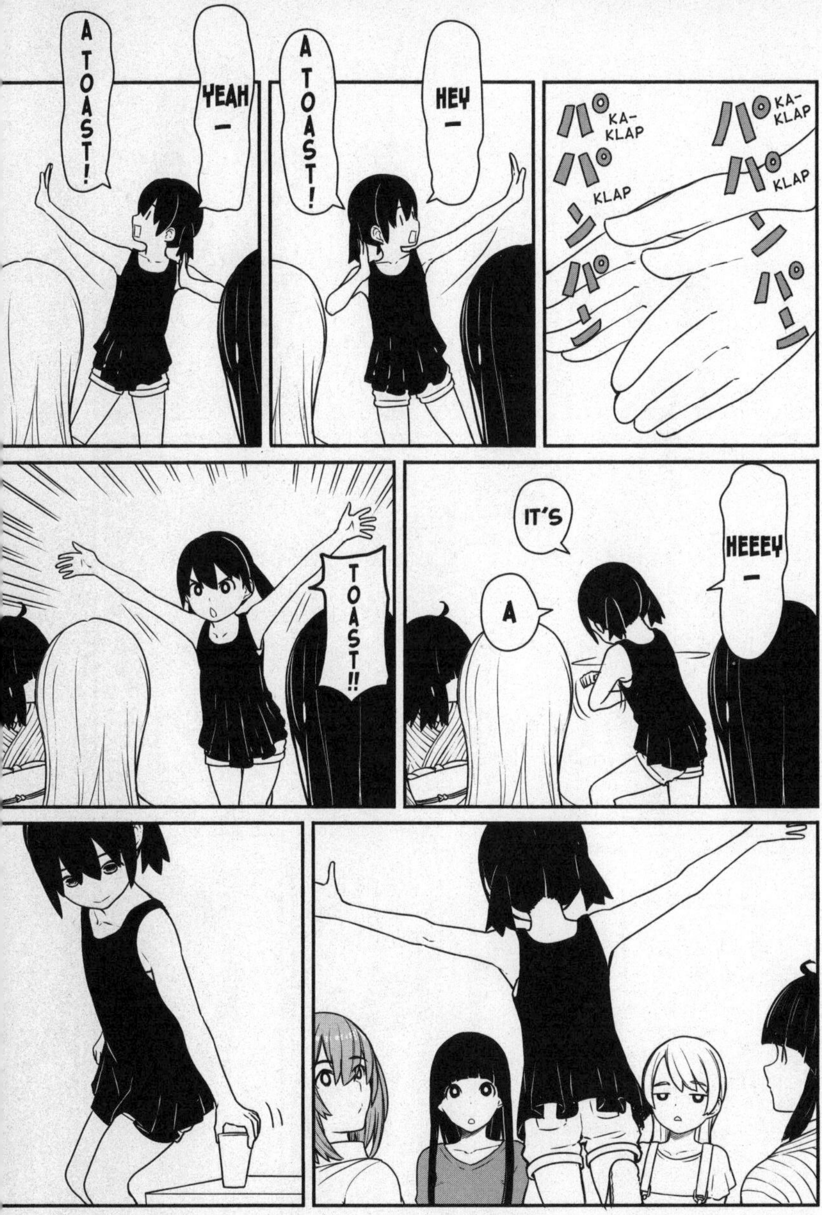
パパンパン
KA-KLAP
KLAP
パパンパン
KA-KLAP
KLAP
HEY —
A TOAST!
YEAH —
A TOAST!
HEEEY —
IT'S
A
TOAST!!

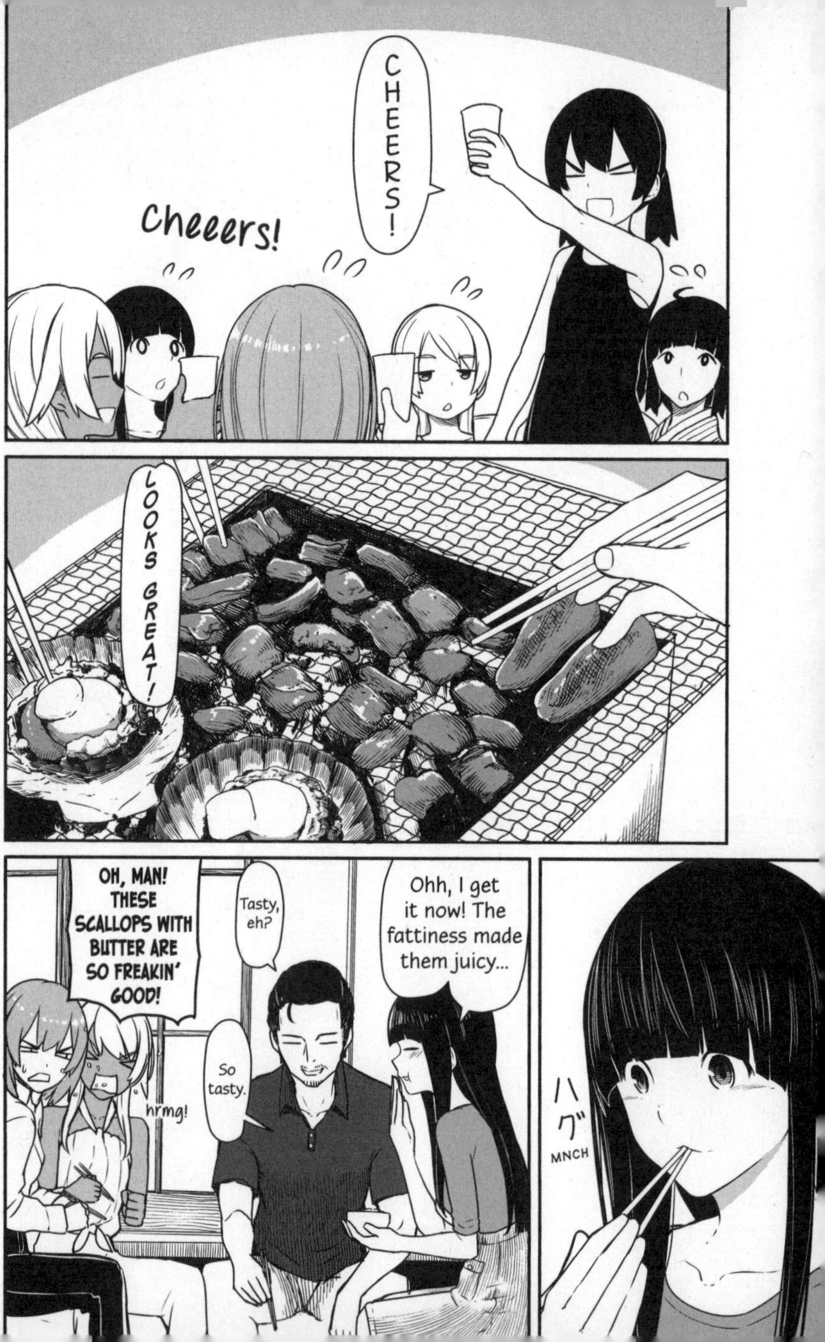
CHEERS!
Cheeers!
LOOKS GREAT!
ハグ
MNCH
Ohh, I get it now! The fattiness made them juicy...
Tasty, eh?
OH, MAN! THESE SCALLOPS WITH BUTTER ARE SO FREAKIN' GOOD!
So tasty.
hrmg!

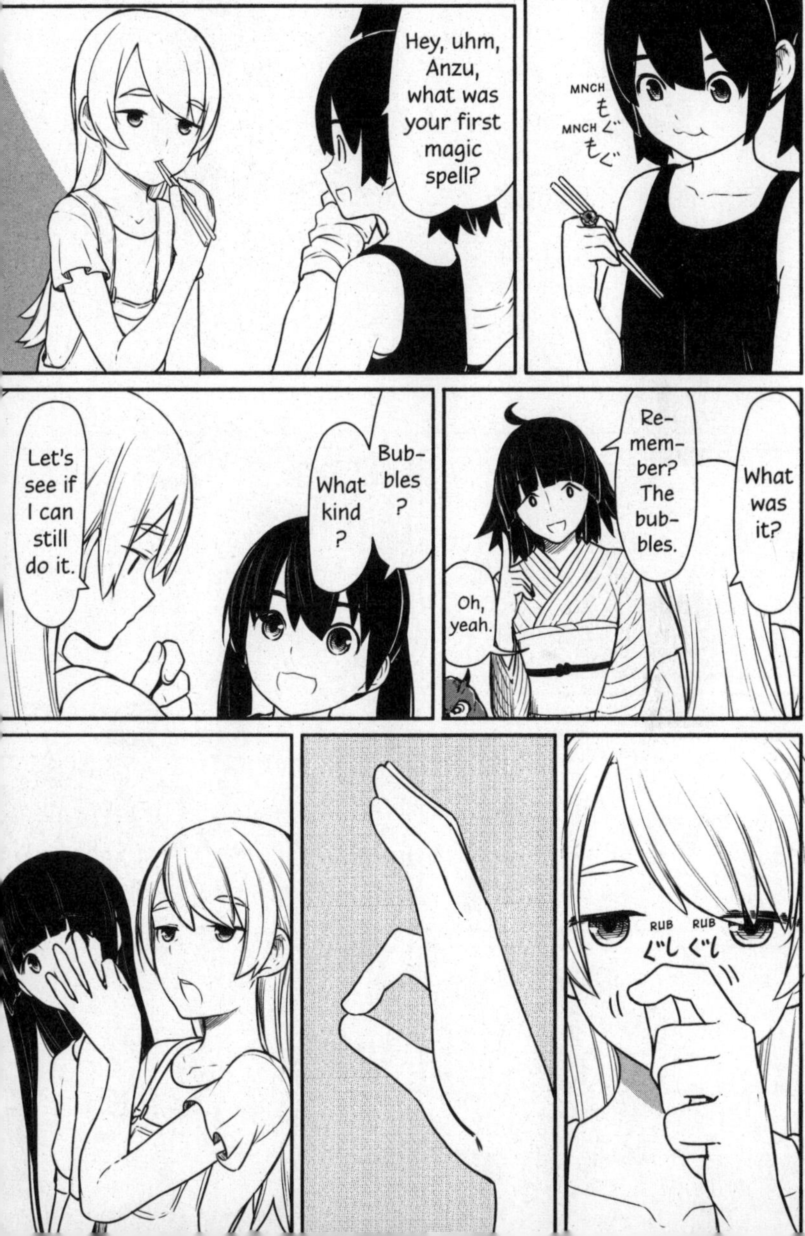
MNCH もぐ
MNCH もぐ
Hey, uhm, Anzu, what was your first magic spell?
What was it?
Re-member? The bub-bles.
Oh, yeah.
Bub-bles?
What kind?
Let's see if I can still do it.
RUB RUB ぐしぐし

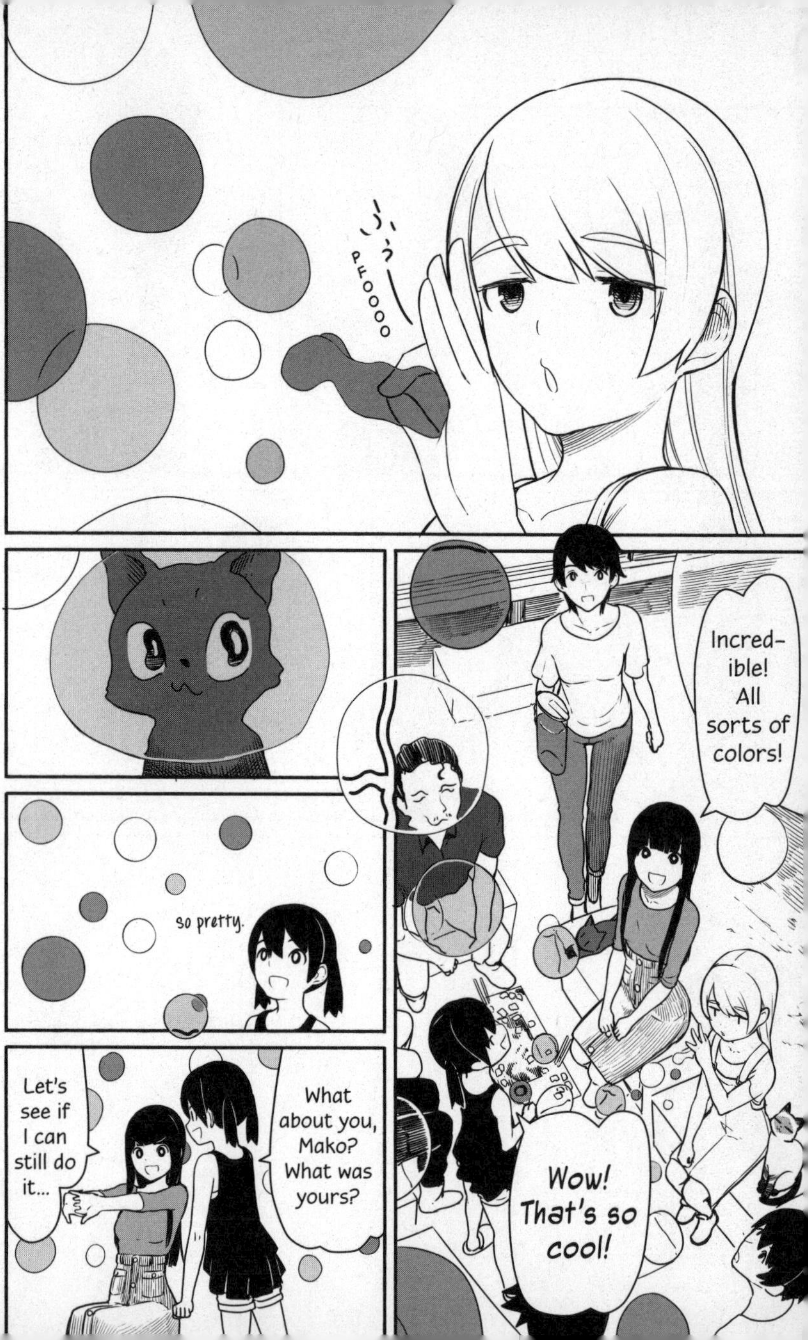
ふぅ
PFOOOO
Incred-ible! All sorts of colors!
Wow! That's so cool!
so pretty.
What about you, Mako? What was yours?
Let's see if I can still do it...

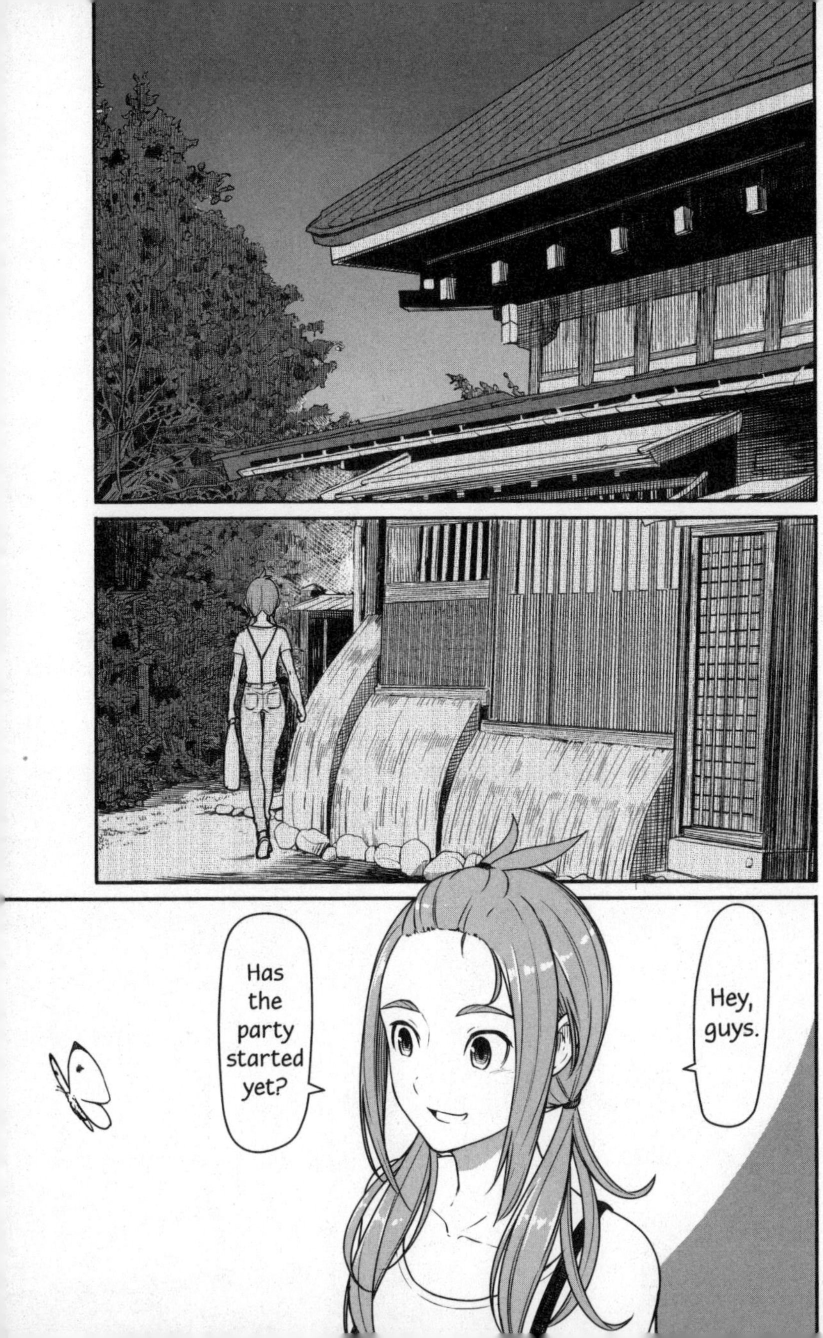
Hey, guys.
Has the party started yet?

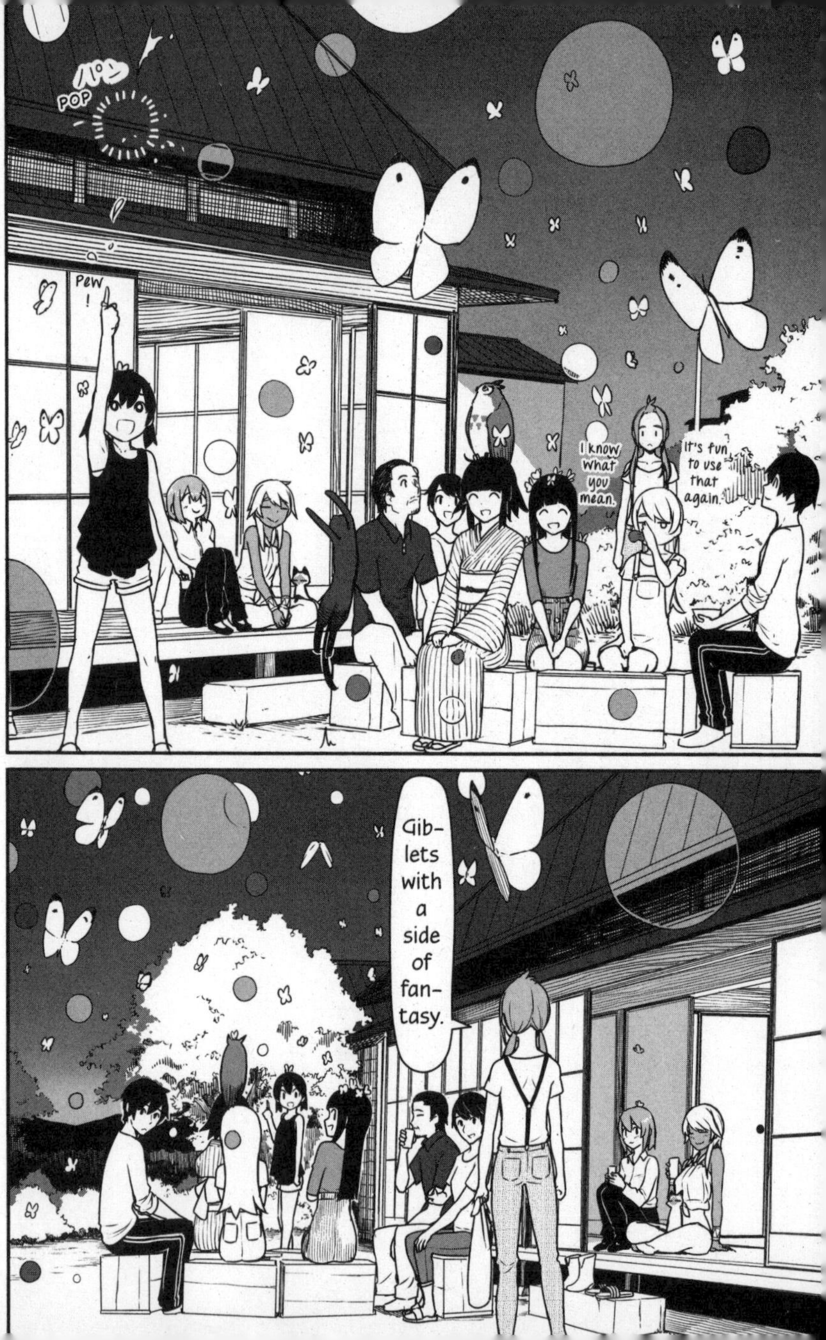
It's fun to use that again.
I know what you mean.
パン
POP
Pew!
Gib-lets with a side of fan-tasy.

Flying
Witch

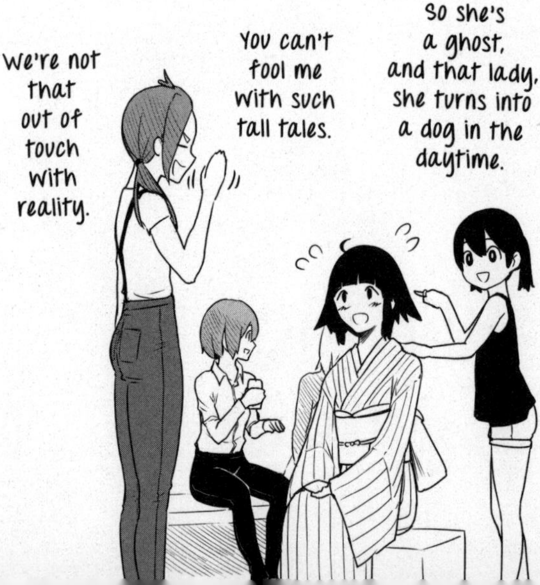
So she's a ghost, and that lady, she turns into a dog in the daytime.
You can't fool me with such tall tales.
We're not that out of touch with reality.

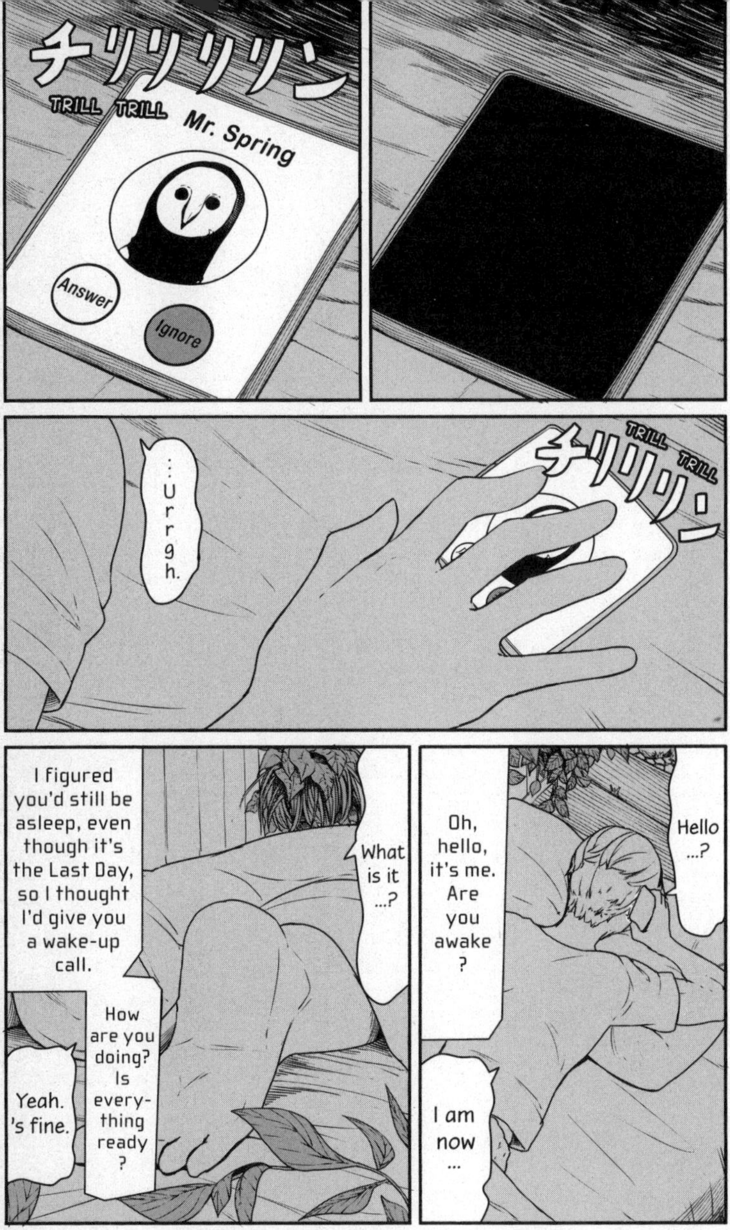
チリリリリン
TRILL TRILL
Mr. Spring
Answer
Ignore
チリリリン
TRILL TRILL
...Urrgh.
Hello ...?
Oh, hello, it's me. Are you awake?
I am now ...
What is it ...?
I figured you'd still be asleep, even though it's the Last Day, so I thought I'd give you a wake-up call.
How are you doing? Is everything ready?
Yeah. 's fine.

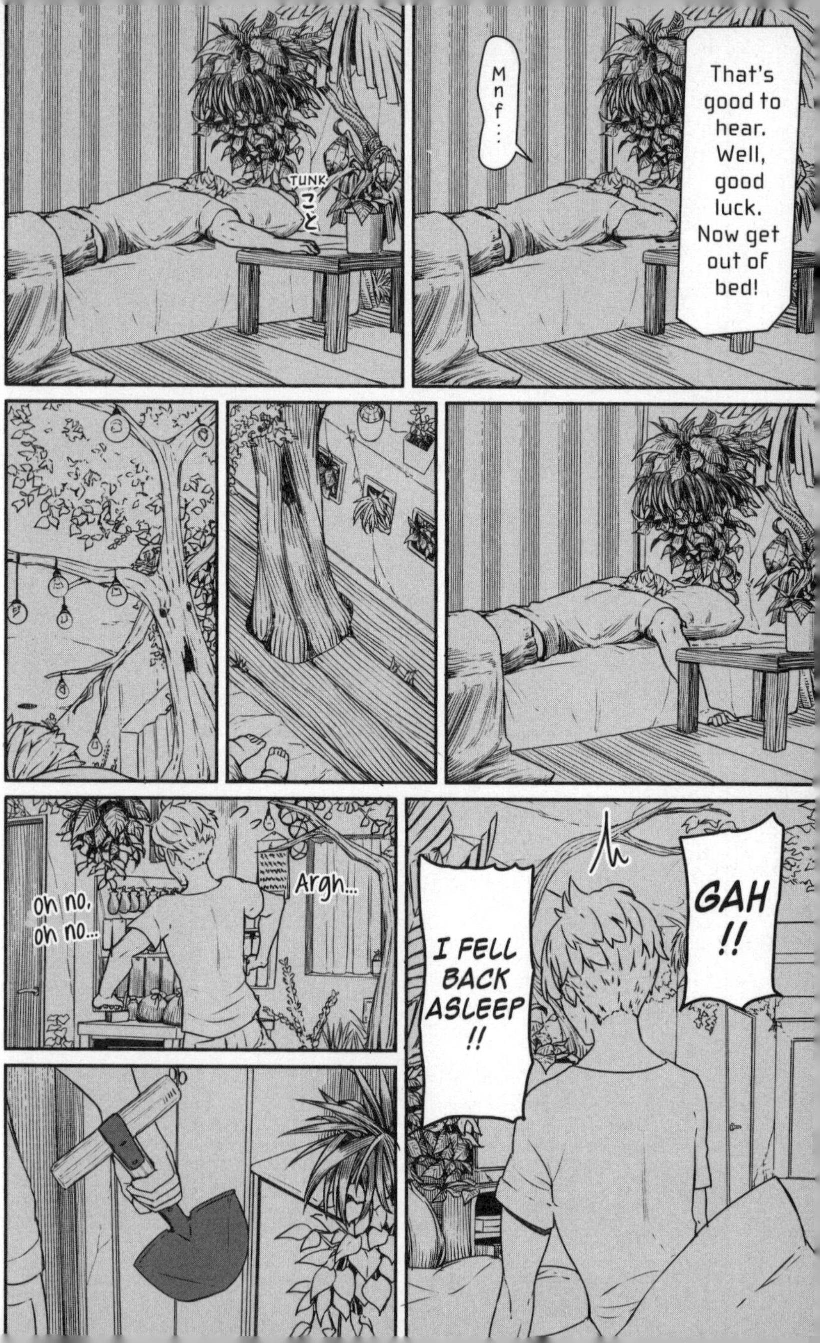
That's good to hear. Well, good luck. Now get out of bed!
Mnf...
TUNK
こと
GAH !!
I FELL BACK ASLEEP !!
Argh...
oh no, oh no...

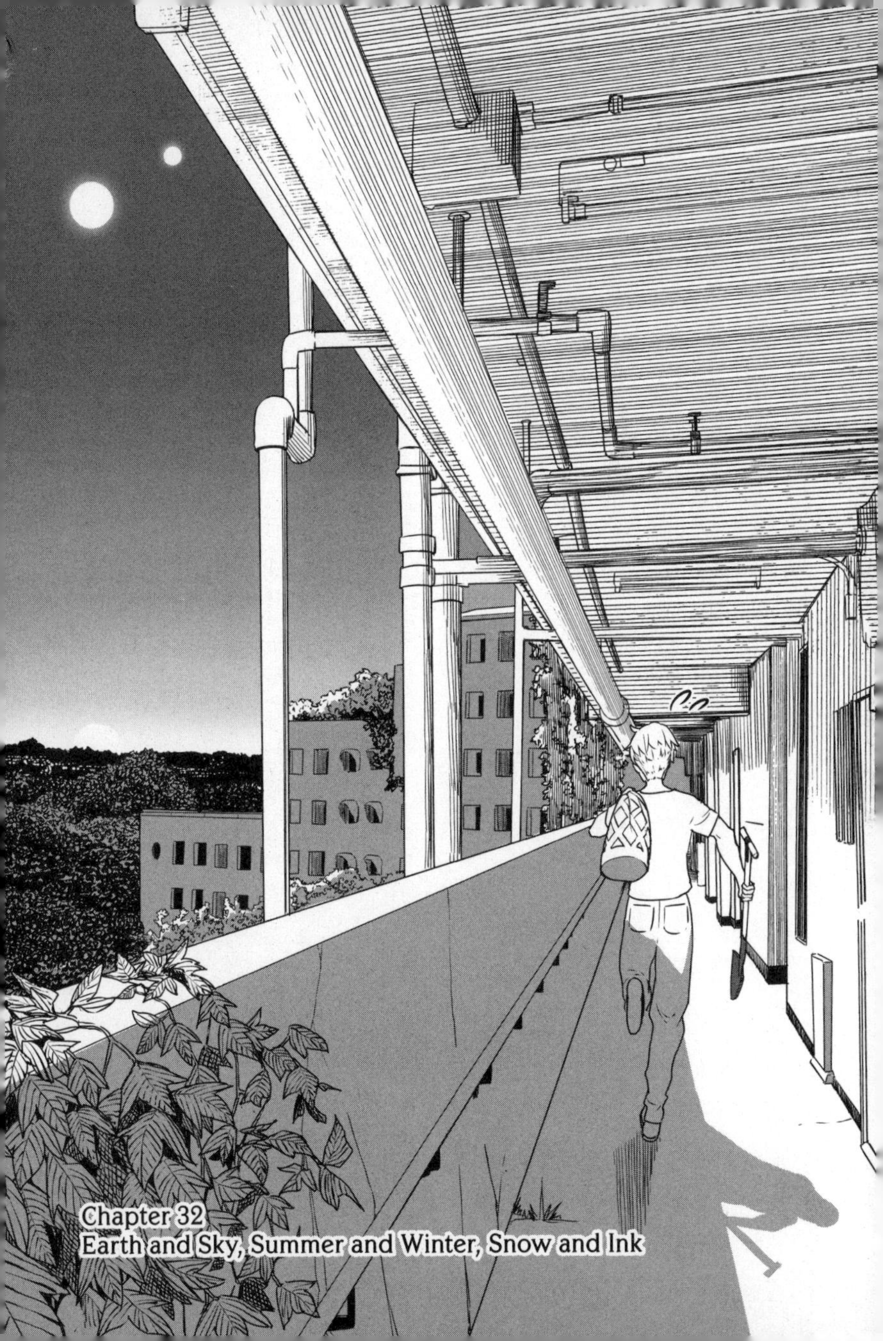

Chapter 32
Earth and Sky, Summer and Winter, Snow and Ink

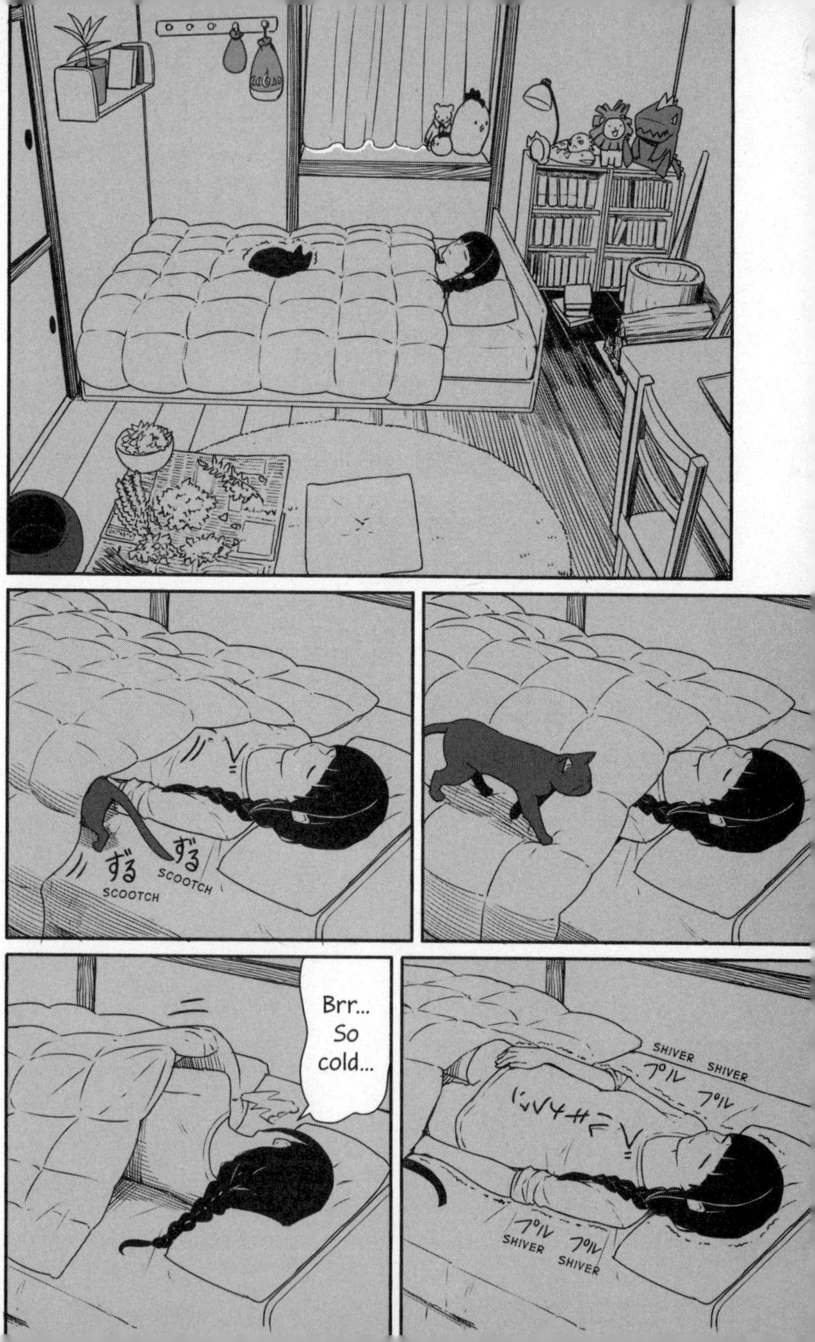
ずる
SCOOTCH
ずる
SCOOTCH
プル
SHIVER
プル
SHIVER
プル
SHIVER
プル
SHIVER
Brr... So cold...

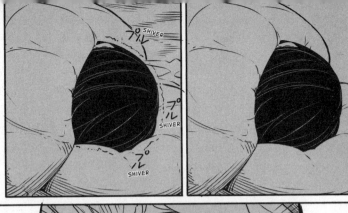

SHIVER
SHIVER
SHIVER

WHY IS MY HEAD SO COLD !?!

COLD !!

RUMBLE
RUMBLE
RUMBLE
RUMBLE
RUMBLE

BWUH ?!

What's going on? It shouldn't be this cold...!

Meoww!

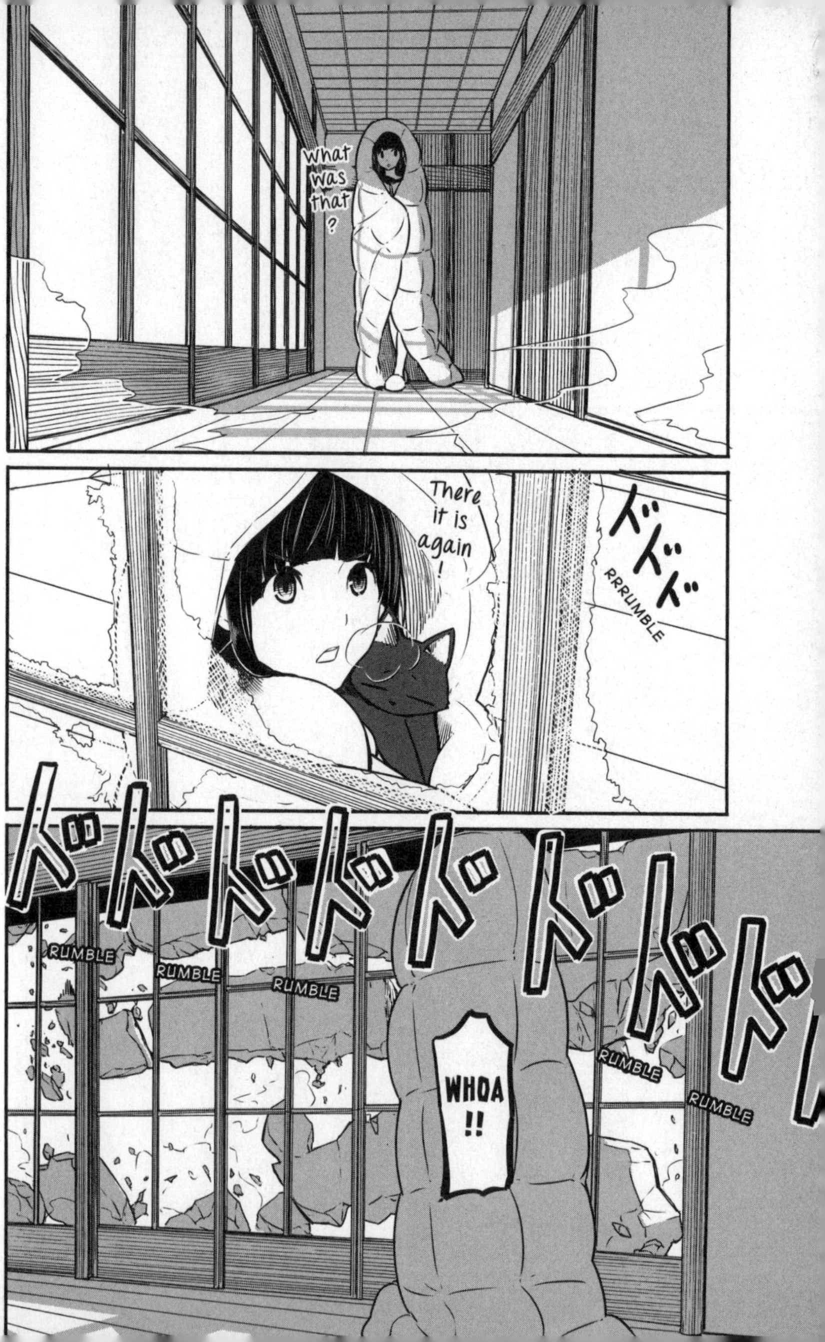
What was that?
ドドド
RRRUMBLE
There it is again!
ドドドドドドドド
RUMBLE
RUMBLE
WHOA!!
RUMBLE
RUMBLE
RUMBLE

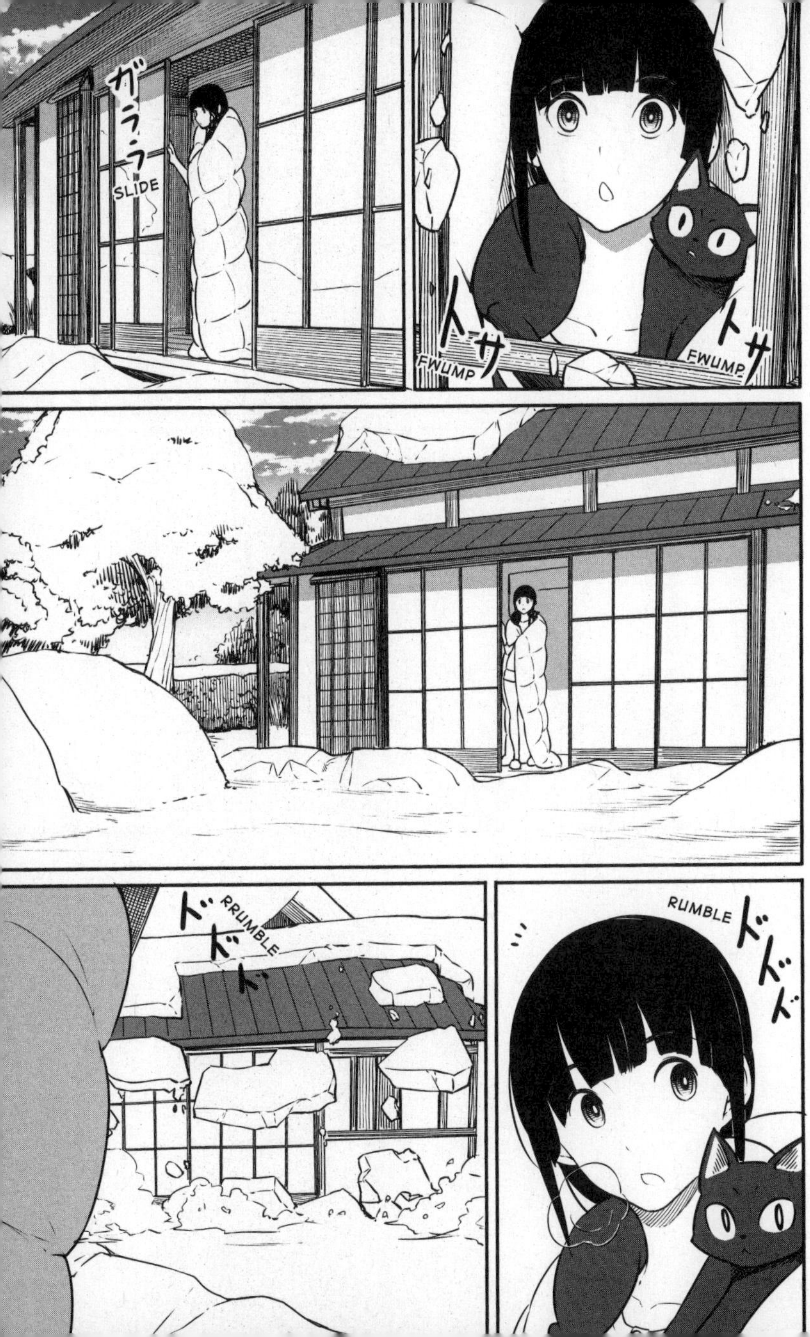
トサ
FWUMP
トサ
FWUMP
ガラ・ラ
SLIDE
ドドド
RUMBLE
…
ドドド
RRUMBLE

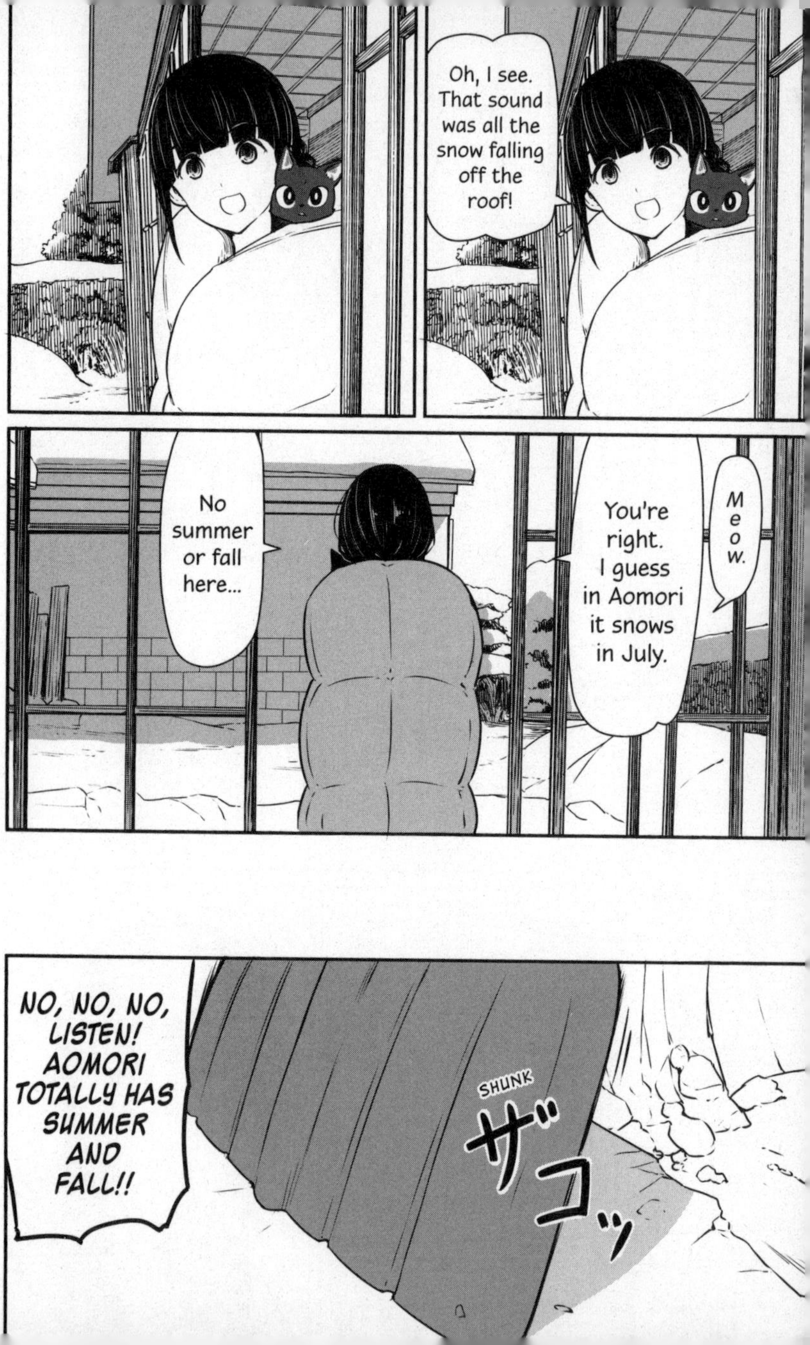
Oh, I see. That sound was all the snow falling off the roof!
Meow.
You're right. I guess in Aomori it snows in July.
No summer or fall here...
SHUNK
ザコッ
NO, NO, NO, LISTEN! AOMORI TOTALLY HAS SUMMER AND FALL!!

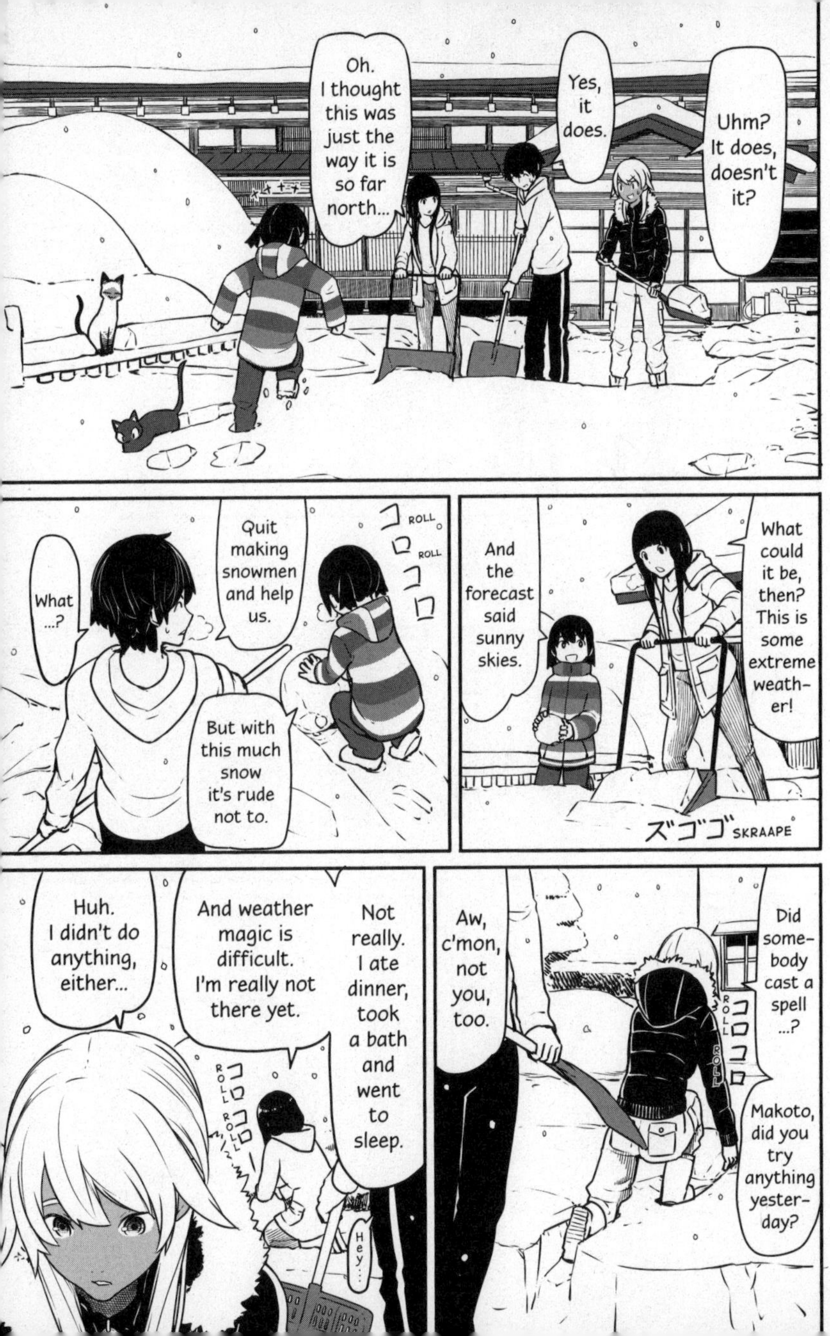

Uhm? It does, doesn't it?
Yes, it does.
Oh. I thought this was just the way it is so far north...
What could it be, then? This is some extreme weather!
And the forecast said sunny skies.
ズゴゴ SKRAAPE
コロコロ ROLL ROLL
Quit making snowmen and help us.
What ...?
But with this much snow it's rude not to.
Did somebody cast a spell ...?
Makoto, did you try anything yesterday?
コロコロ ROLL ROLL
Aw, c'mon, not you, too.
Not really. I ate dinner, took a bath and went to sleep.
And weather magic is difficult. I'm really not there yet.
Huh. I didn't do anything, either...
コロコロ ROLL ROLL
Hey...

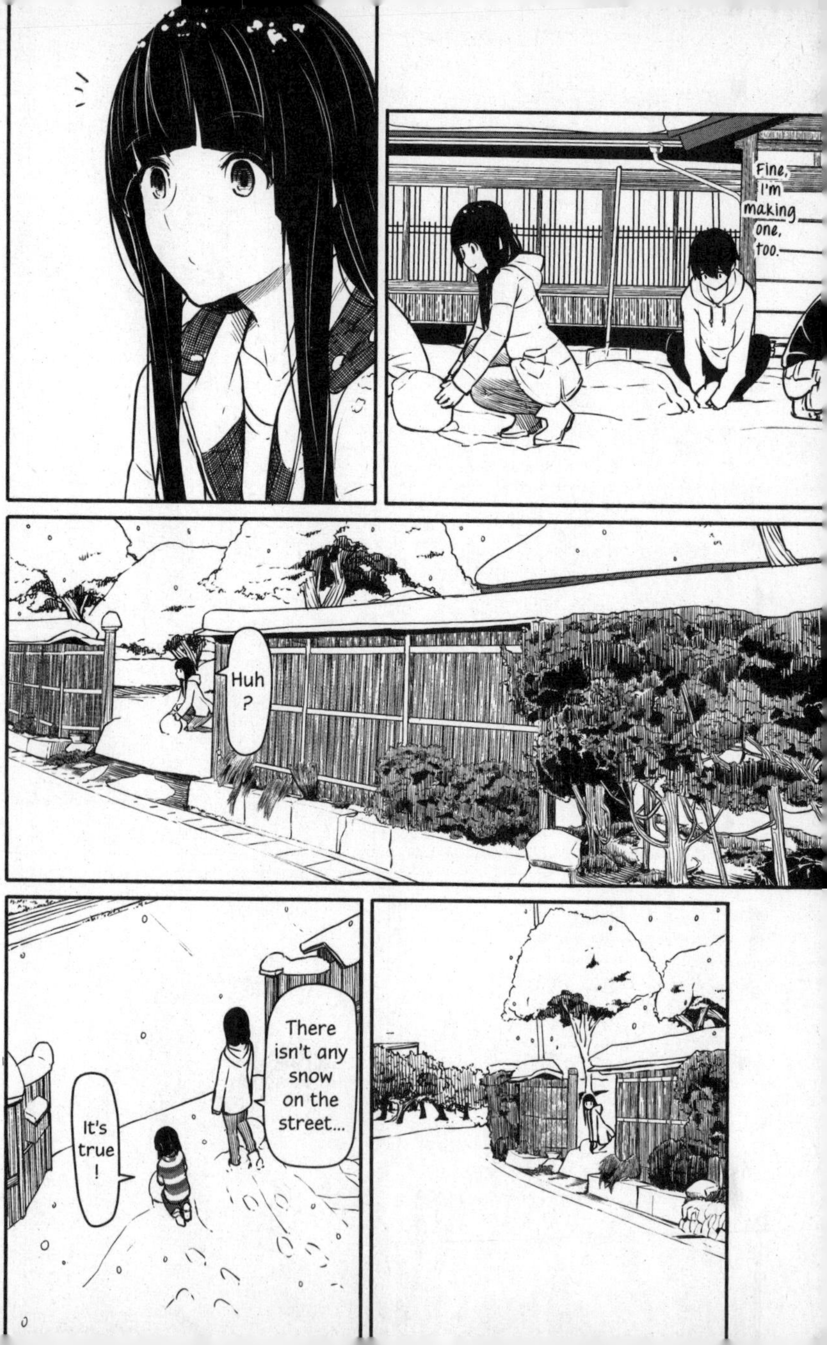
Fine, I'm making one, too.
Huh?
There isn't any snow on the street...
It's true!

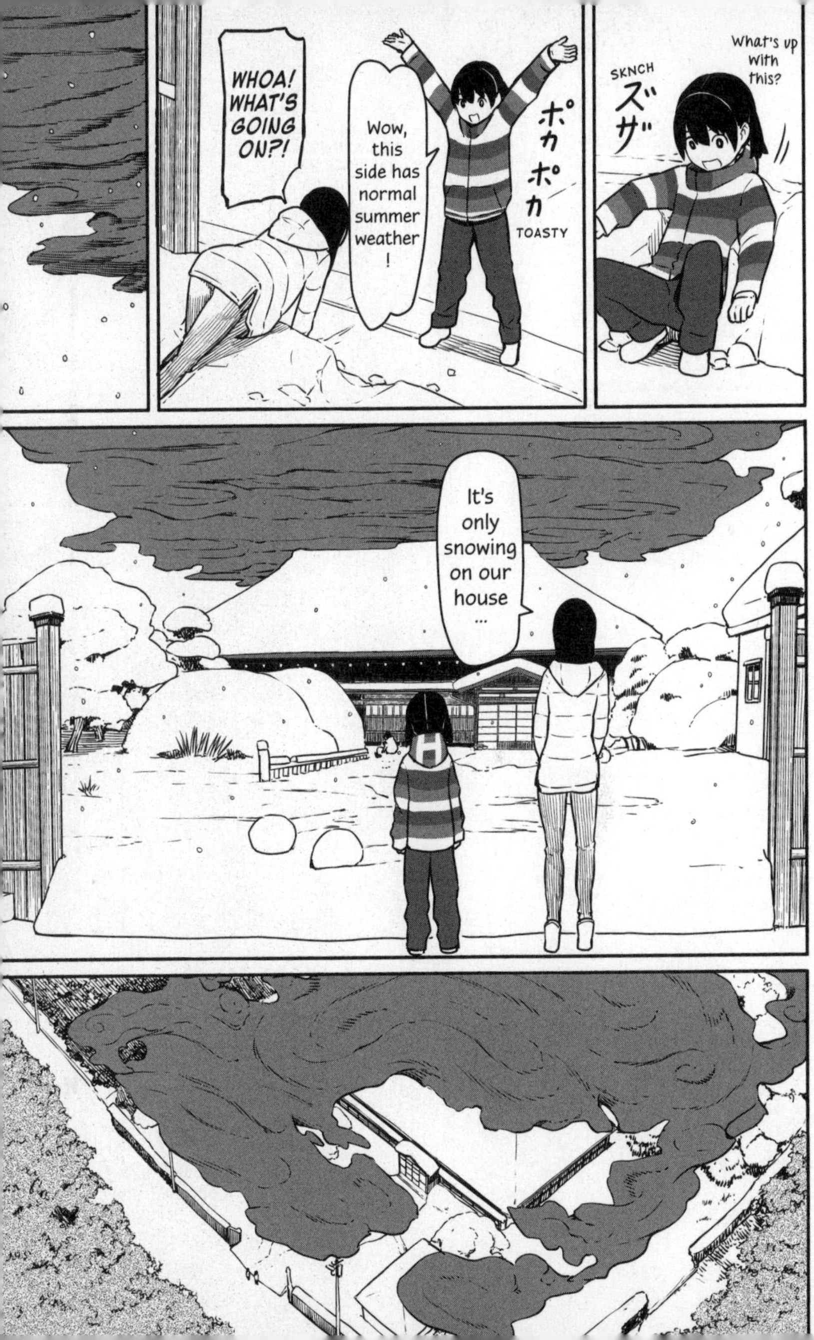
What's up with this?
SKNCH
ズザ
Wow, this side has normal summer weather!
ポカポカ
TOASTY
WHOA! WHAT'S GOING ON?!
It's only snowing on our house...

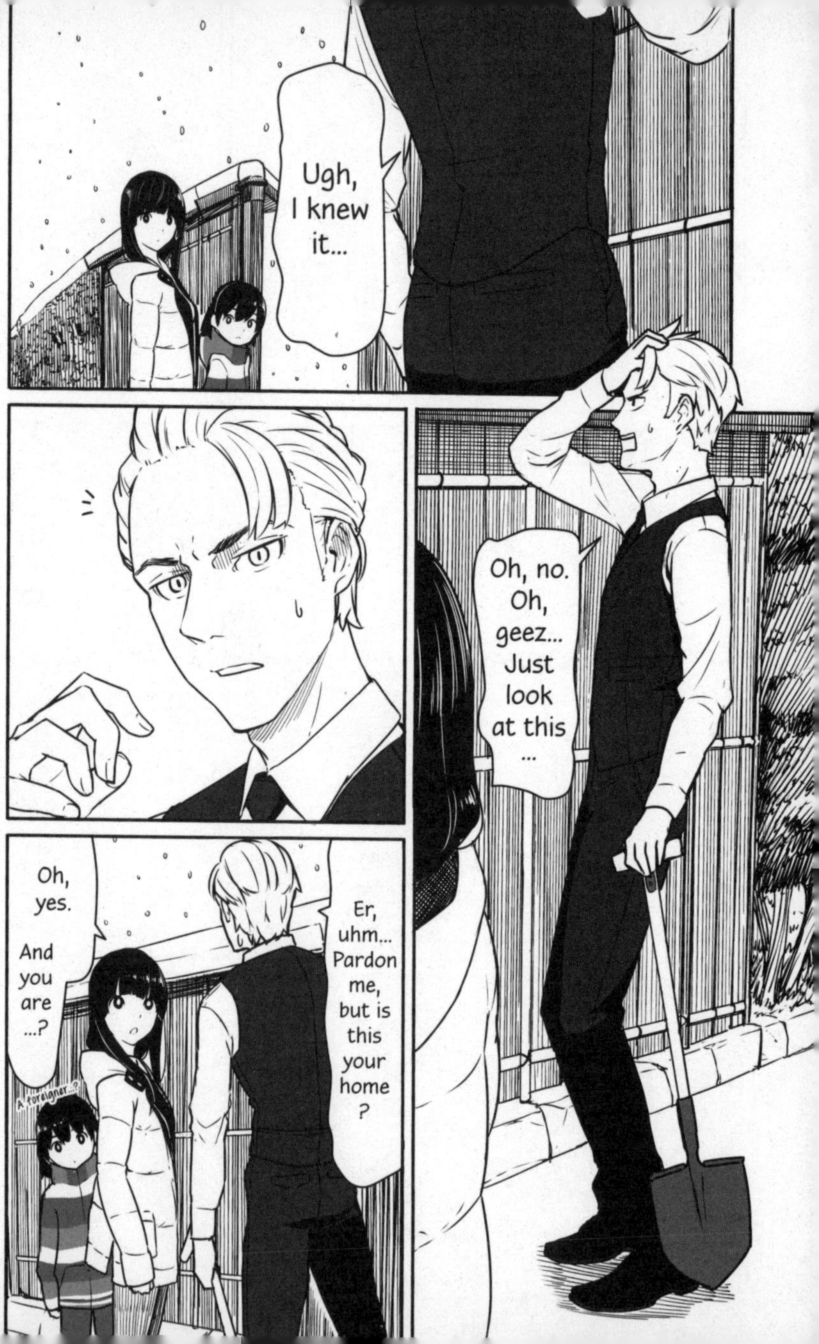
Ugh, I knew it...
Oh, no. Oh, geez... Just look at this ...
Er, uhm... Pardon me, but is this your home ?
Oh, yes.
And you are ...?
A foreigner...?

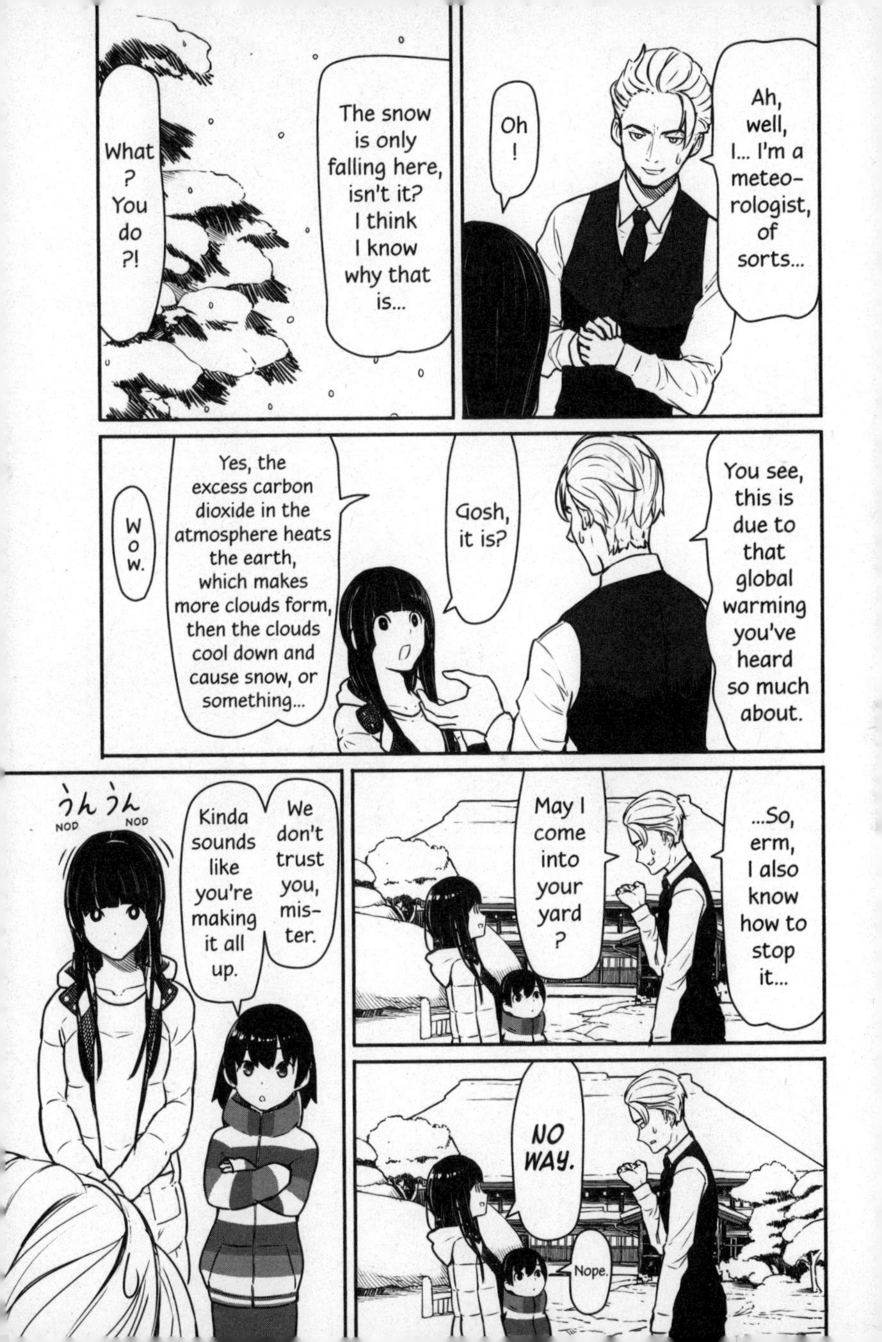
Ah, well, I... I'm a meteorologist, of sorts...
Oh!
The snow is only falling here, isn't it? I think I know why that is...
What? You do?!
You see, this is due to that global warming you've heard so much about.
Gosh, it is?
Yes, the excess carbon dioxide in the atmosphere heats the earth, which makes more clouds form, then the clouds cool down and cause snow, or something...
Wow.
...So, erm, I also know how to stop it...
May I come into your yard?
NO WAY.
Nope.
We don't trust you, mister.
Kinda sounds like you're making it all up.
うんうん
NOD NOD

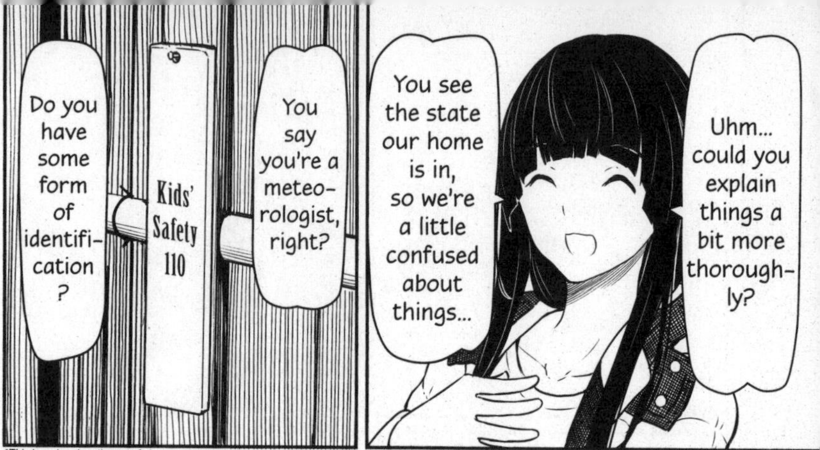
Uhm... could you explain things a bit more thoroughly?
You see the state our home is in, so we're a little confused about things...
You say you're a meteorologist, right?
Kids' Safety 110
Do you have some form of identification?

*This is a sign denoting a safe house where kids who are in danger can enter and call 110 (Japan's 911).

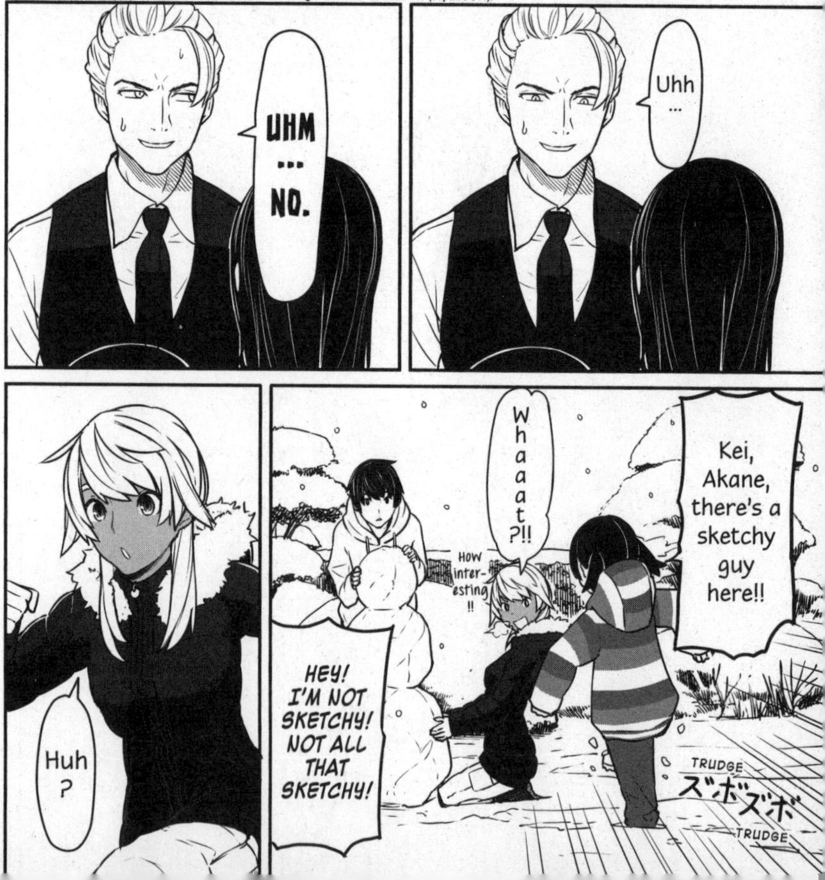
Uhh ...
UHM ... NO.
Kei, Akane, there's a sketchy guy here!!
Whaaaat?!!
HOW interesting !!
HEY! I'M NOT SKETCHY! NOT ALL THAT SKETCHY!
TRUDGE
ズボズボ
TRUDGE
Huh?

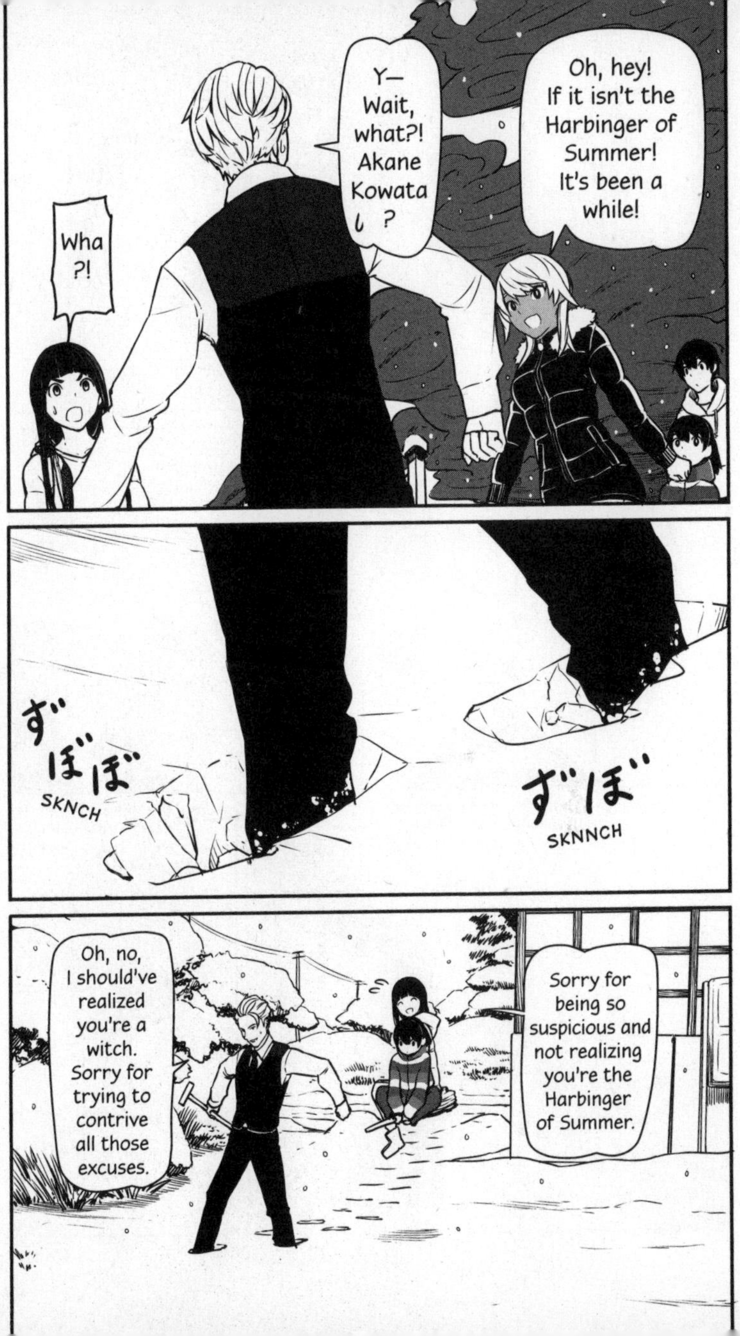
Oh, hey! If it isn't the Harbinger of Summer! It's been a while!
Y— Wait, what?! Akane Kowata し ?
Wha ?!
ずぼ
SKNNCH
ずぼぼ
SKNCH
Sorry for being so suspicious and not realizing you're the Harbinger of Summer.
Oh, no, I should've realized you're a witch. Sorry for trying to contrive all those excuses.

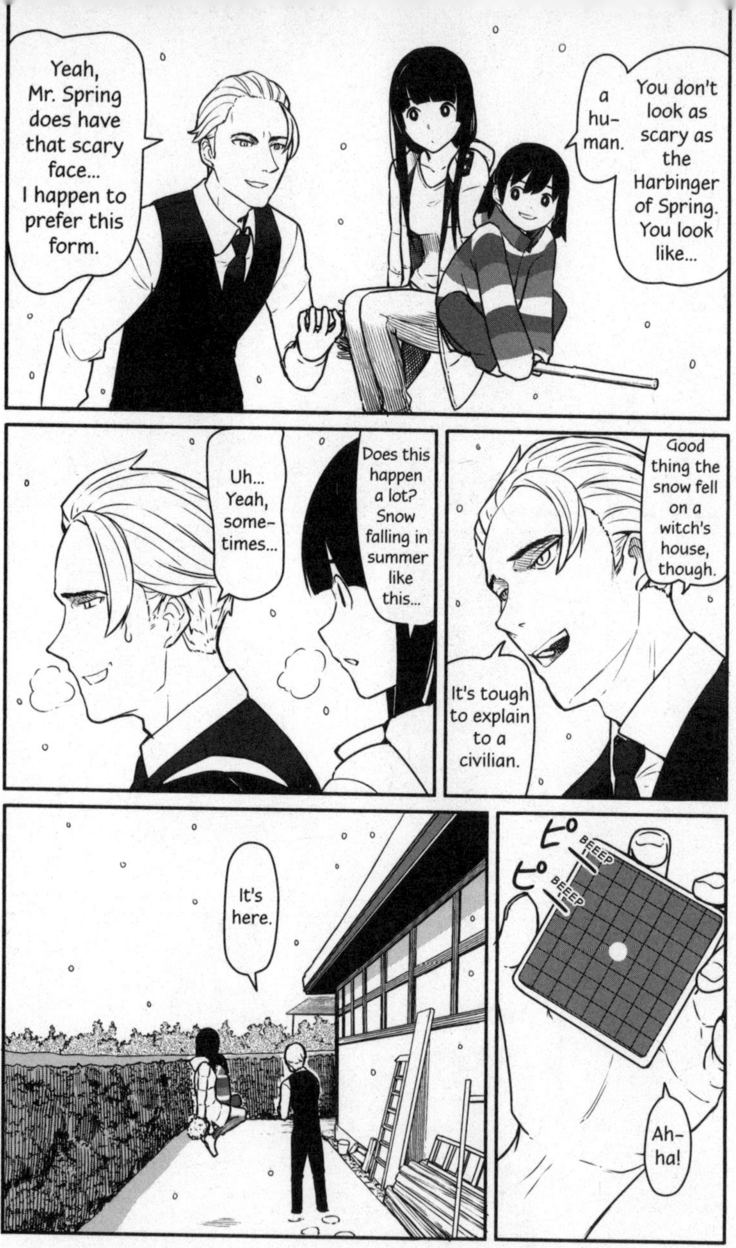
You don't look as scary as the Harbinger of Spring. You look like...
a human.
Yeah, Mr. Spring does have that scary face... I happen to prefer this form.
Good thing the snow fell on a witch's house, though.
It's tough to explain to a civilian.
Does this happen a lot? Snow falling in summer like this...
Uh... Yeah, sometimes...
ピ BEEEP
ピ BEEEP
Ah-ha!
It's here.

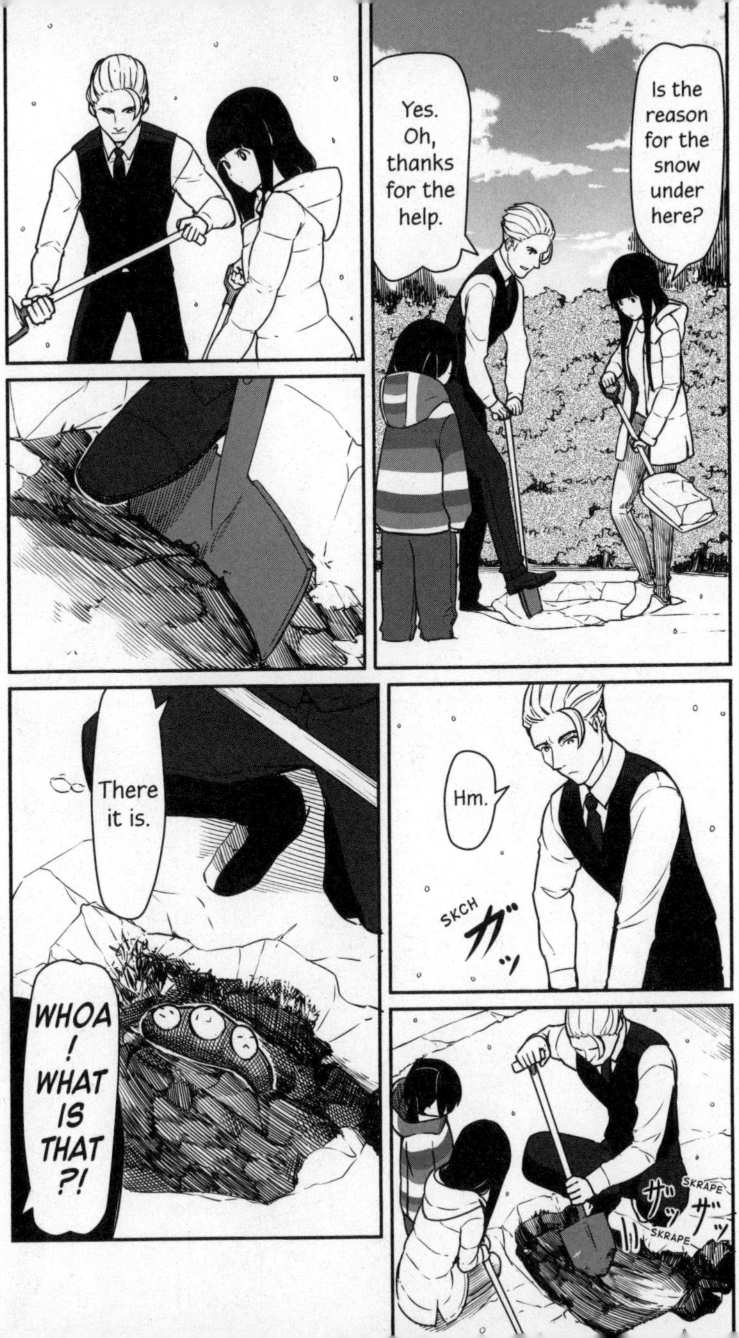
Is the reason for the snow under here?
Yes. Oh, thanks for the help.
Hm.
SKCH
ガッ
ザッ
SKRAPE
ザッ
SKRAPE
There it is.
WHOA! WHAT IS THAT?!

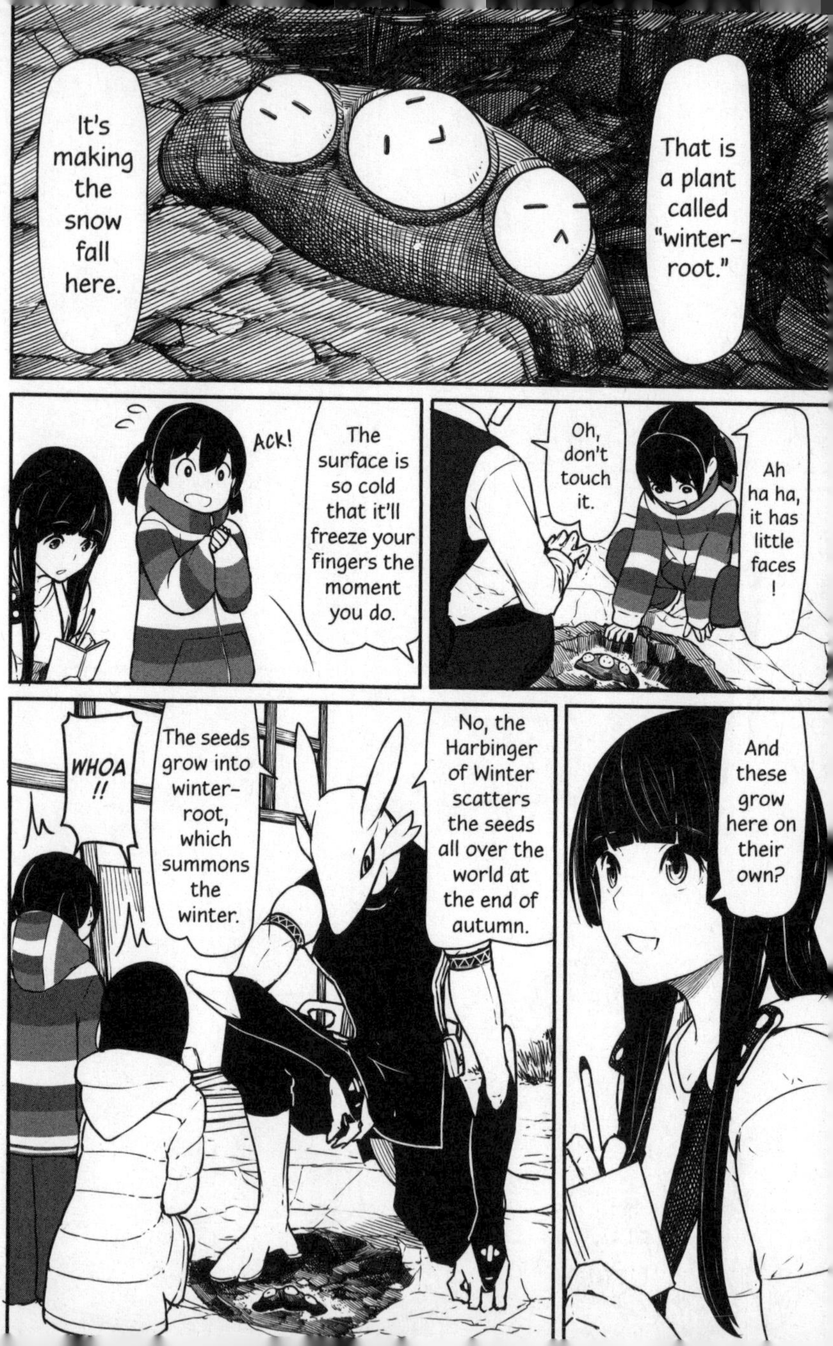

That is a plant called "winter-root."
It's making the snow fall here.
Ah ha ha, it has little faces!
Oh, don't touch it.
The surface is so cold that it'll freeze your fingers the moment you do.
ACK!
And these grow here on their own?
No, the Harbinger of Winter scatters the seeds all over the world at the end of autumn.
The seeds grow into winter-root, which summons the winter.
WHOA!!

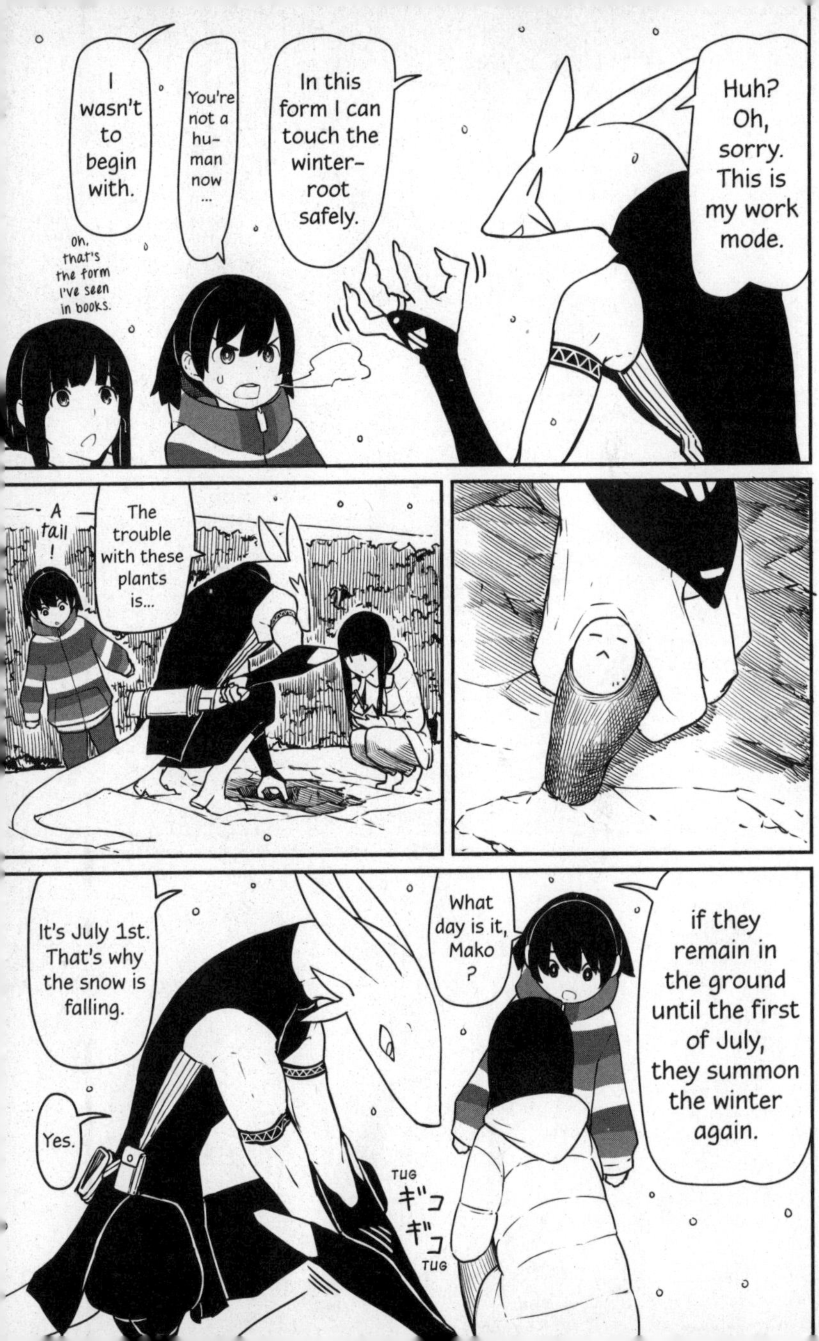
Huh? Oh, sorry. This is my work mode.
In this form I can touch the winter-root safely.
You're not a human now...
I wasn't to begin with.
Oh, that's the form I've seen in books.
The trouble with these plants is...
A tail!
if they remain in the ground until the first of July, they summon the winter again.
What day is it, Mako?
It's July 1st. That's why the snow is falling.
Yes.
TUG ギコ
ギコ TUG

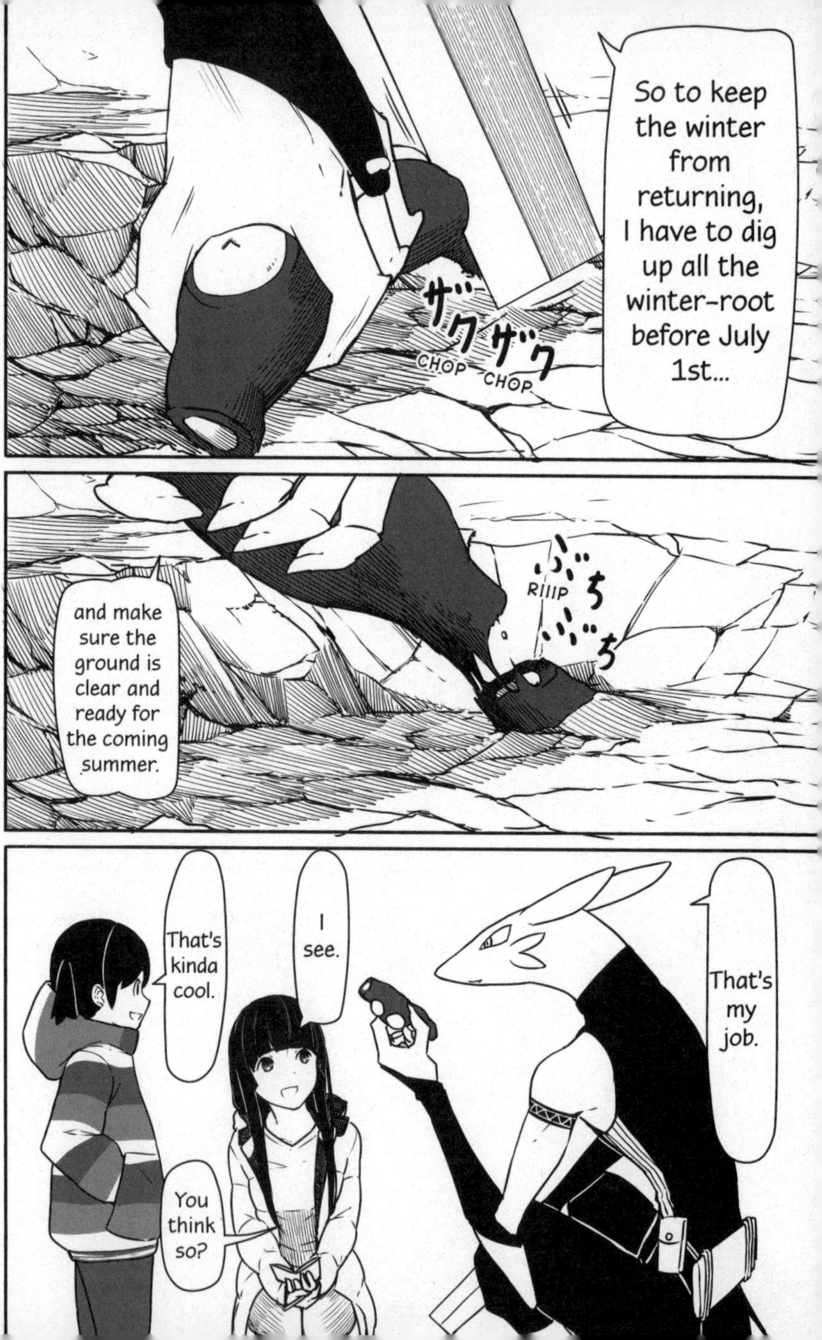
So to keep the winter from returning, I have to dig up all the winter-root before July 1st...
ザクザク
CHOP CHOP
ぶちぶち
RIIIP
and make sure the ground is clear and ready for the coming summer.
That's my job.
I see.
That's kinda cool.
You think so?

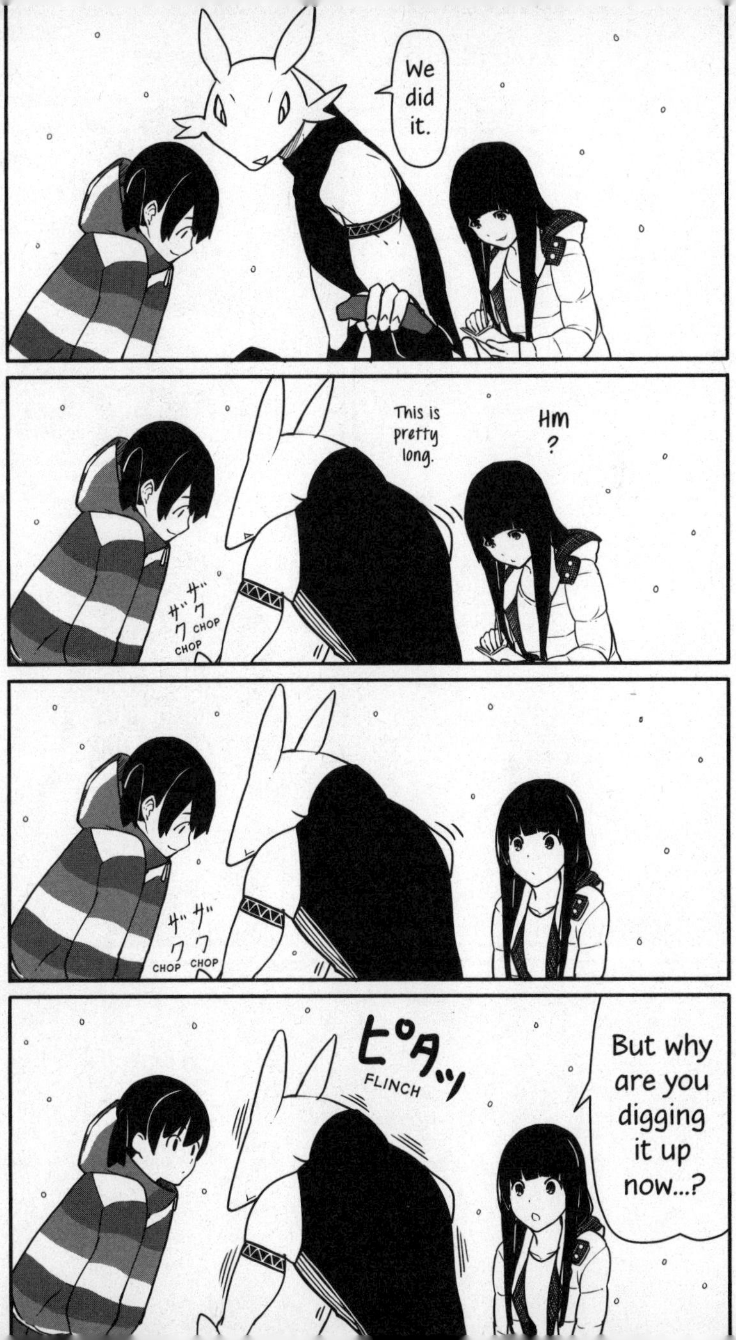
We did it.
Hm?
This is pretty long.
ザクザク
CHOP CHOP
ザクザク
CHOP CHOP
But why are you digging it up now...?
ピタッ
FLINCH

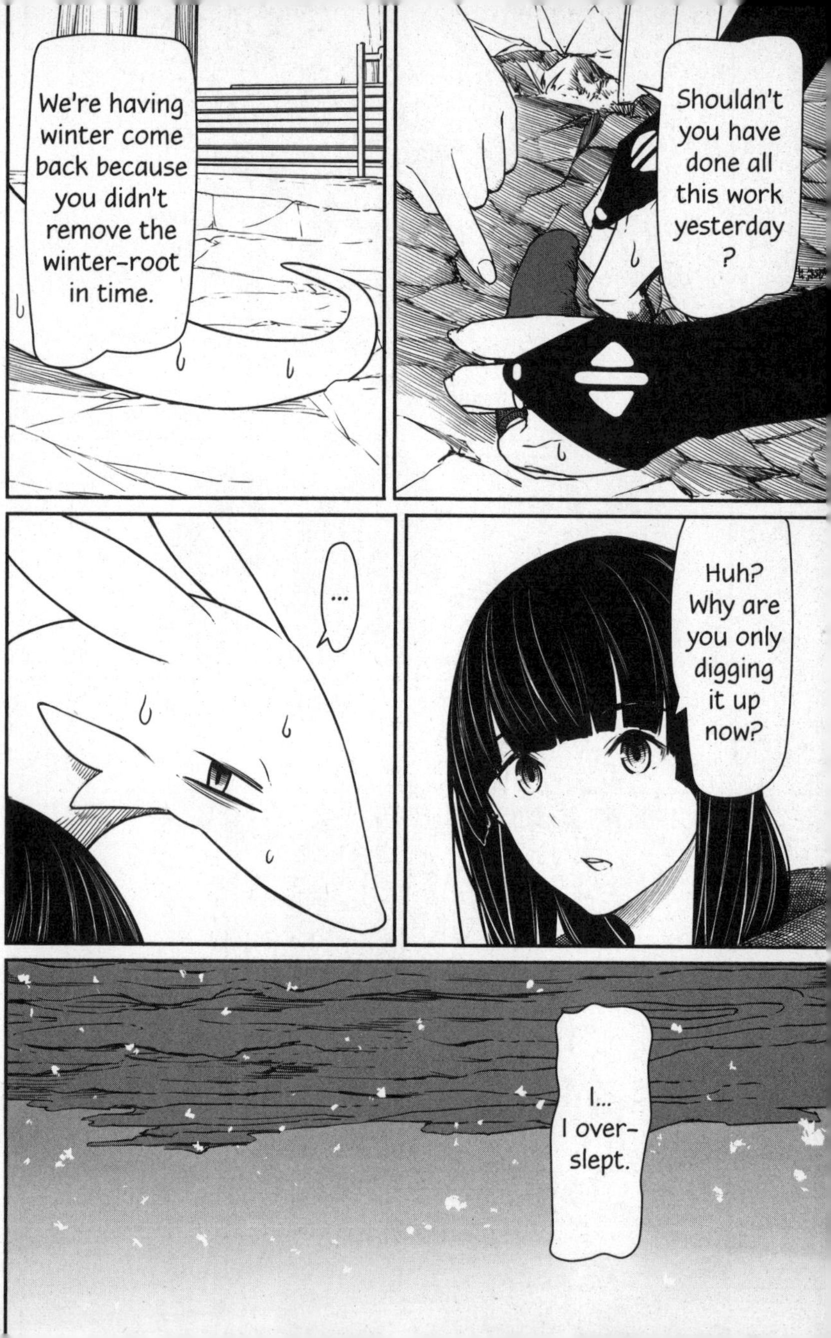
Shouldn't you have done all this work yesterday?
We're having winter come back because you didn't remove the winter-root in time.
Huh? Why are you only digging it up now?
...
I... I over-slept.

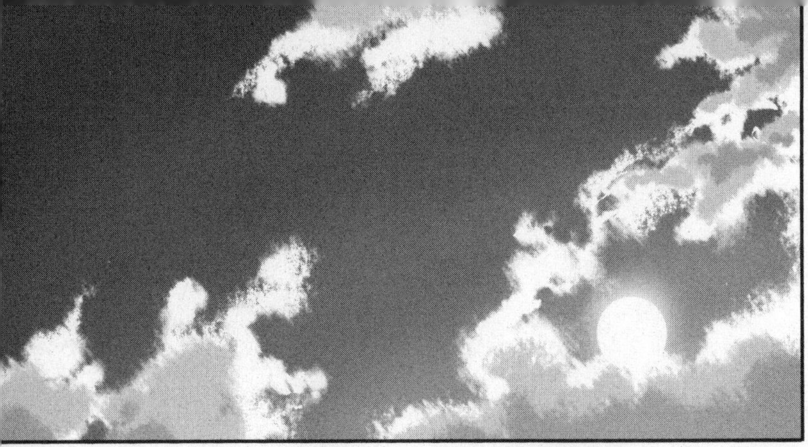

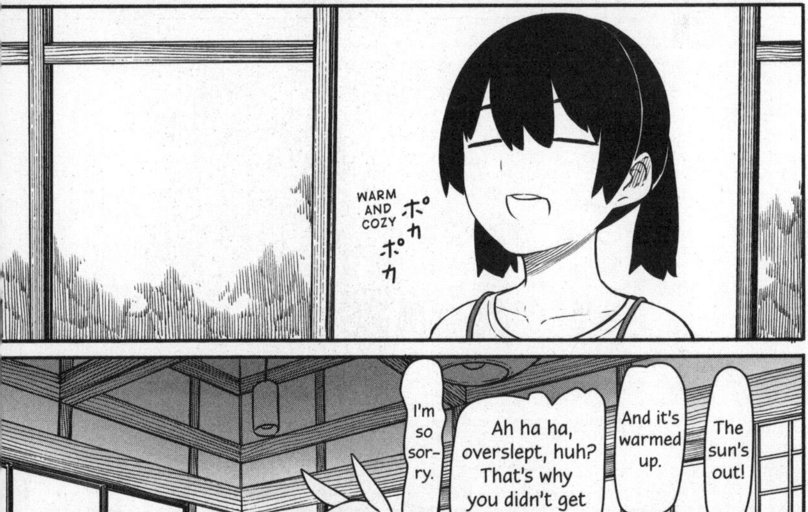
WARM AND COZY
ポカポカ

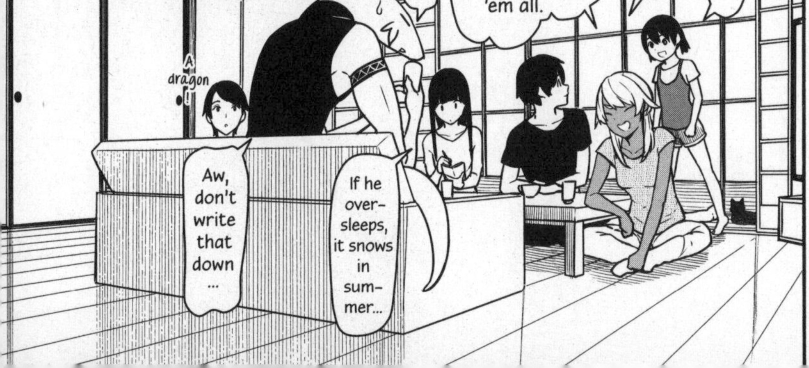
The sun's out!
And it's warmed up.
Ah ha ha, overslept, huh? That's why you didn't get 'em all.
I'm so sor-ry.
A dragon!
If he over-sleeps, it snows in summ-mer...
Aw, don't write that down ...

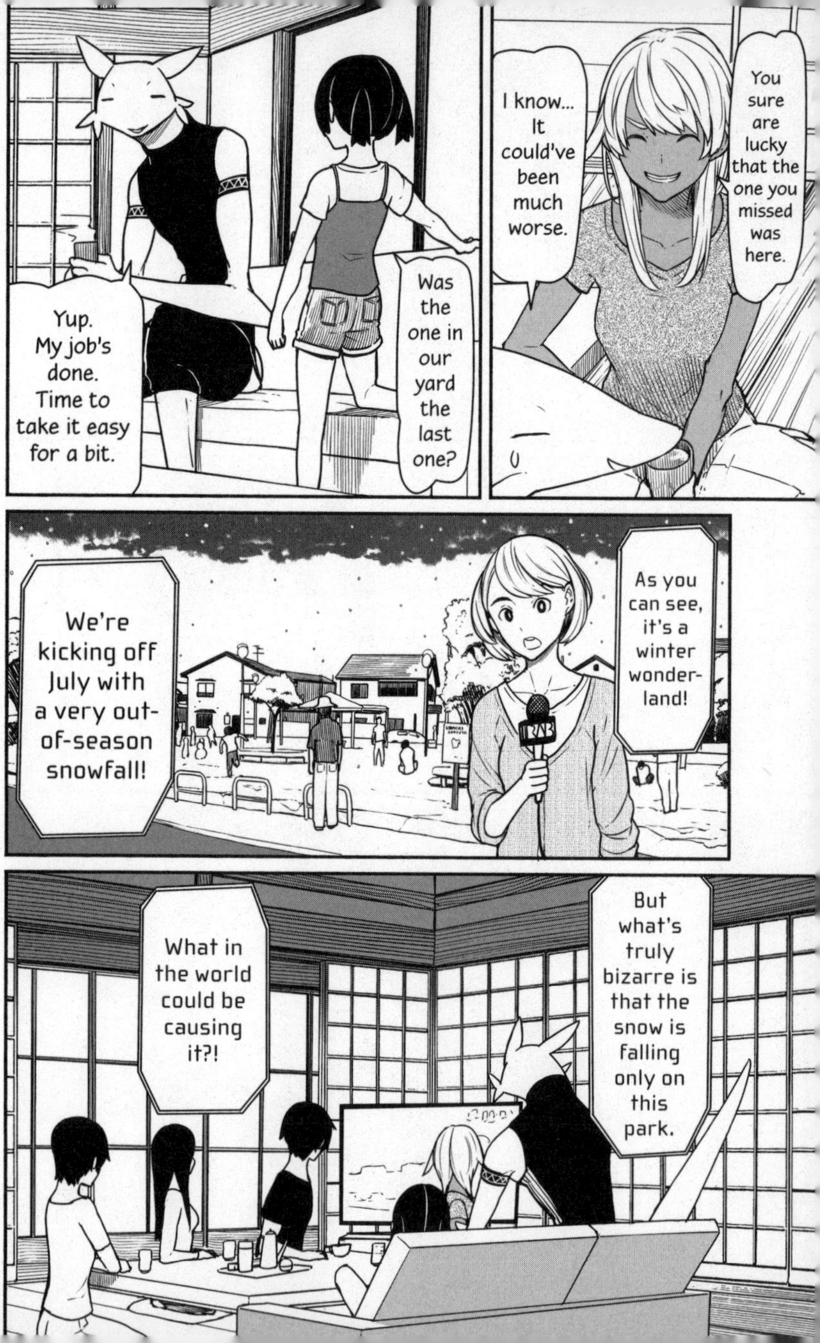
You sure are lucky that the one you missed was here.
I know... It could've been much worse.
Was the one in our yard the last one?
Yup. My job's done. Time to take it easy for a bit.
As you can see, it's a winter wonderland!
We're kicking off July with a very out-of-season snowfall!
But what's truly bizarre is that the snow is falling only on this park.
What in the world could be causing it?!

Flying
Witch

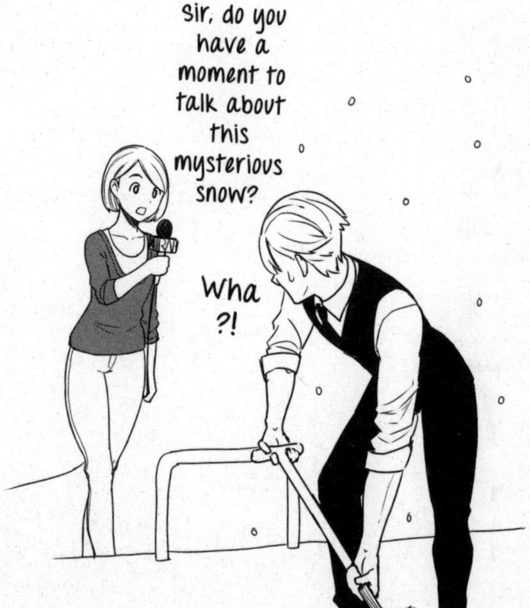
Sir, do you have a moment to talk about this mysterious snow?
Wha ?!

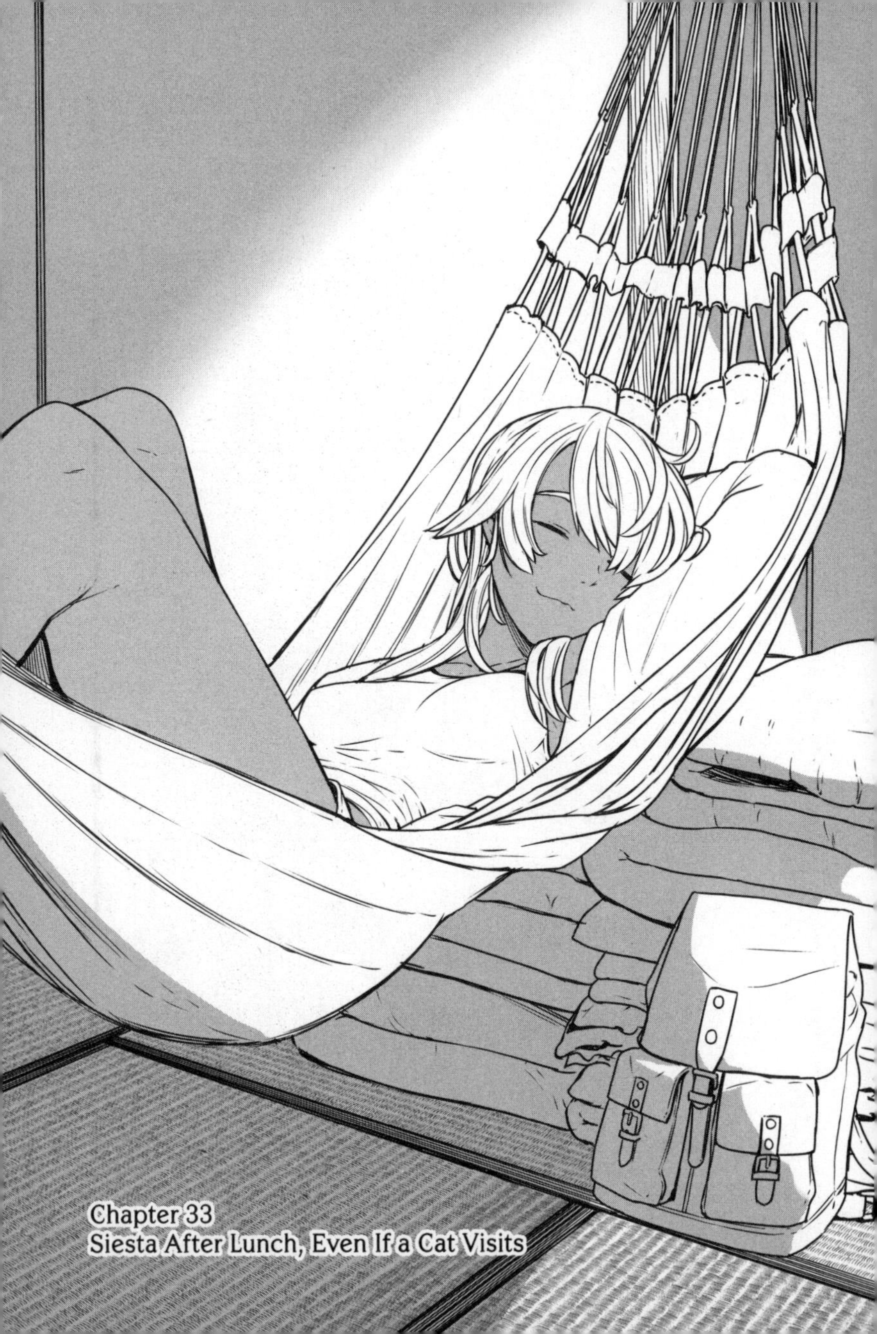

Chapter 33
Siesta After Lunch, Even If a Cat Visits

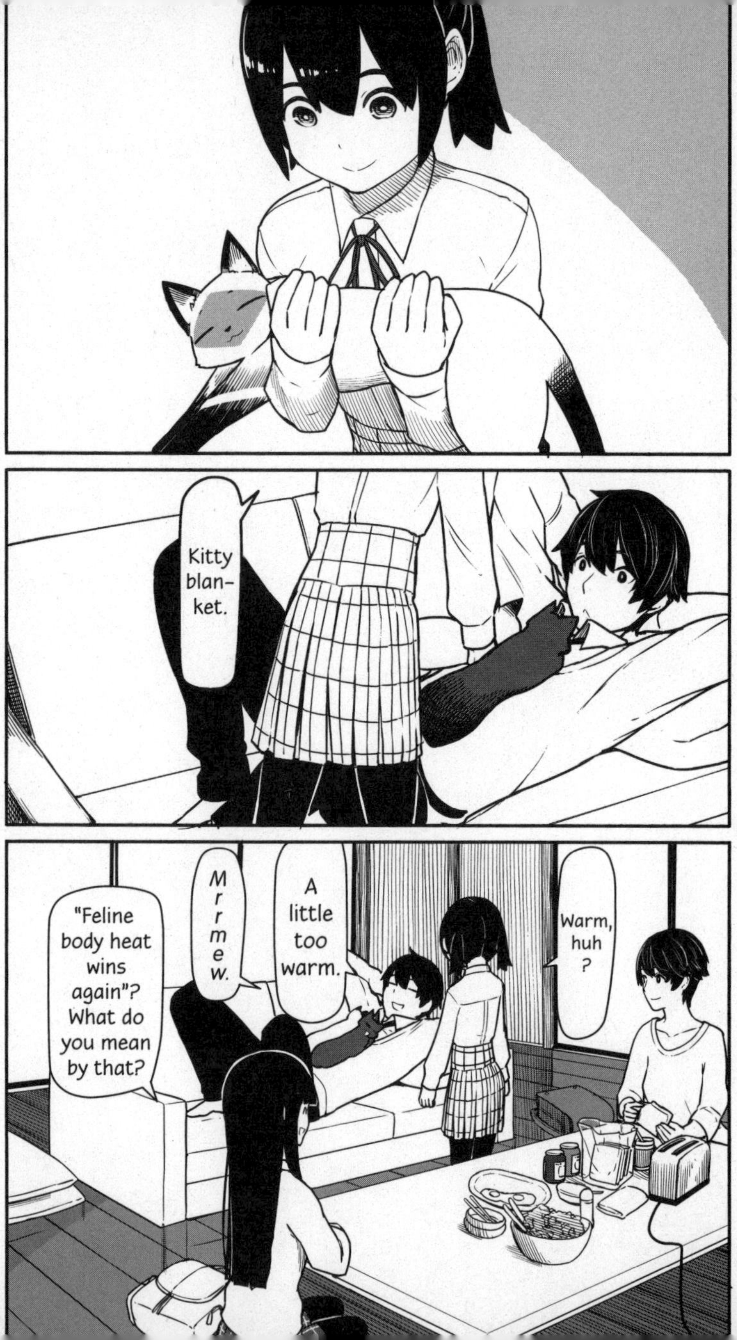
Kitty blan-ket.
Warm, huh?
A little too warm.
Mrrmew.
"Feline body heat wins again"? What do you mean by that?

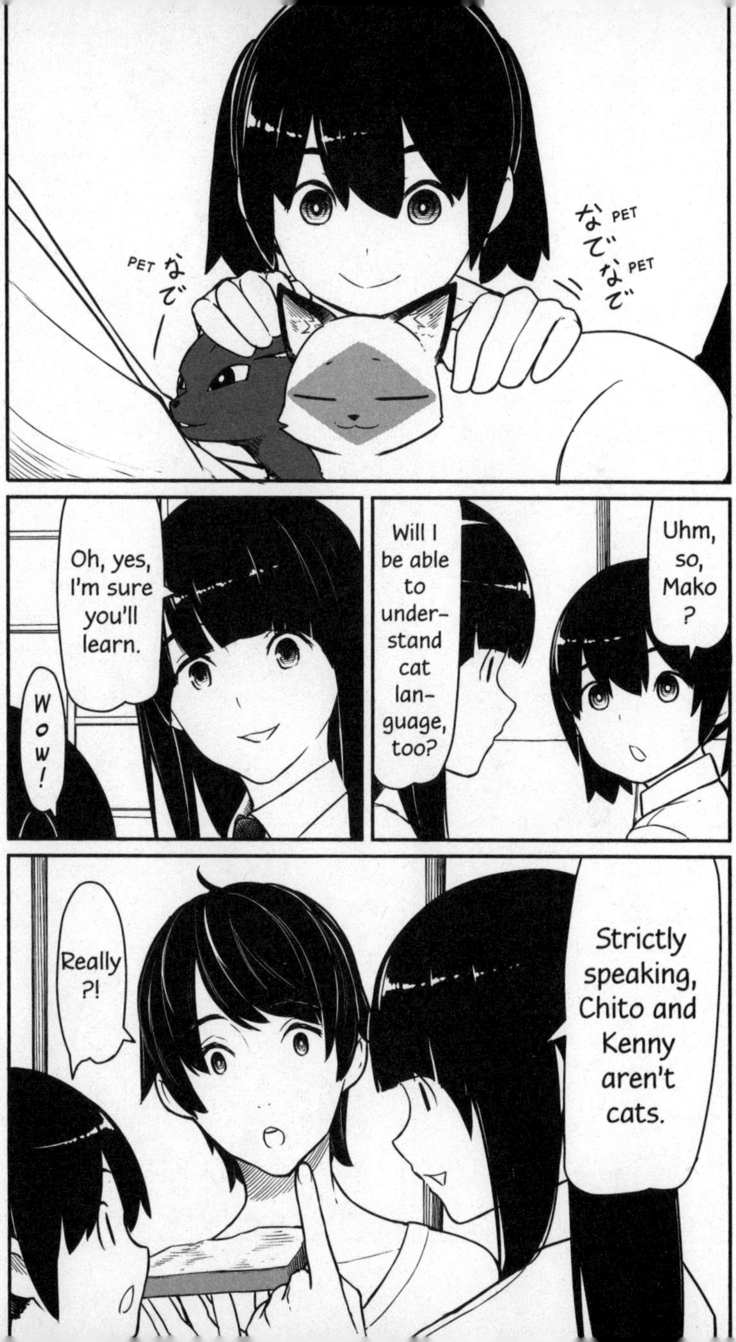
なでなで
PET PET
なで
PET
Uhm, so, Mako?
Will I be able to understand cat language, too?
Oh, yes, I'm sure you'll learn.
Wow!
Strictly speaking, Chito and Kenny aren't cats.
Really?!

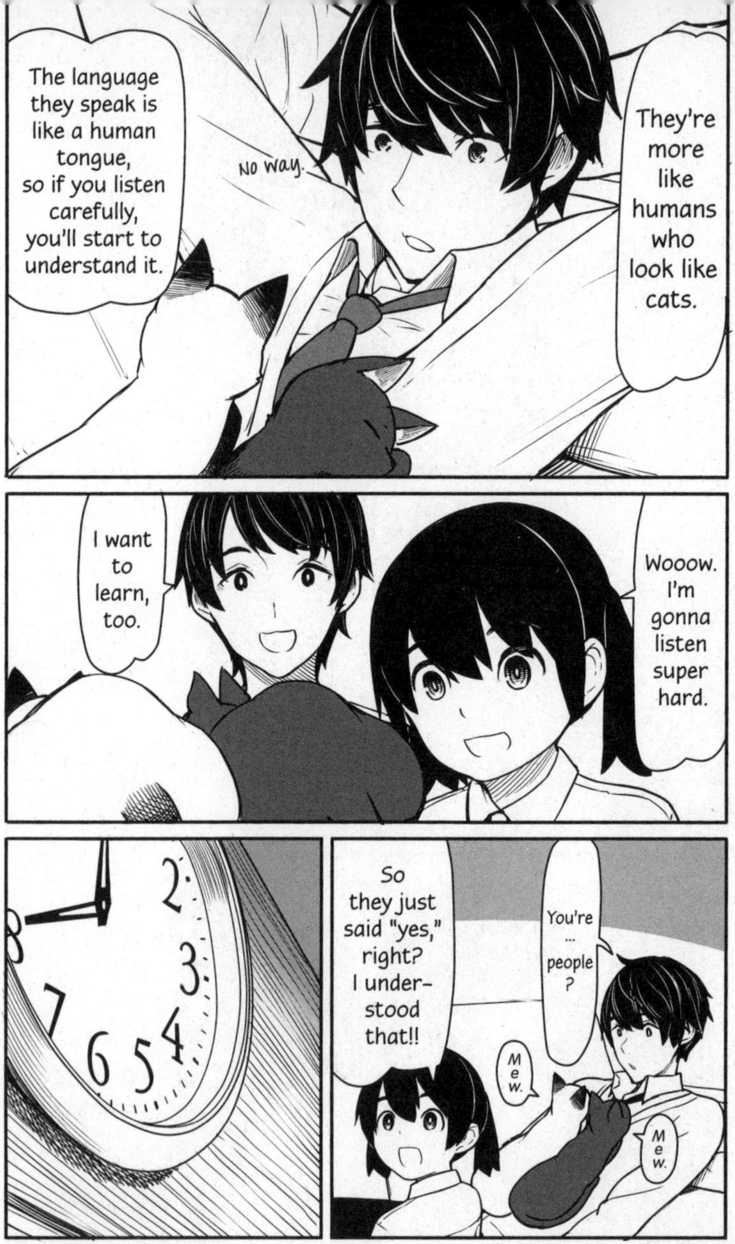
They're more like humans who look like cats.
No way.
The language they speak is like a human tongue, so if you listen carefully, you'll start to understand it.
Wooow. I'm gonna listen super hard.
I want to learn, too.
You're ... people?
Mew.
Mew.
So they just said "yes," right? I under-stood that!!

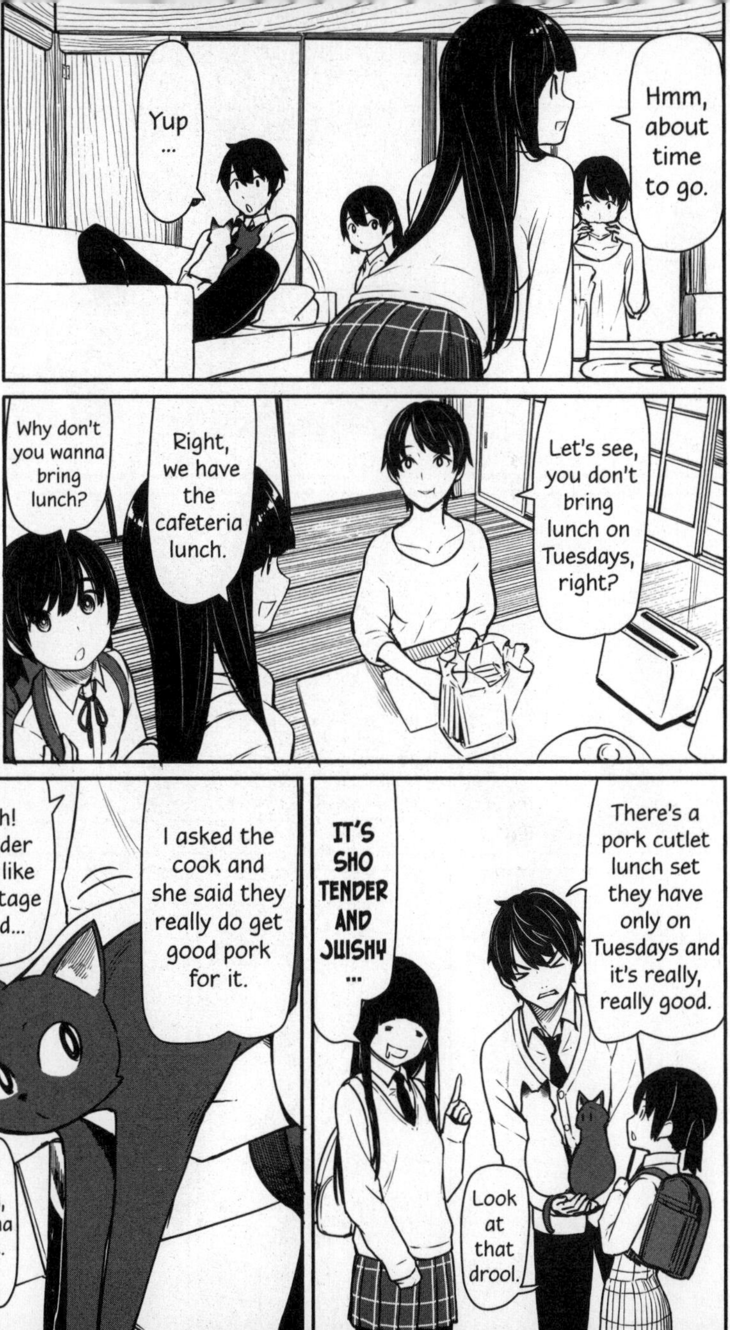

Hmm, about time to go.
Yup ...
Let's see, you don't bring lunch on Tuesdays, right?
Right, we have the cafeteria lunch.
Why don't you wanna bring lunch?
There's a pork cutlet lunch set they have only on Tuesdays and it's really, really good.
IT'S SHO TENDER AND JUISHY ...
Look at that drool.
I asked the cook and she said they really do get good pork for it.
Yeah! I wonder if it's like a heritage breed...
Whoa, I wanna try it.

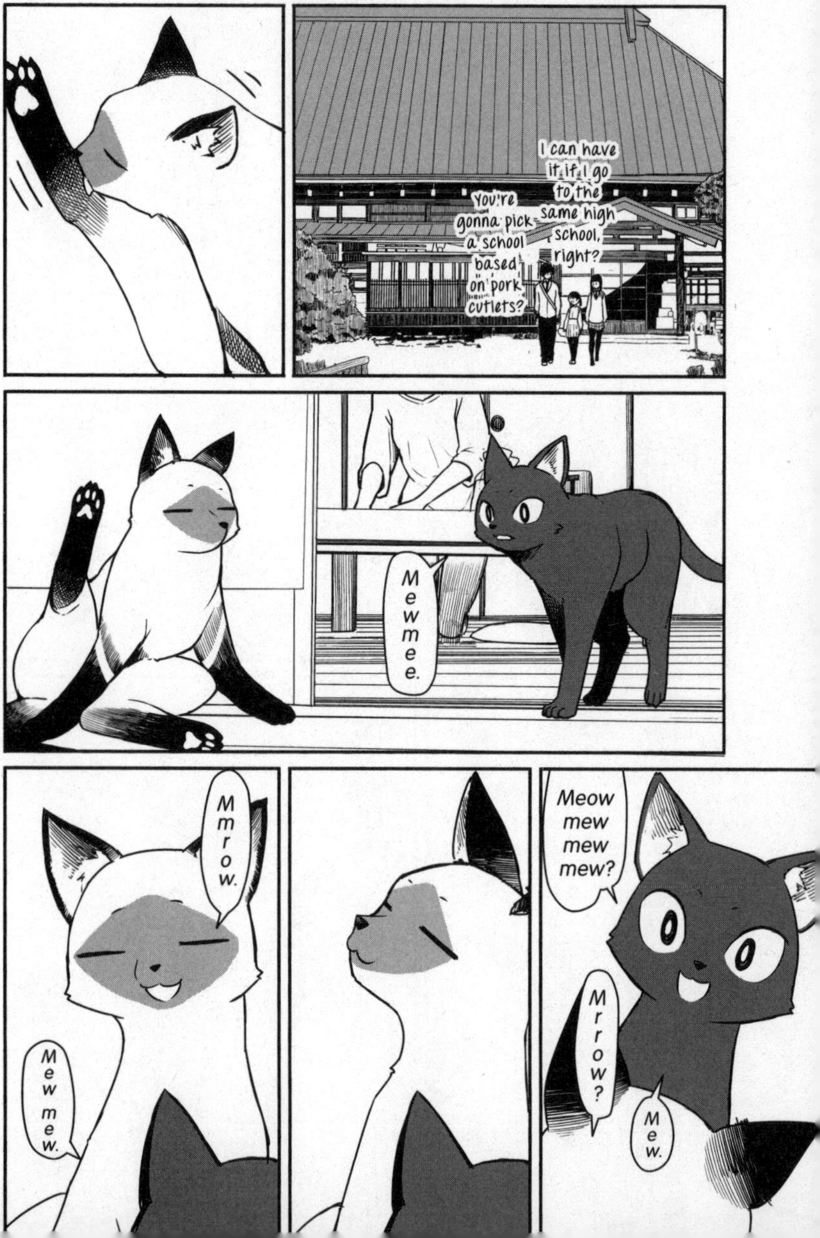
I can have it if I go to the same high school, right?
You're gonna pick a school based on pork cutlets?
Mewmee.
Meow mew mew mew?
Mrrow?
Mew.
Mmrow.
Mew mew.

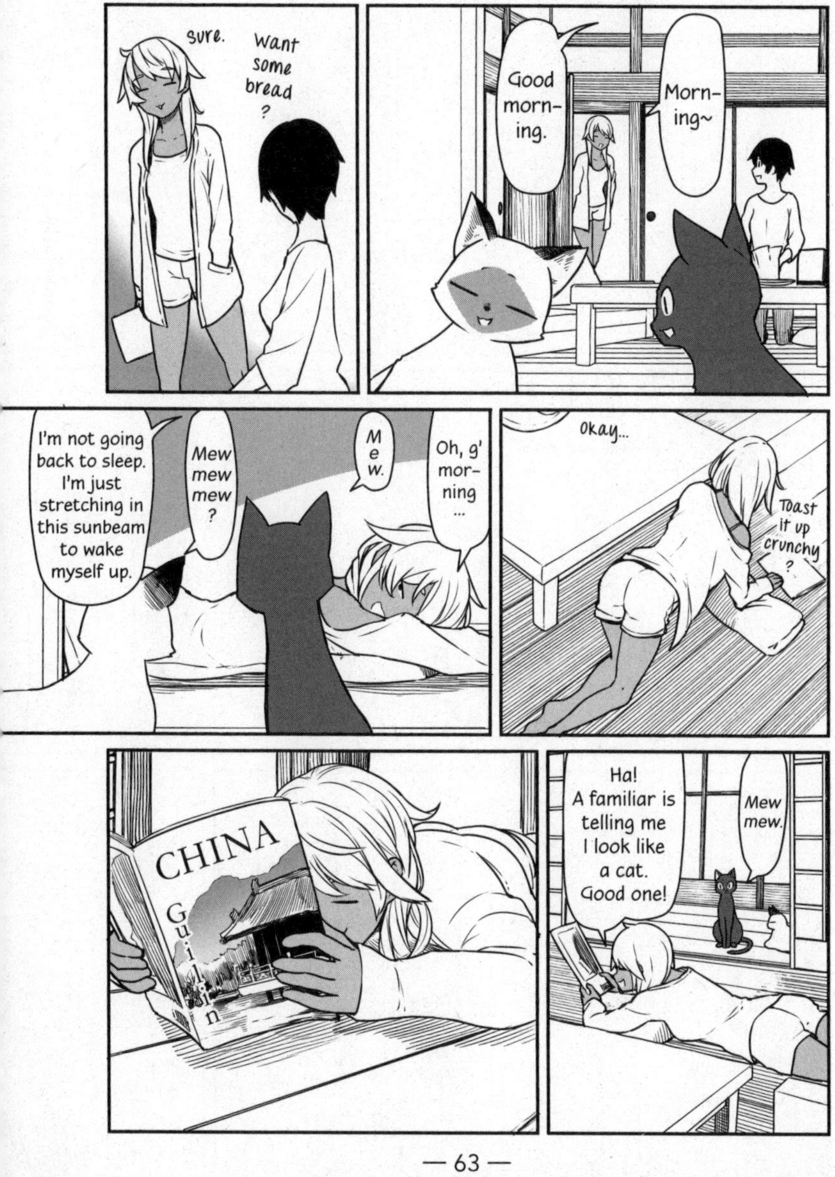
Morn-ing~
Good morn-ing.
Want some bread?
Sure.
Toast it up crunchy?
Okay...
Oh, g' mor-ning...
Mew.
Mew mew mew?
I'm not going back to sleep. I'm just stretching in this sunbeam to wake myself up.
Mew mew.
Ha! A familiar is telling me I look like a cat. Good one!
CHINA
Guilin

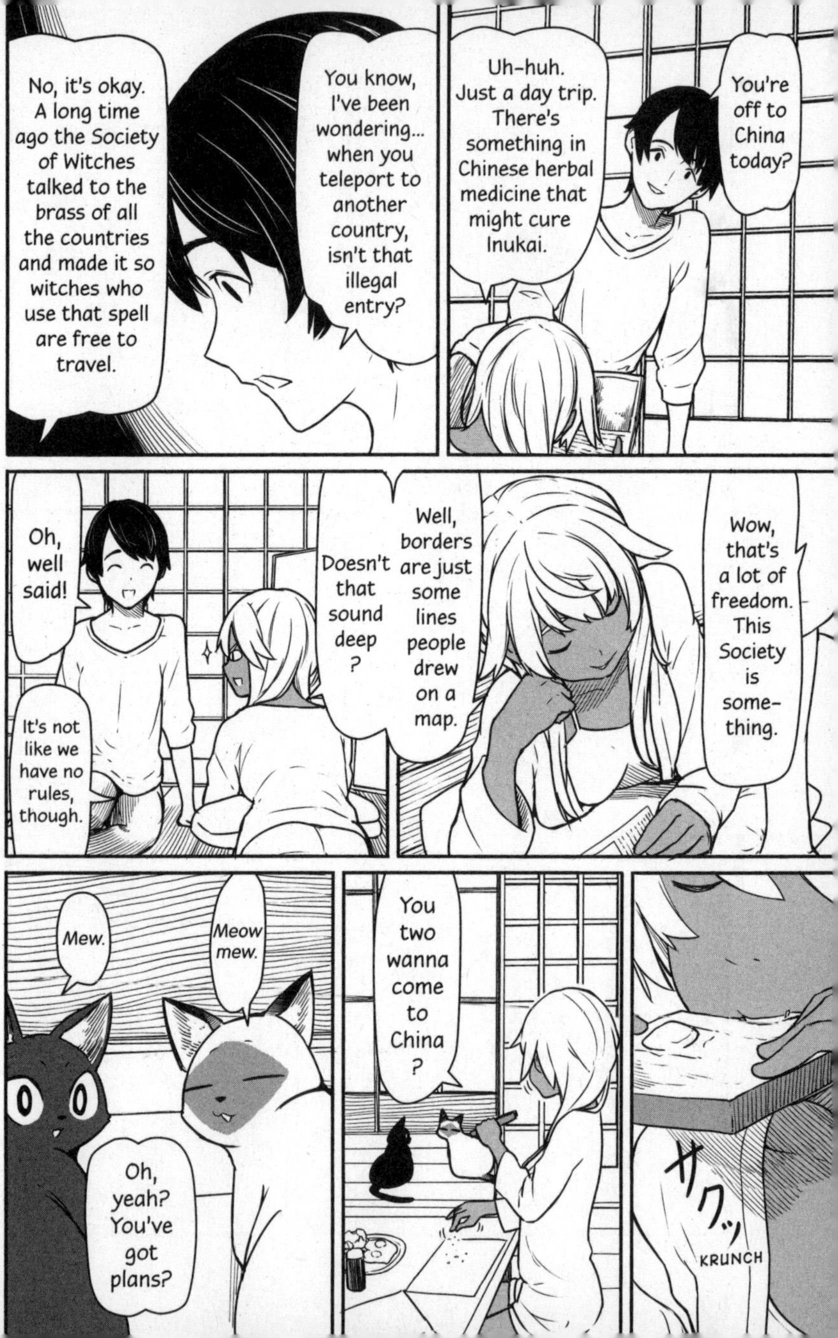
You're off to China today?
Uh-huh. Just a day trip. There's something in Chinese herbal medicine that might cure Inukai.
You know, I've been wondering... when you teleport to another country, isn't that illegal entry?
No, it's okay. A long time ago the Society of Witches talked to the brass of all the countries and made it so witches who use that spell are free to travel.
Wow, that's a lot of freedom. This Society is some-thing.
Well, borders are just some lines people drew on a map.
Doesn't that sound deep?
Oh, well said!
It's not like we have no rules, though.
サクッ
KRUNCH
You two wanna come to China?
Meow mew.
Mew.
Oh, yeah? You've got plans?

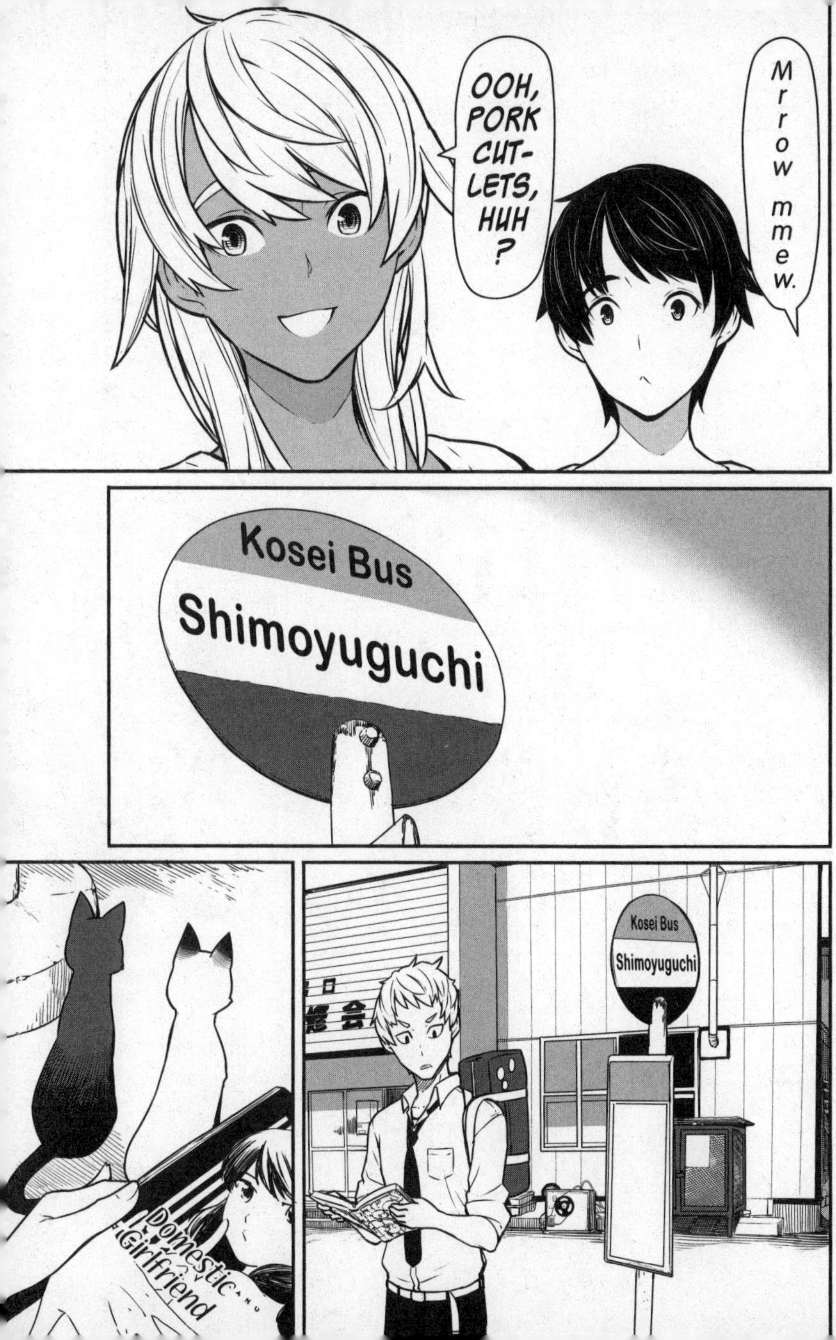
Mrrow mmew.
OOH, PORK CUT-LETS, HUH?
Kosei Bus
Shimoyuguchi
Kosei Bus
Shimoyuguchi
Domestic
Girlfriend

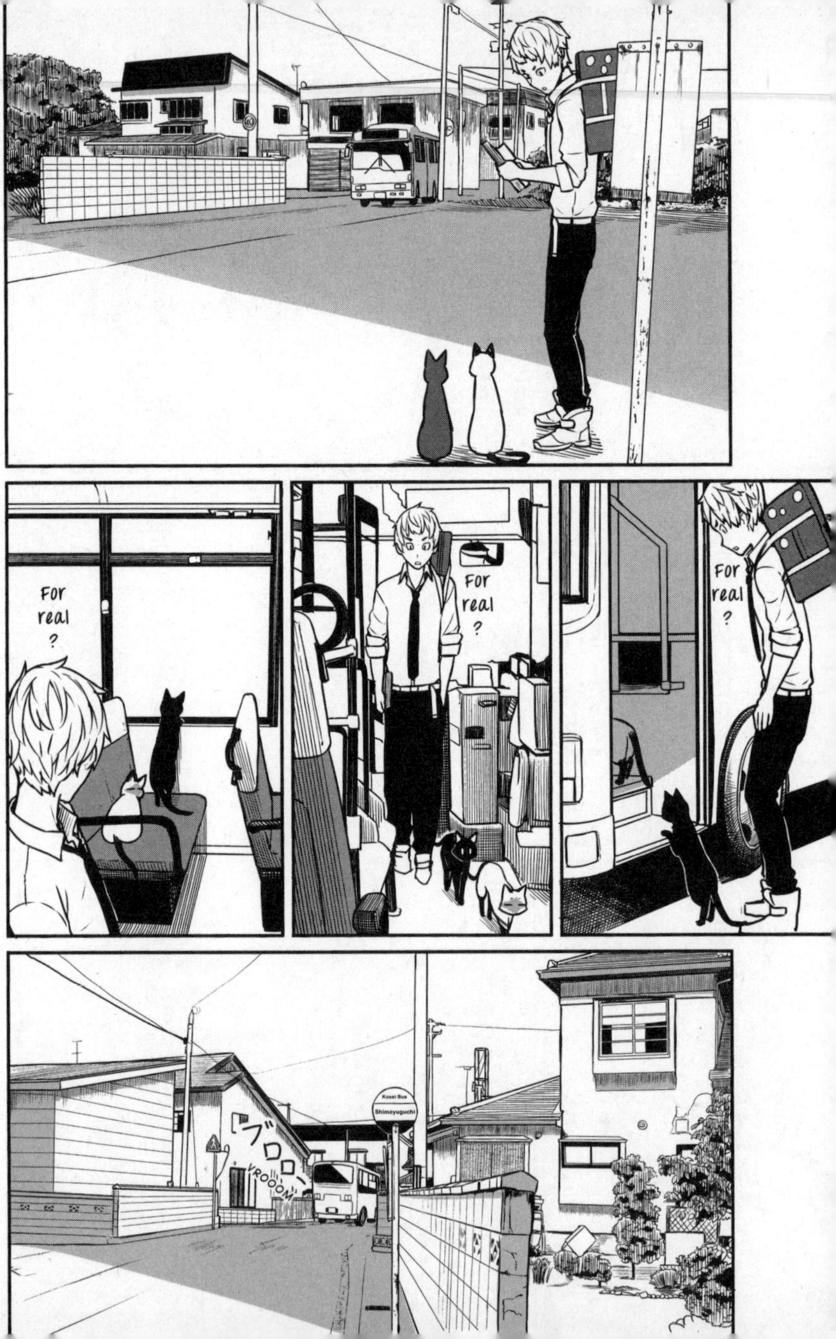
For real?
For real?
For real?
Kosei Bus
Shimoyuguchi
ブロロー
VROOOM

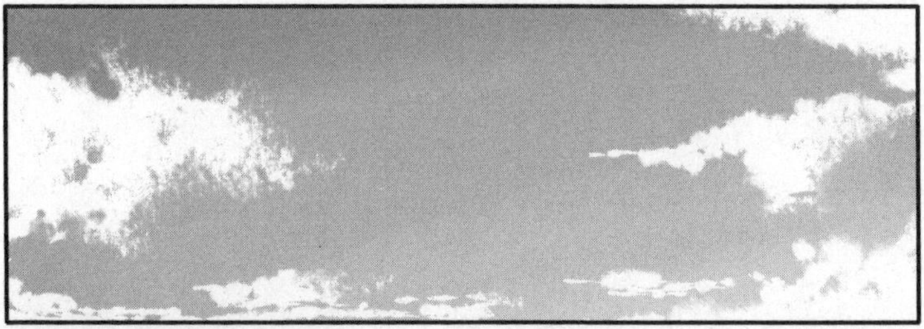

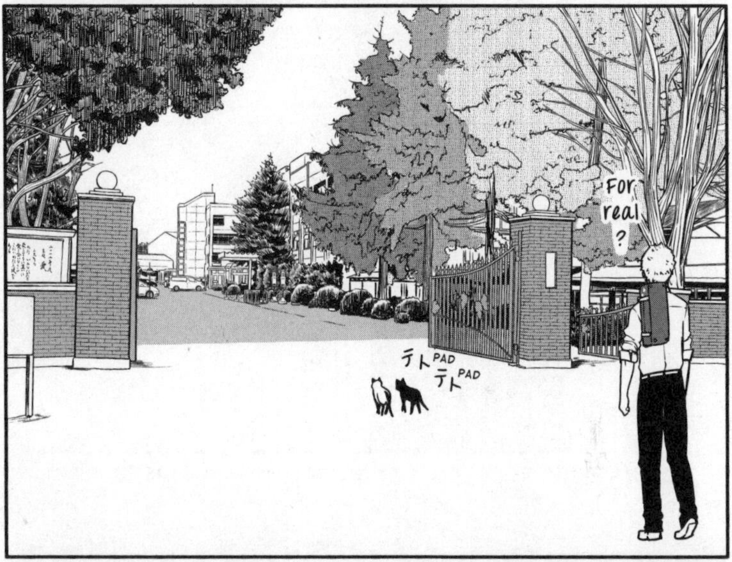
For real ?
テト PAD
テト PAD

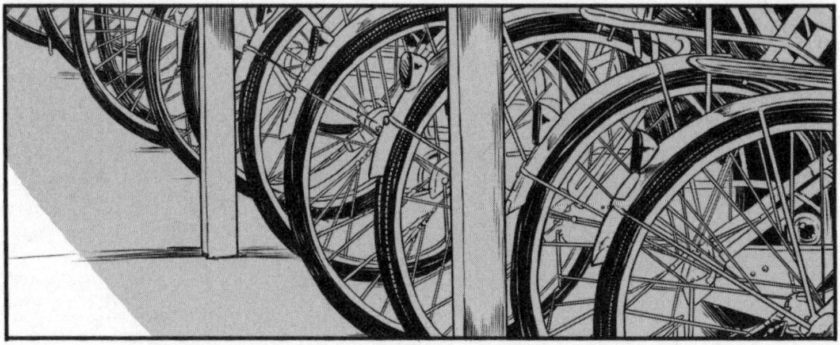

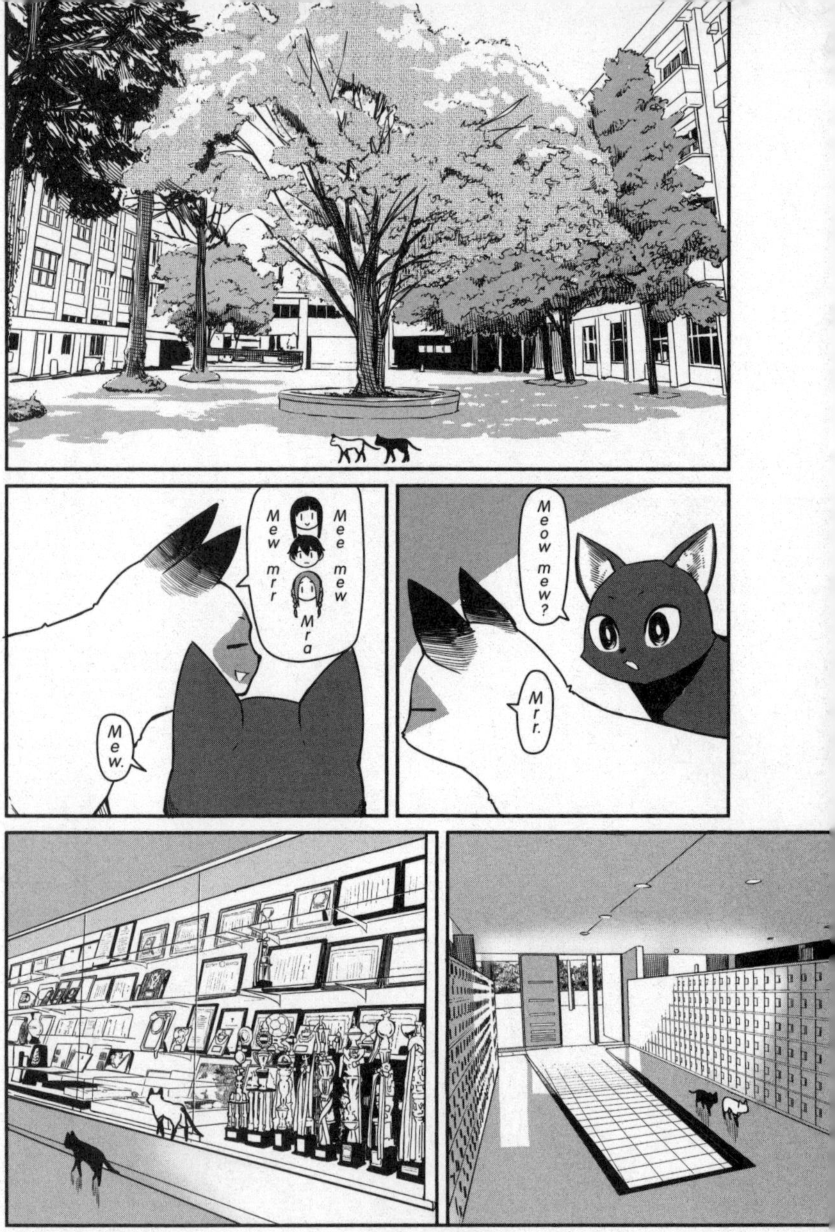
Meow mew?
Mrr.
Mee mew Mra
Mew mrr
Mew.

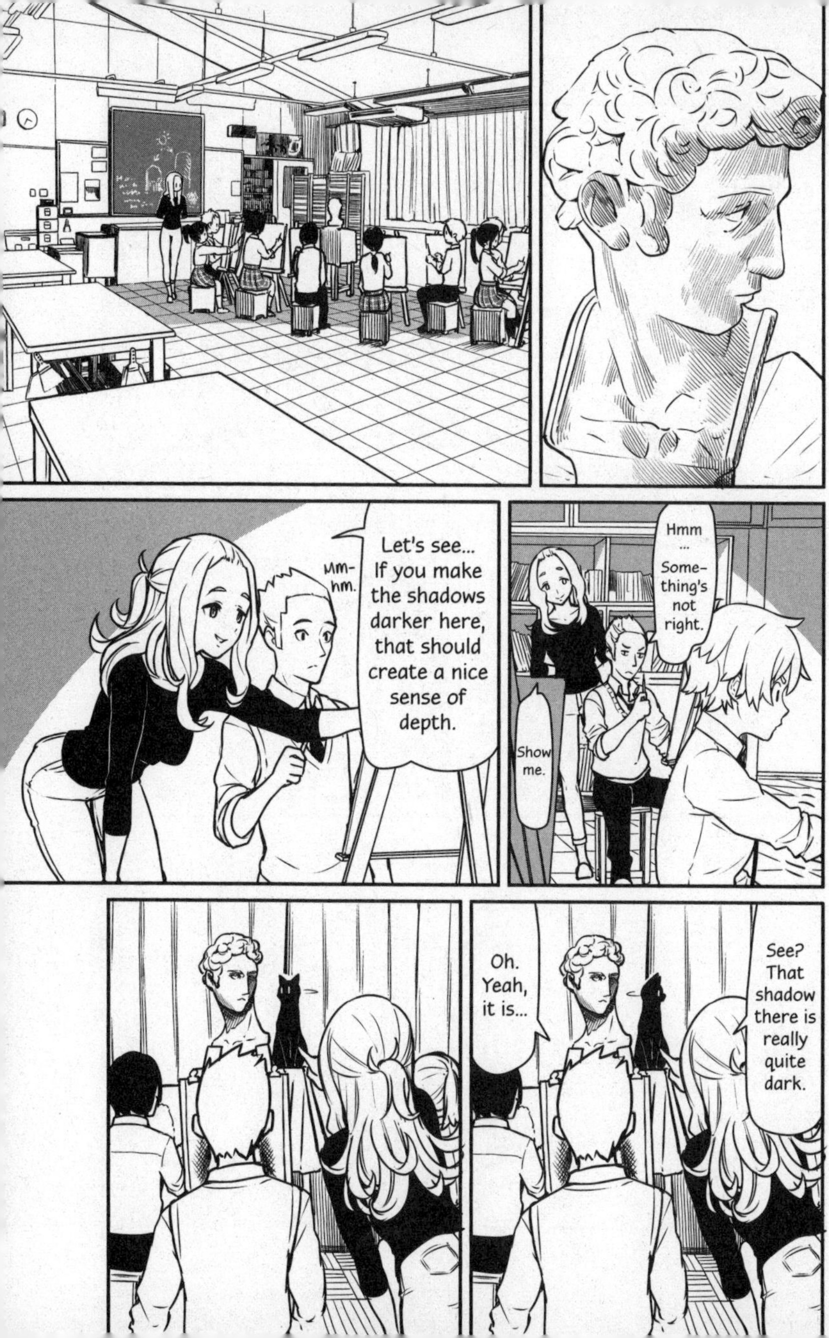
Hmm ... Something's not right.
Show me.
Let's see... If you make the shadows darker here, that should create a nice sense of depth.
Mm-hm.
See? That shadow there is really quite dark.
Oh. Yeah, it is...

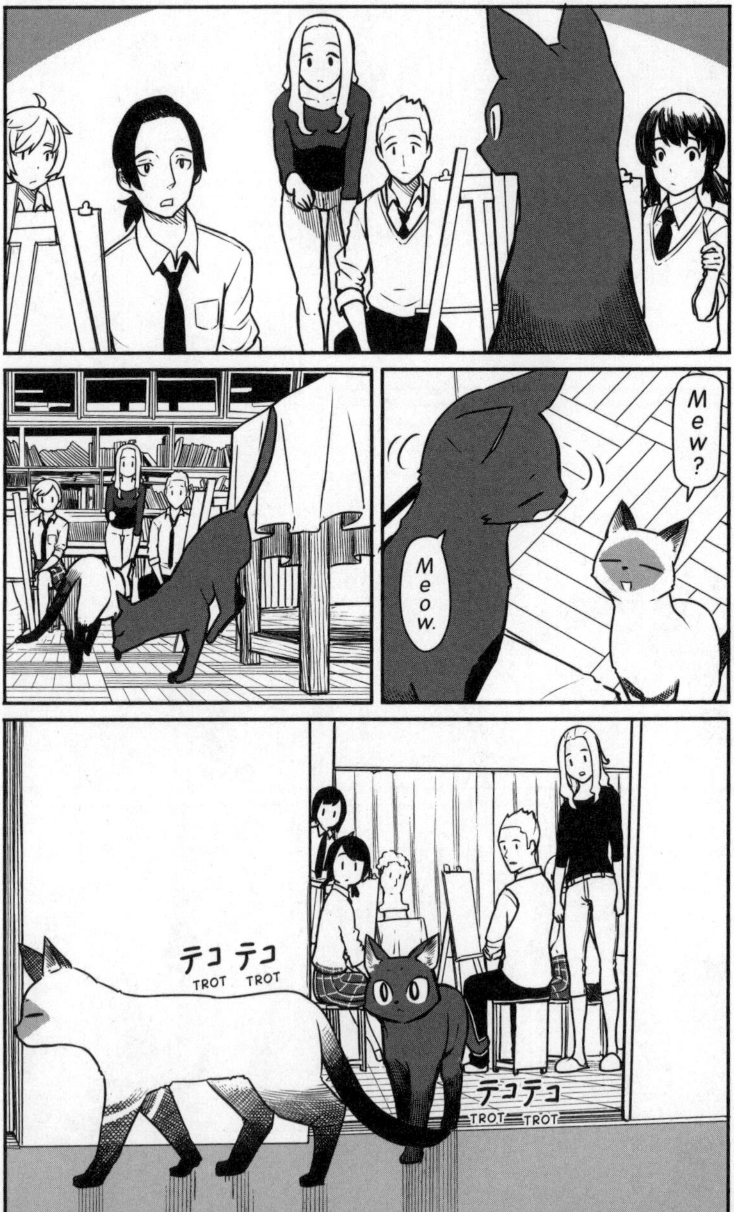
Mew?
Meow.
テコ テコ
TROT TROT
テコテコ
TROT TROT

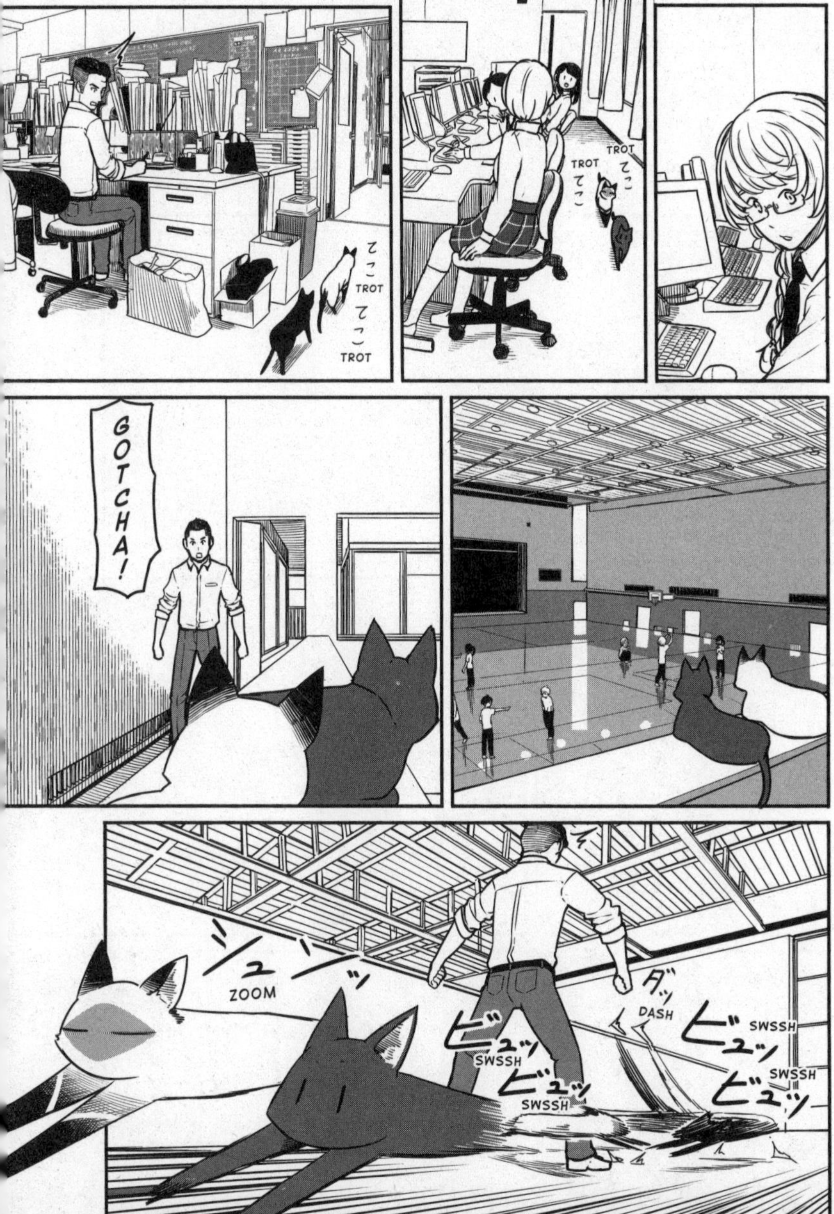
TROT
てこ
TROT
てこ
てこ
TROT
てこ
TROT
GOTCHA!
ビュッ
SWSSH
ビュッ
SWSSH
ダッ
DASH
ビュッ
SWSSH
ビュッ
SWSSH
シュンッ
ZOOM

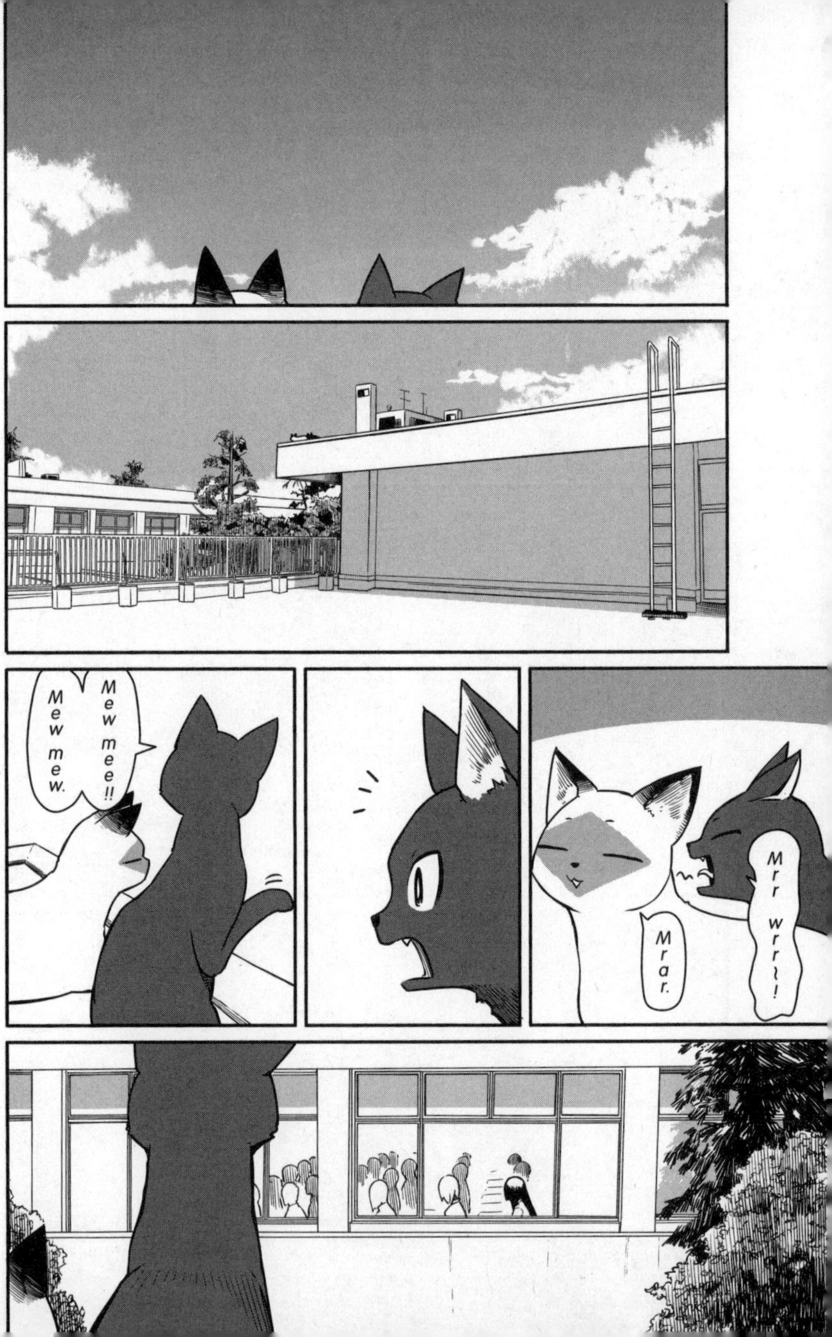
Mrr wrr~!
Mrar.
Mew mee!!
Mew mew.

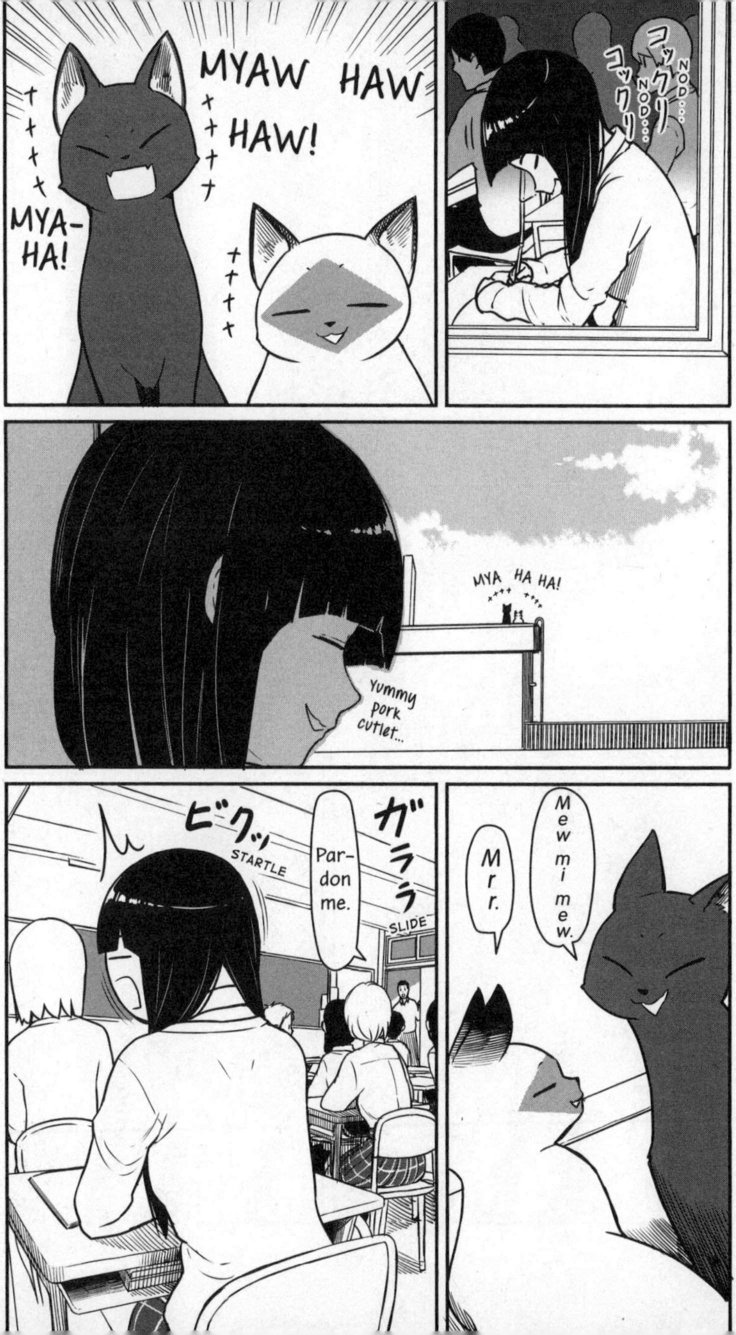

コックリ
コックリ
NOD...
NOD...
MYAW HAW HAW!
MYA-HA!
MYA HA HA!
Yummy pork cutlet...
Mew mi mew.
Mrr.
ガララ
SLIDE
Par-don me.
ビクッ
STARTLE

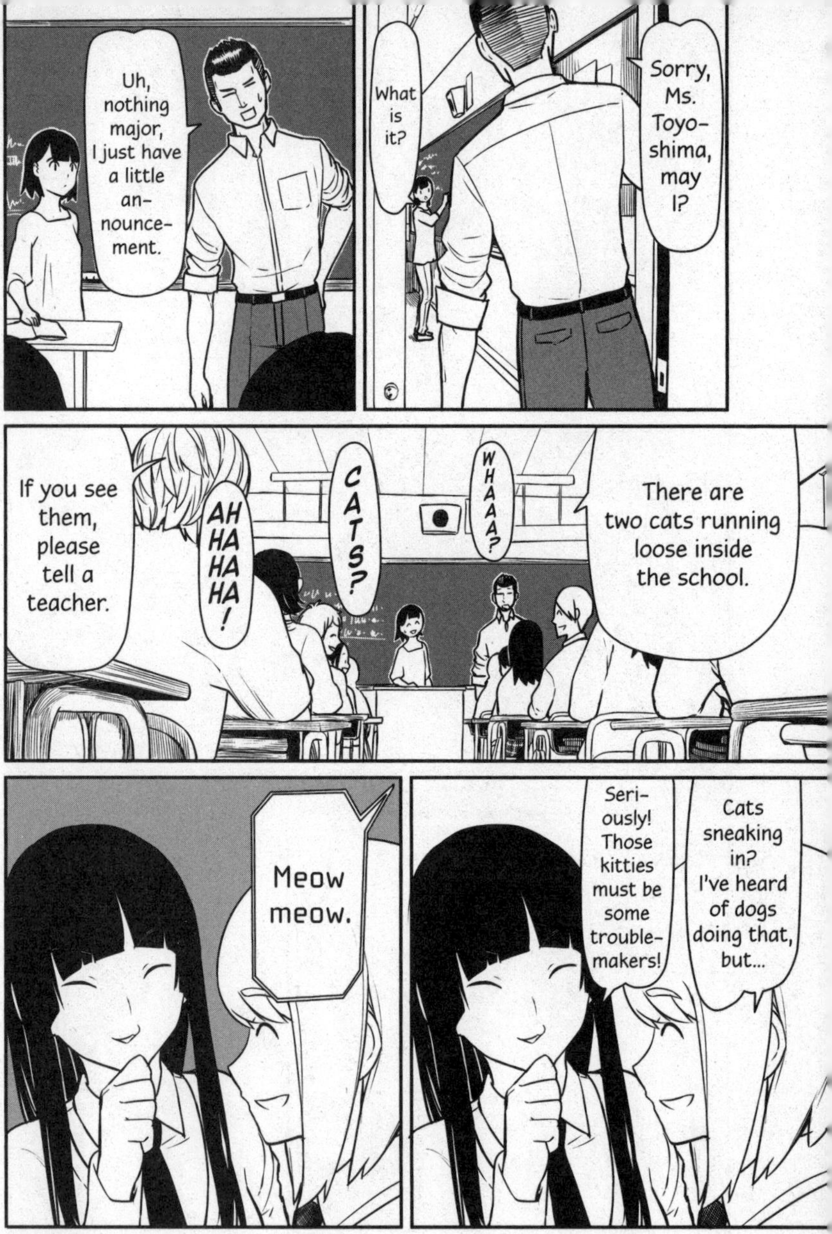
Sorry, Ms. Toyoshima, may I?
What is it?
Uh, nothing major, I just have a little announcement.
There are two cats running loose inside the school.
WHAAAA?
CATS?
AHHAHAHA!
If you see them, please tell a teacher.
Cats sneaking in? I've heard of dogs doing that, but...
Seriously! Those kitties must be some troublemakers!
Meow meow.

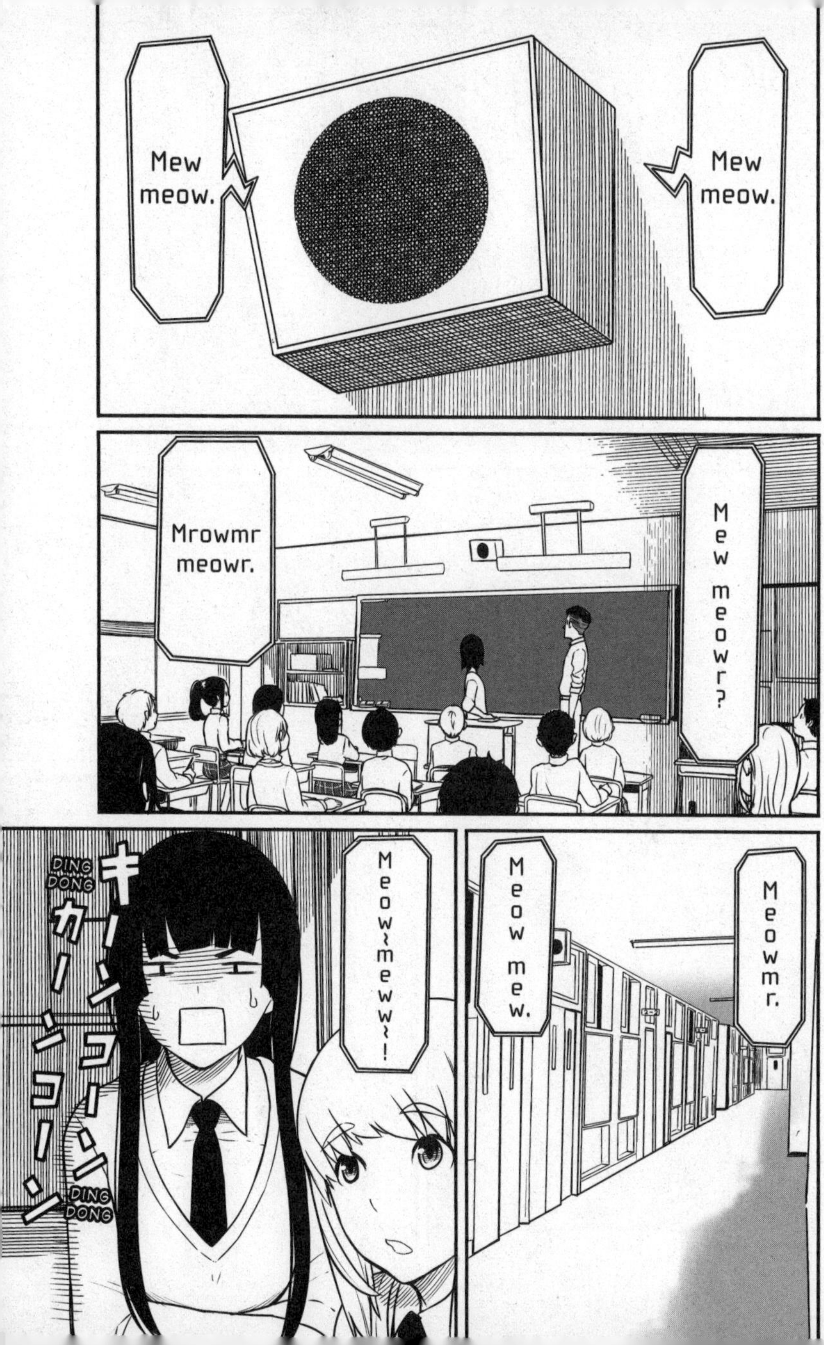
Mew meow.
Mew meow.
Mew meowr?
Mrowmr meowr.
Meowmr.
Meow mew.
Meow~meww~!
DING DONG
DING DONG

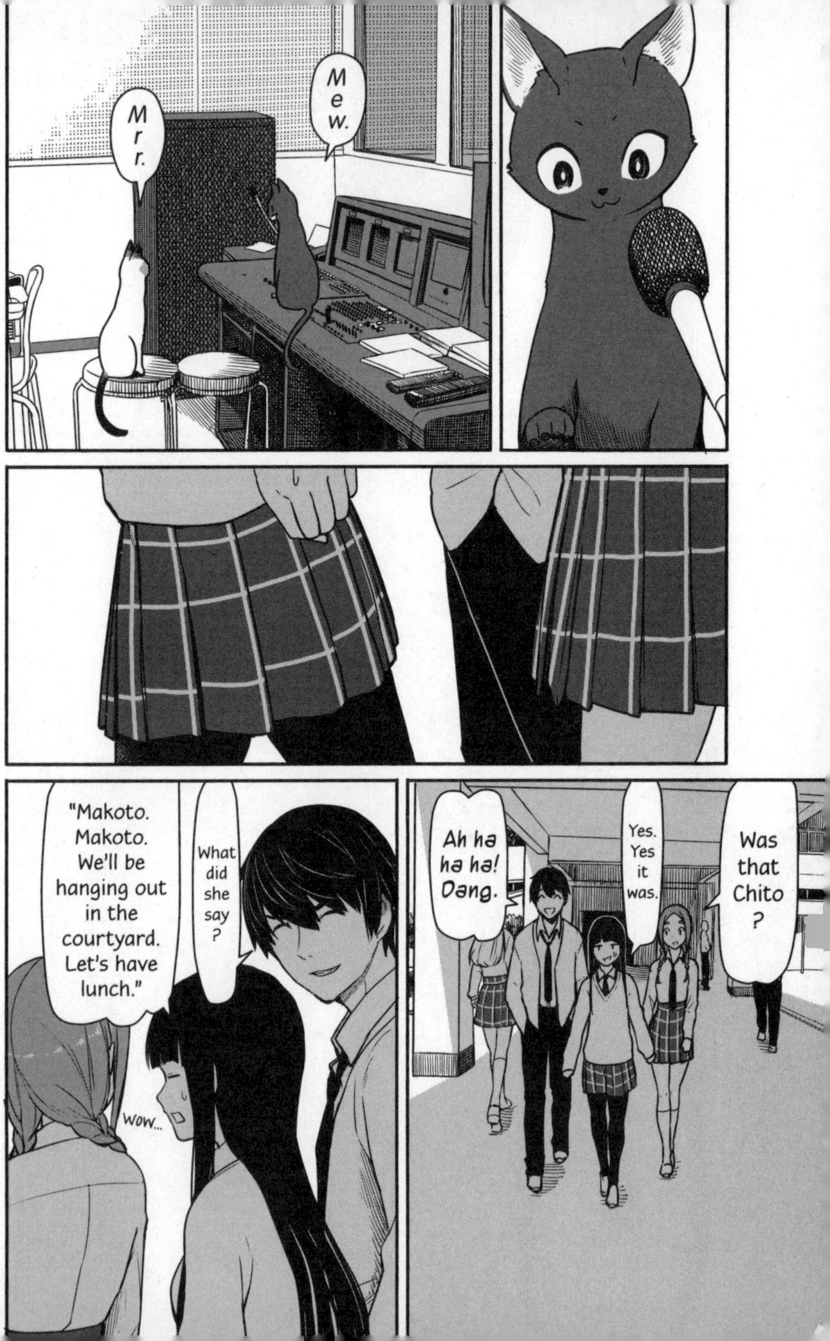
Mew.
Mrr.
Was that Chito?
Yes. Yes it was.
Ah ha ha ha! Dang.
What did she say?
"Makoto. Makoto. We'll be hanging out in the courtyard. Let's have lunch."
Wow...

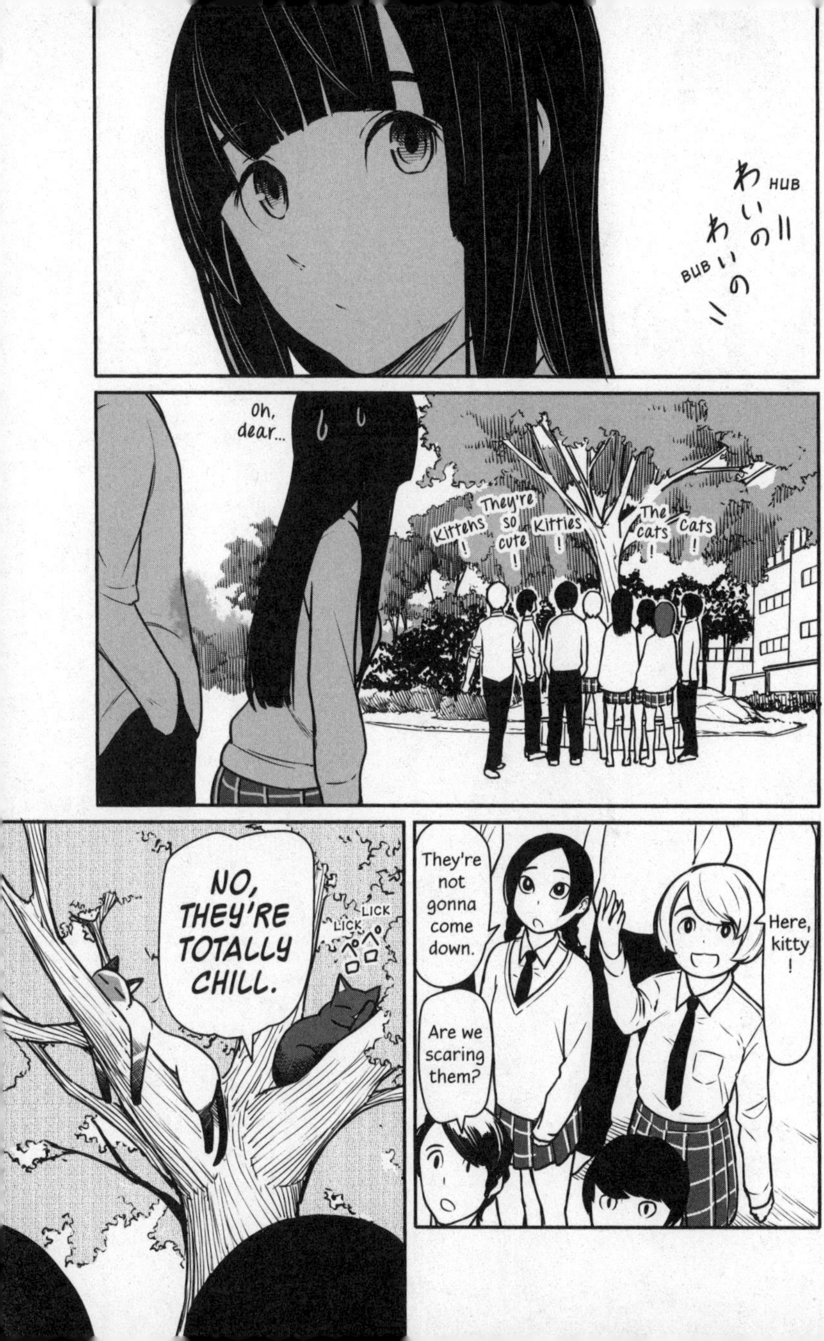

わいのわいの
HUB
BUB
Cats!
The cats!
Kitties!
They're so cute!
Kittens!
Oh, dear...
Here, kitty!
They're not gonna come down.
Are we scaring them?
NO, THEY'RE TOTALLY CHILL.
ペロペロ
LICK
LICK

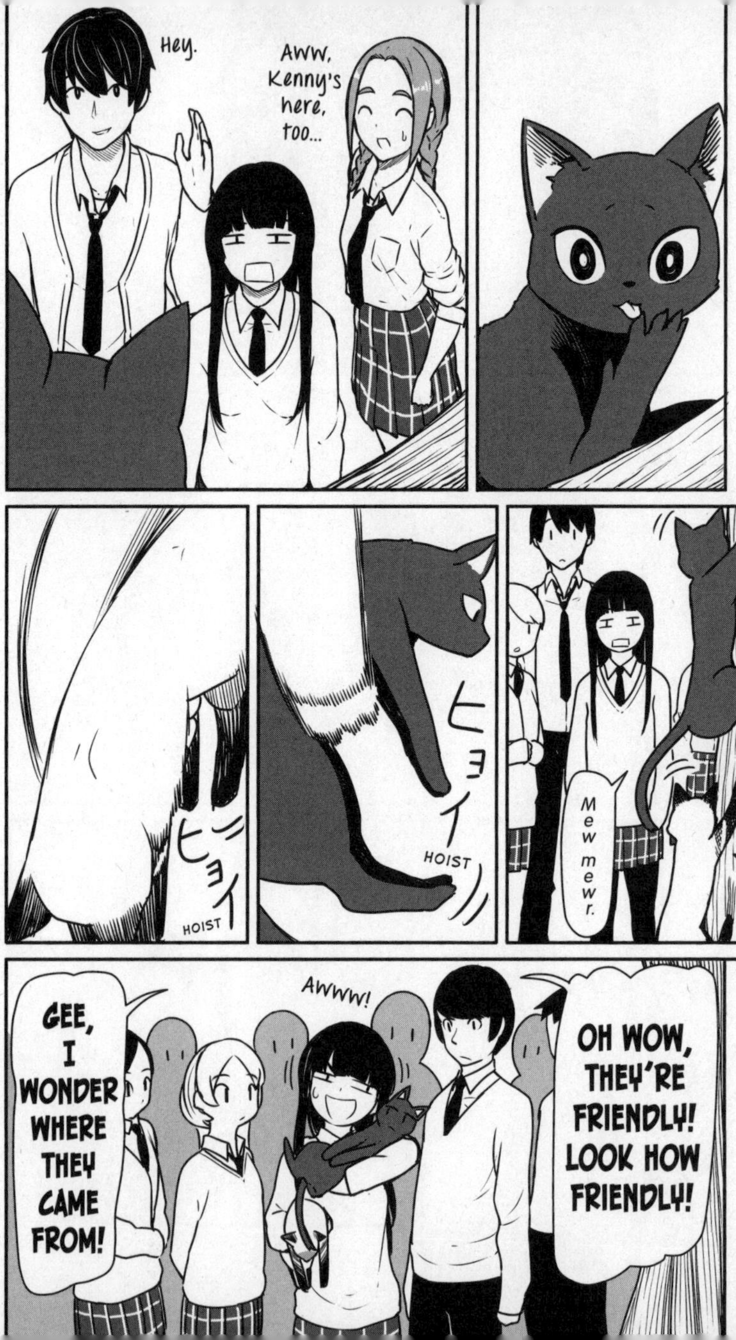
Hey.
Aww, Kenny's here, too...
Meow.
Meow meow mew mew.
Mew mewr.
Mrar.
ヒョイ
HOIST
ヒョイ
HOIST
OH WOW, THEY'RE FRIENDLY! LOOK HOW FRIENDLY!
AWWW!
GEE, I WONDER WHERE THEY CAME FROM!

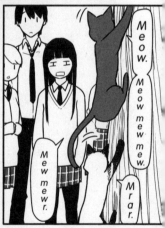

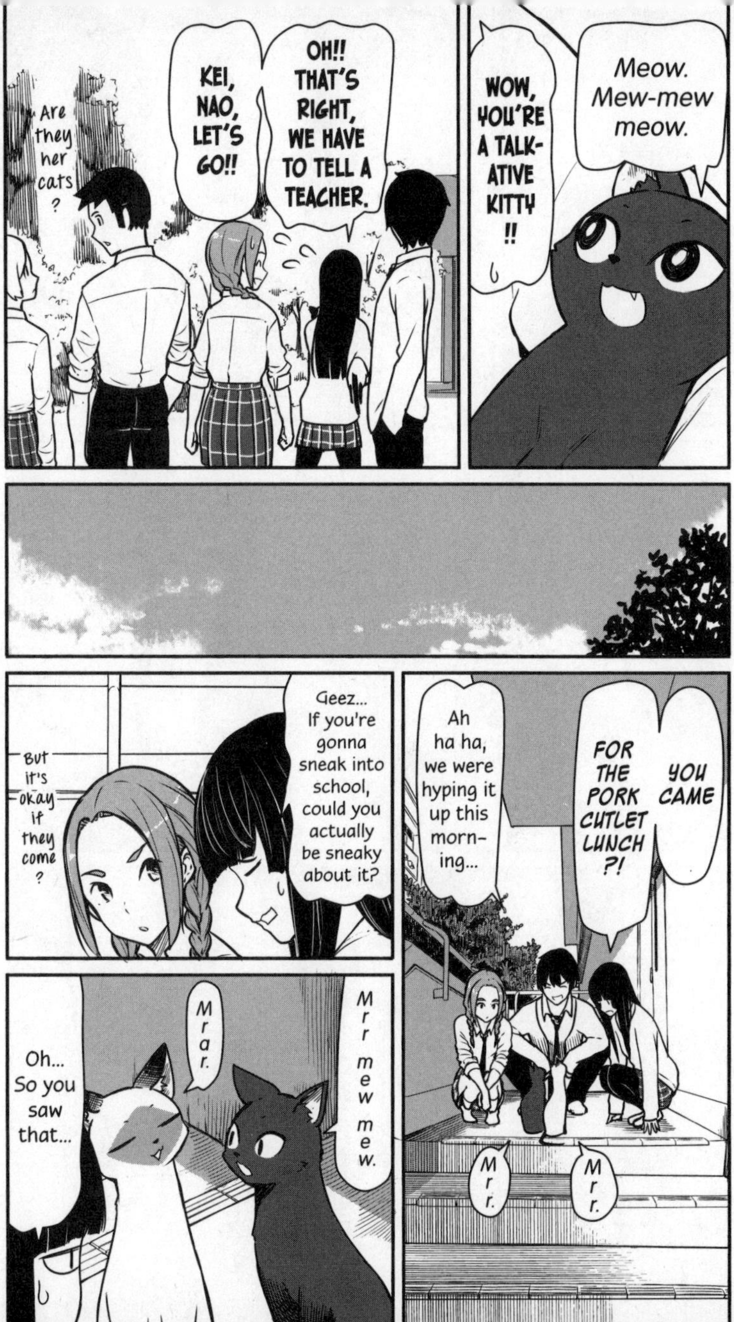
Meow. Mew-mew meow.
WOW, YOU'RE A TALK-ATIVE KITTY!!
OH!! THAT'S RIGHT, WE HAVE TO TELL A TEACHER.
KEI, NAO, LET'S GO!!
Are they her cats?
YOU CAME FOR THE PORK CUTLET LUNCH?!
Ah ha ha, we were hyping it up this morn-ing...
Mrr.
Mrr.
Geez... If you're gonna sneak into school, could you actually be sneaky about it?
But it's okay if they come?
Mrr mew mew mew.
Mrar.
Oh... So you saw that...

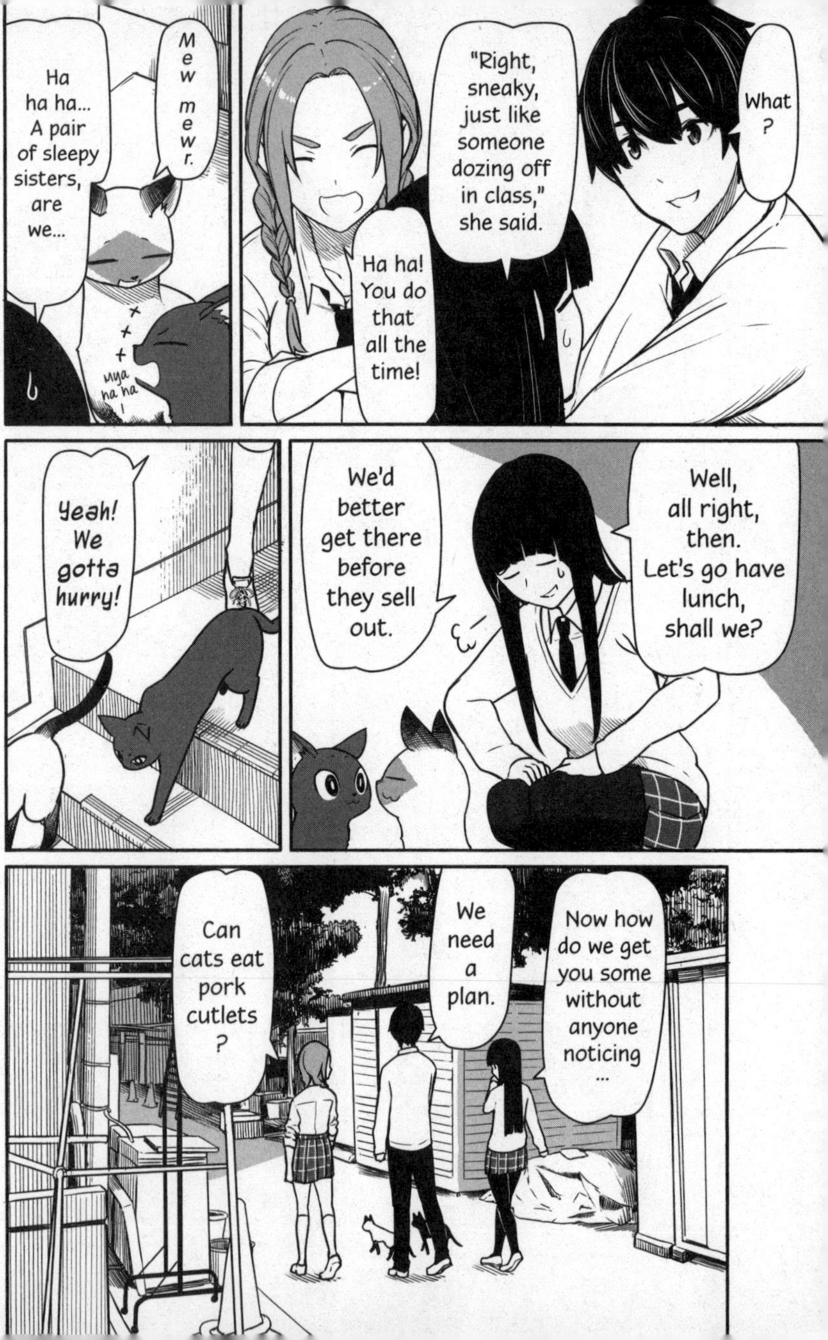
What?
"Right, sneaky, just like someone dozing off in class," she said.
Ha ha! You do that all the time!
Mew mewr.
Ha ha ha... A pair of sleepy sisters, are we...
Mya ha ha!
Well, all right, then. Let's go have lunch, shall we?
We'd better get there before they sell out.
Yeah! We gotta hurry!
Now how do we get you some without anyone noticing...
We need a plan.
Can cats eat pork cutlets?

Flying
Witch

Chapter 34
The Experienced Upperclassman

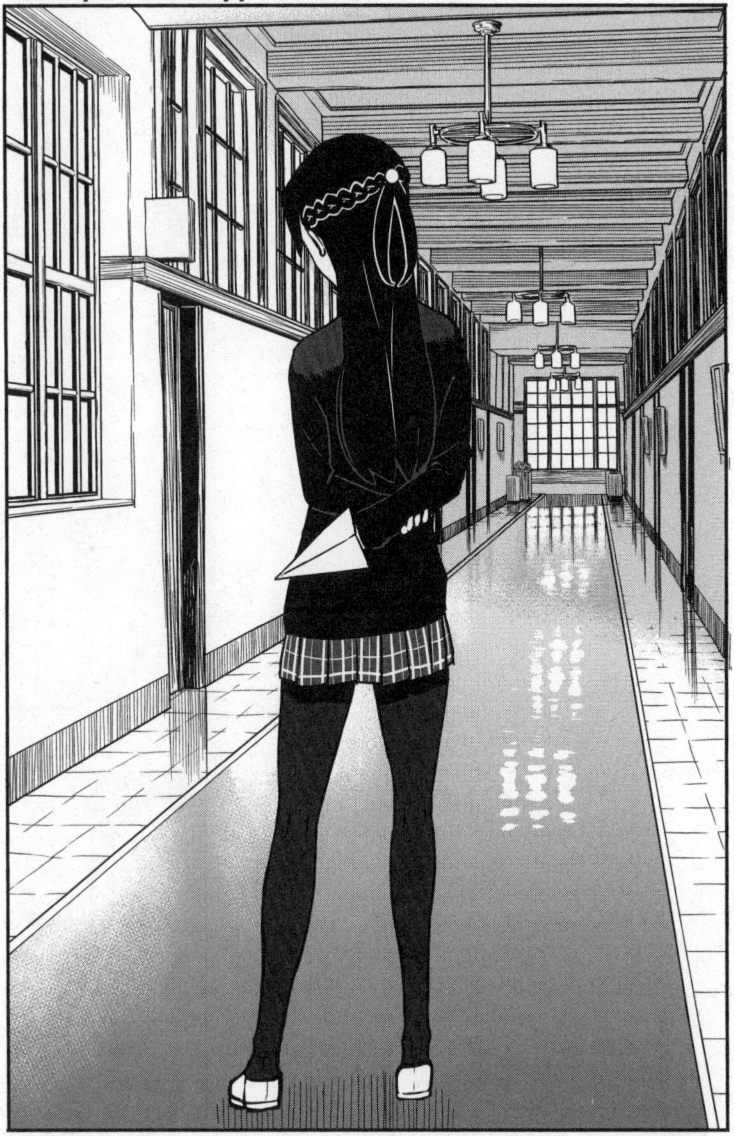

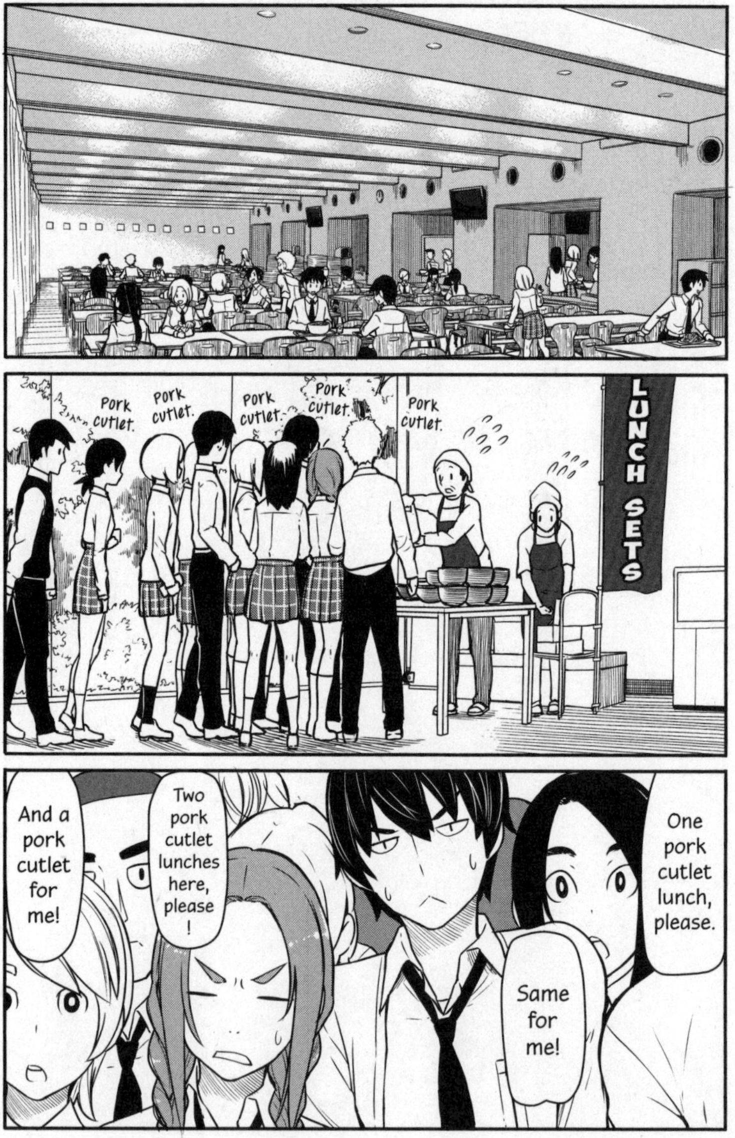
LUNCH SETS
Pork cutlet.
Pork cutlet.
Pork cutlet.
Pork cutlet.
Pork cutlet.
One pork cutlet lunch, please.
Same for me!
Two pork cutlet lunches here, please!
And a pork cutlet for me!

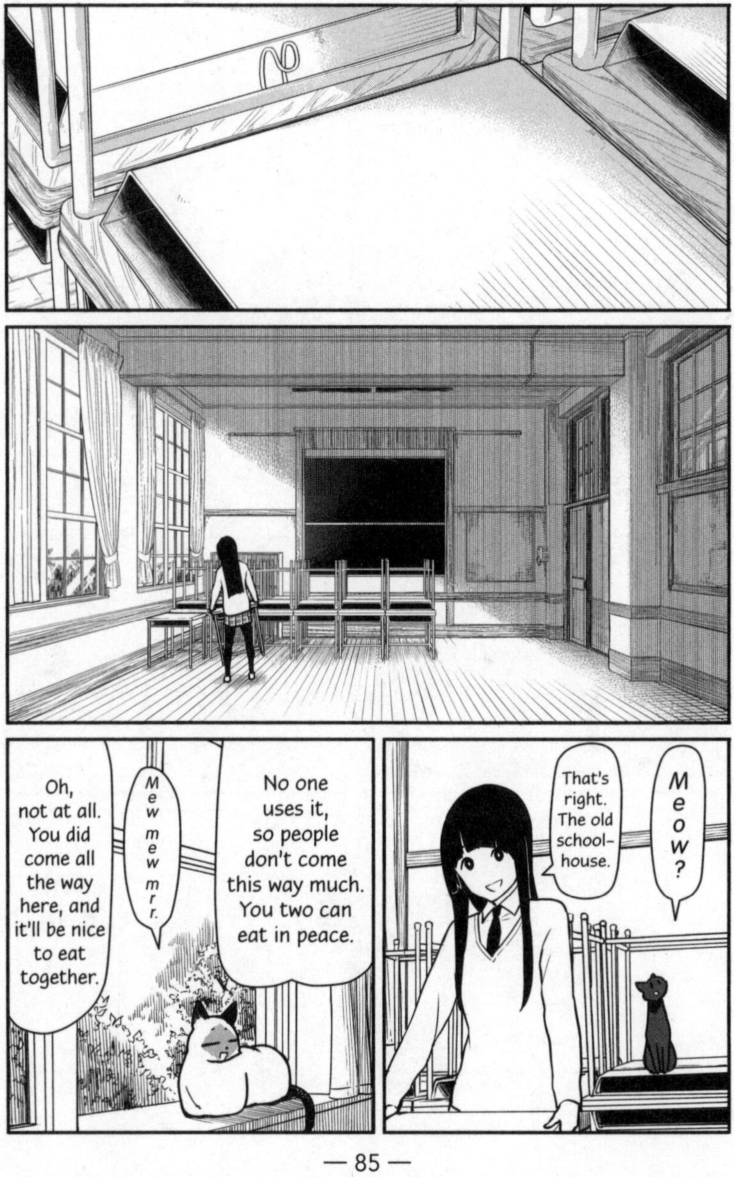
Meow?
That's right. The old school-house.
No one uses it, so people don't come this way much. You two can eat in peace.
Mew mew mrr.
Oh, not at all. You did come all the way here, and it'll be nice to eat together.

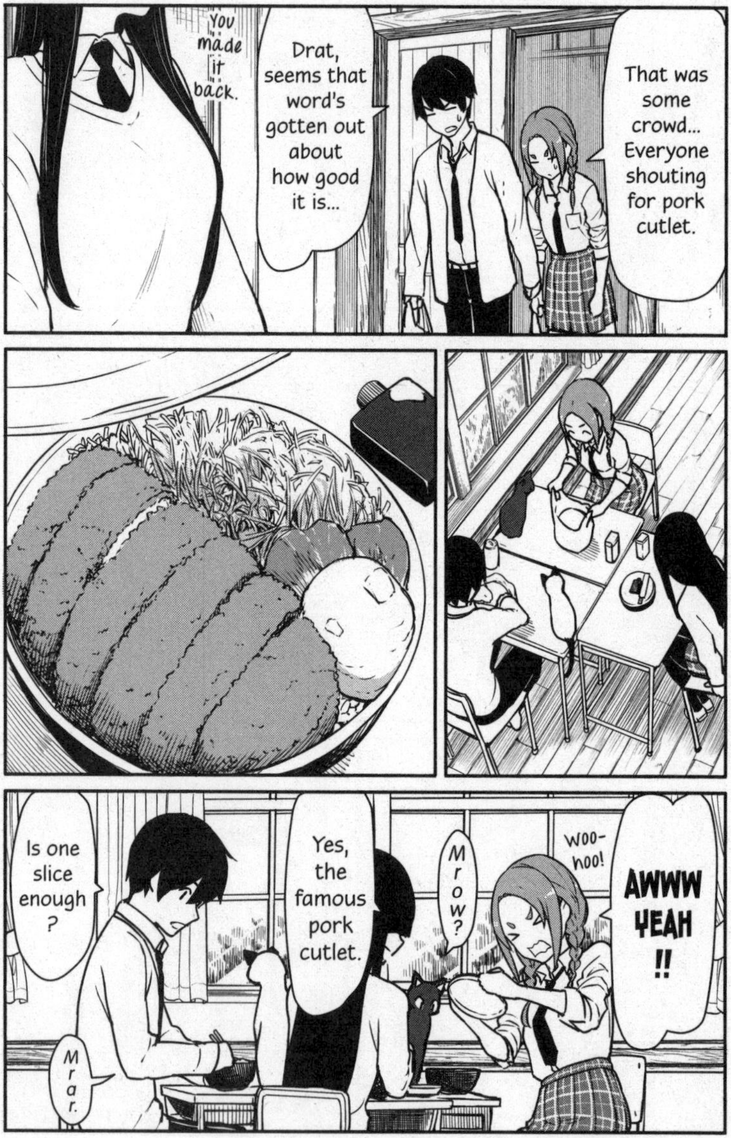
That was some crowd... Everyone shouting for pork cutlet.
Drat, seems that word's gotten out about how good it is...
You made it back.
AWWW YEAH!!
Woo-hoo!
Mrow?
Yes, the famous pork cutlet.
Is one slice enough?
Mrar.

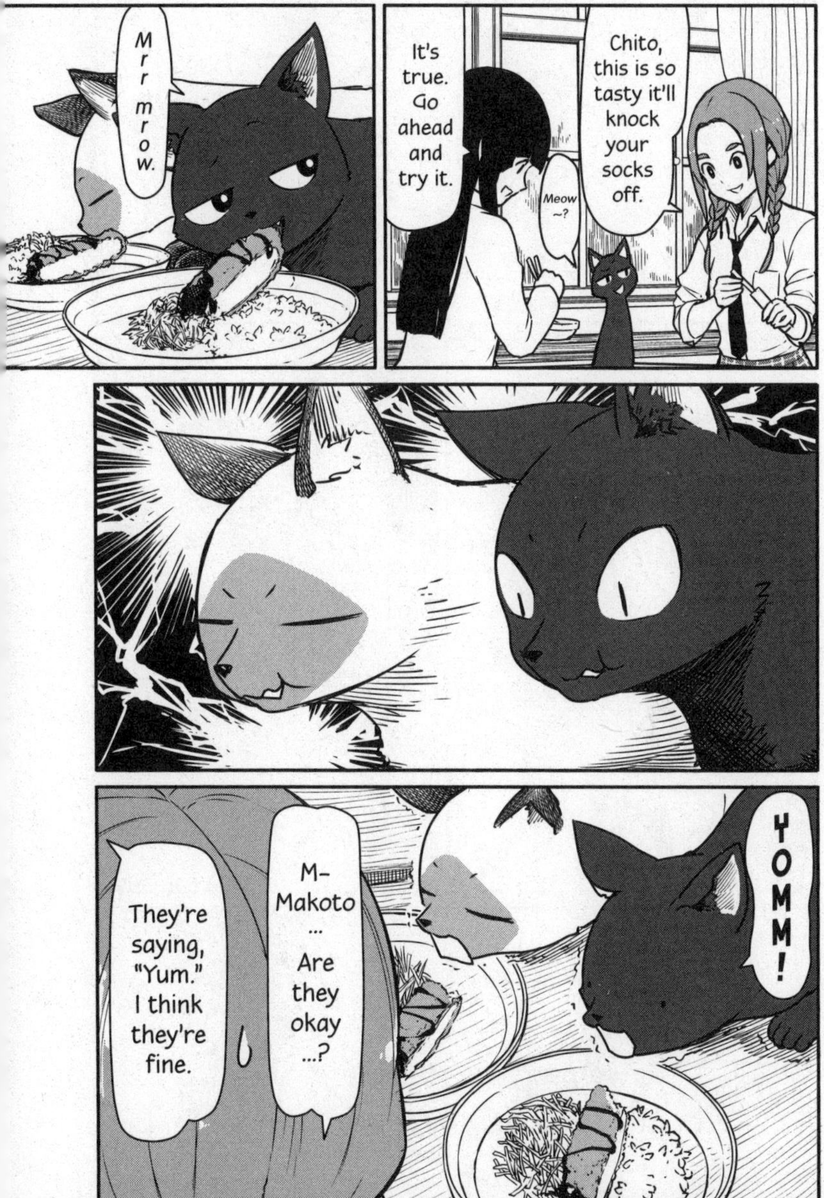
Chito, this is so tasty it'll knock your socks off.
It's true. Go ahead and try it.
Meow ~?
Mrr mrow.
YOMM!
M-Makoto ... Are they okay ...?
They're saying, "Yum." I think they're fine.

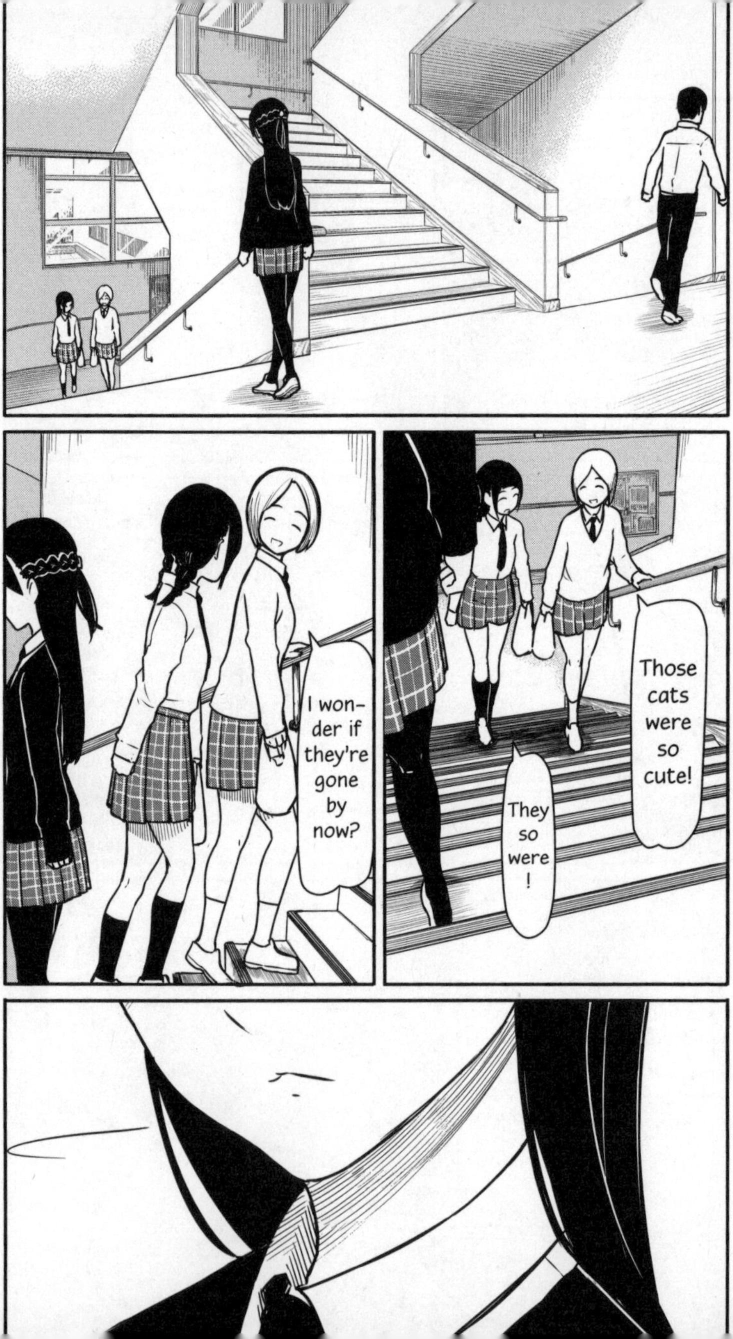
Those cats were so cute!
They so were!
I wonder if they're gone by now?

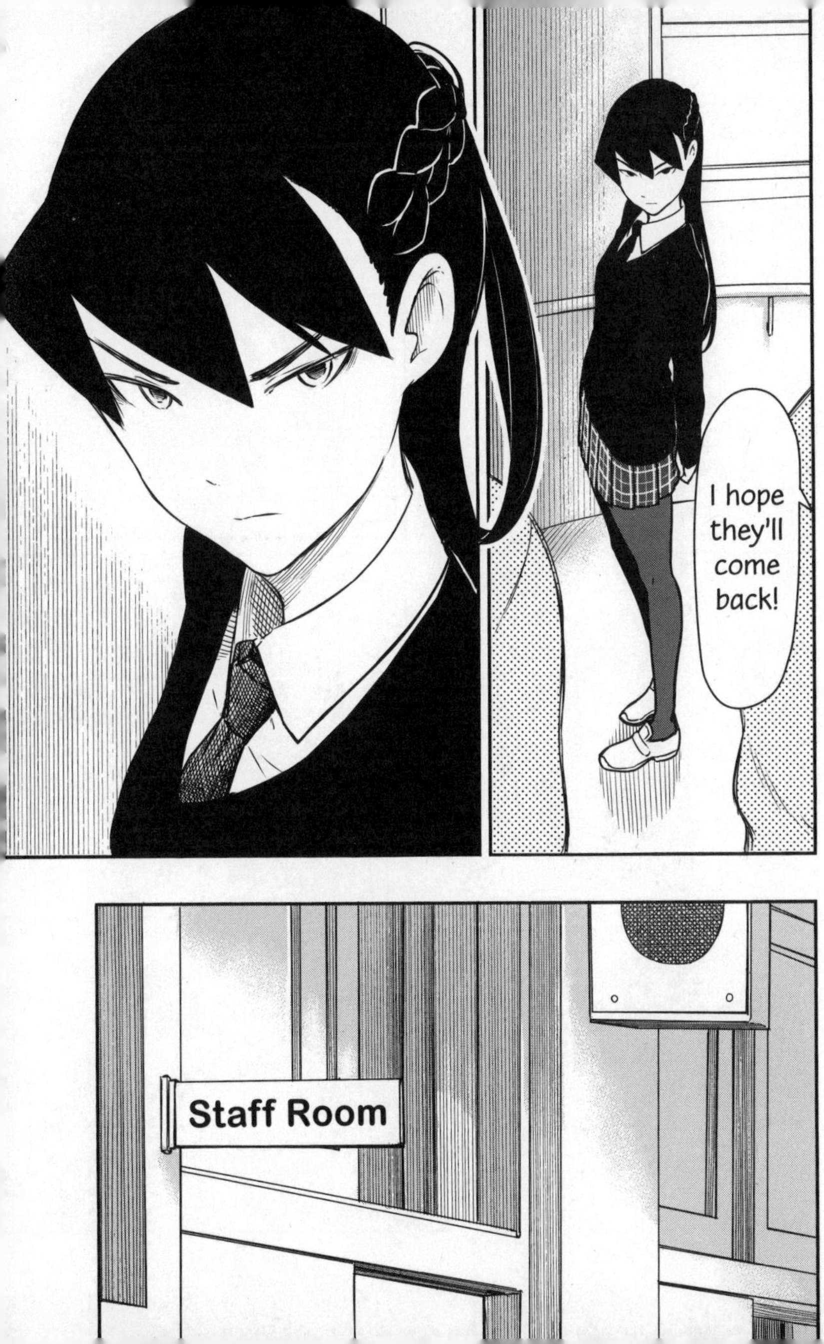
I hope they'll come back!
Staff Room

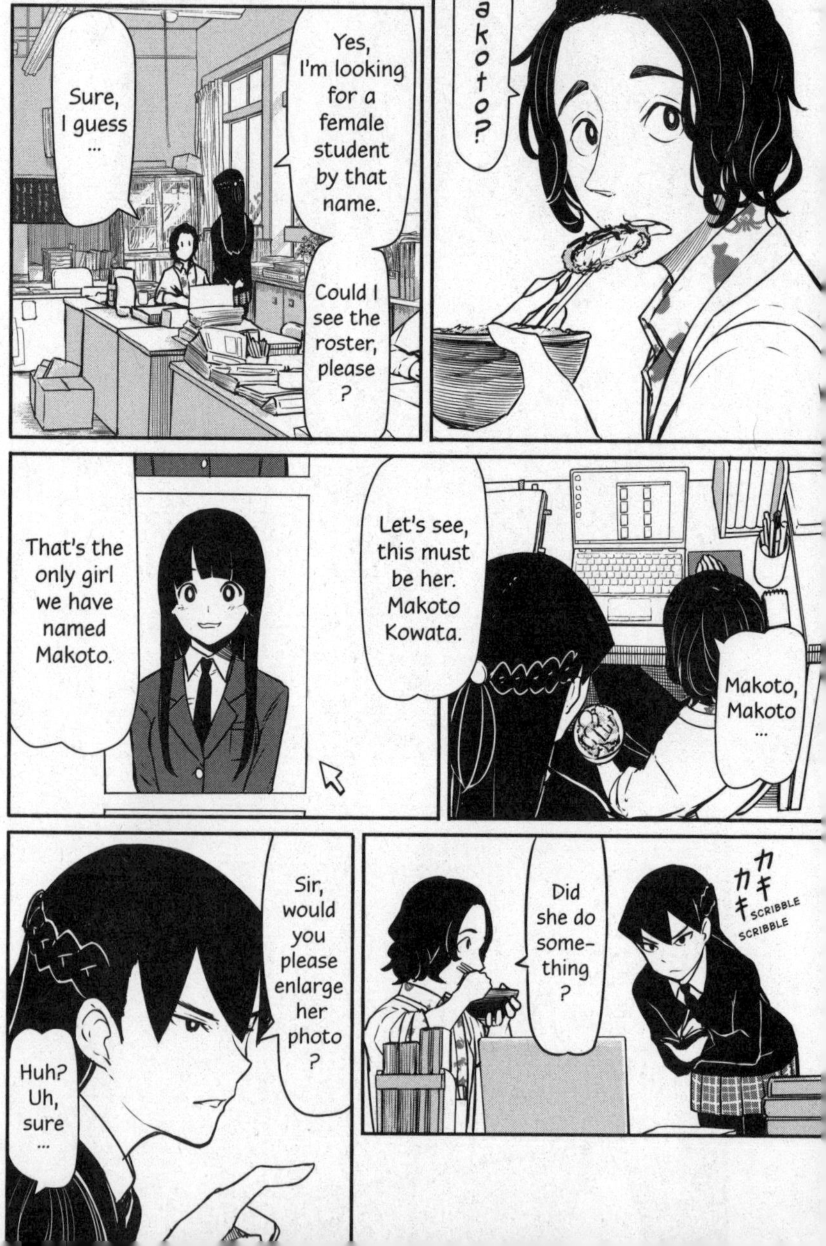
Makoto?
Yes, I'm looking for a female student by that name.
Could I see the roster, please?
Sure, I guess ...
Makoto, Makoto ...
Let's see, this must be her. Makoto Kowata.
That's the only girl we have named Makoto.
カキカキ SCRIBBLE SCRIBBLE
Did she do something?
Sir, would you please enlarge her photo?
Huh? Uh, sure ...

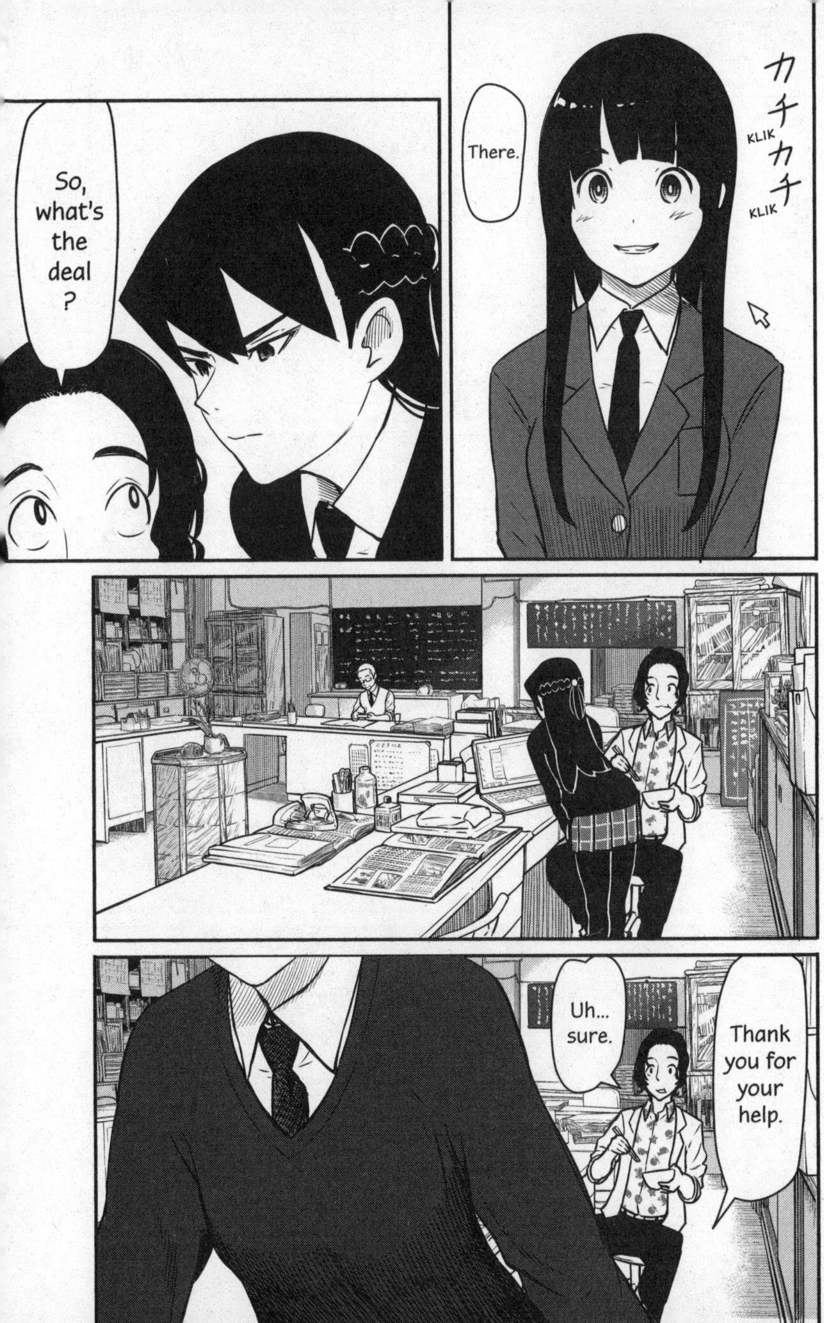

There.
カチ
KLIK
カチ
KLIK
So, what's the deal?
Thank you for your help.
Uh... sure.

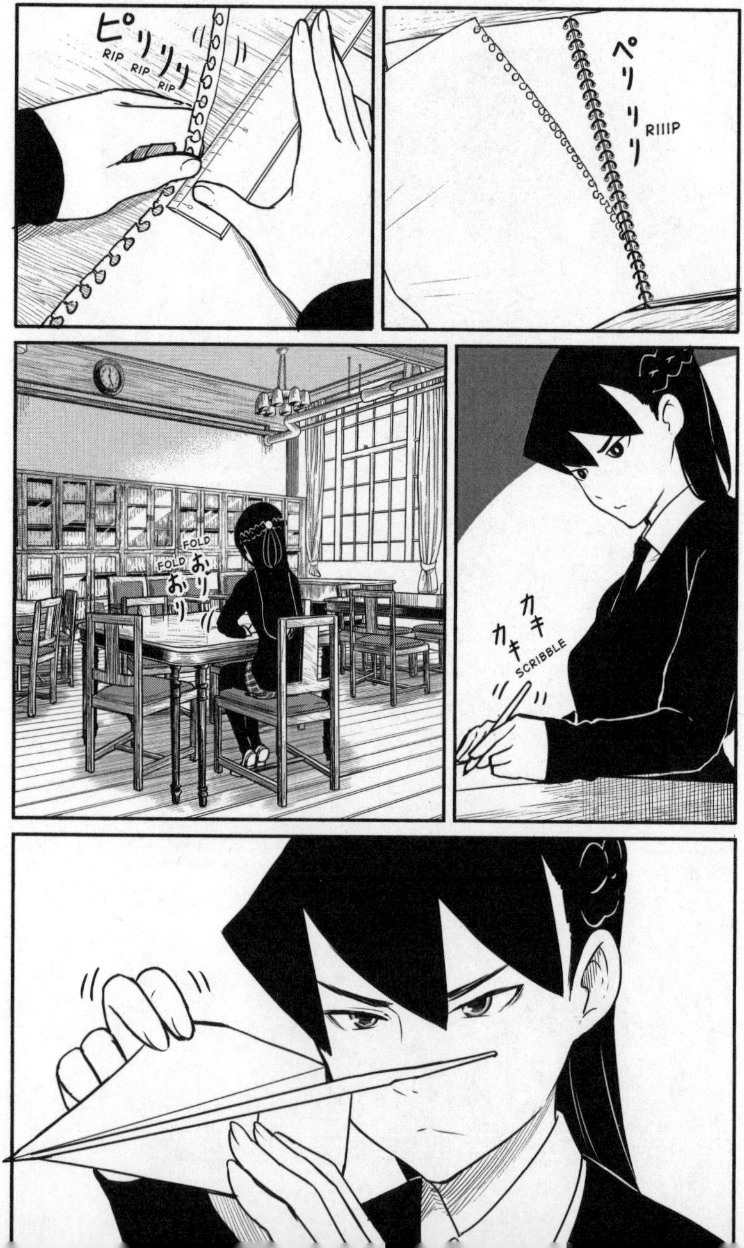
ペリリリ
RIIIP
ピリリリ
RIP RIP RIP
カキカキ
SCRIBBLE
おりおり
FOLD FOLD

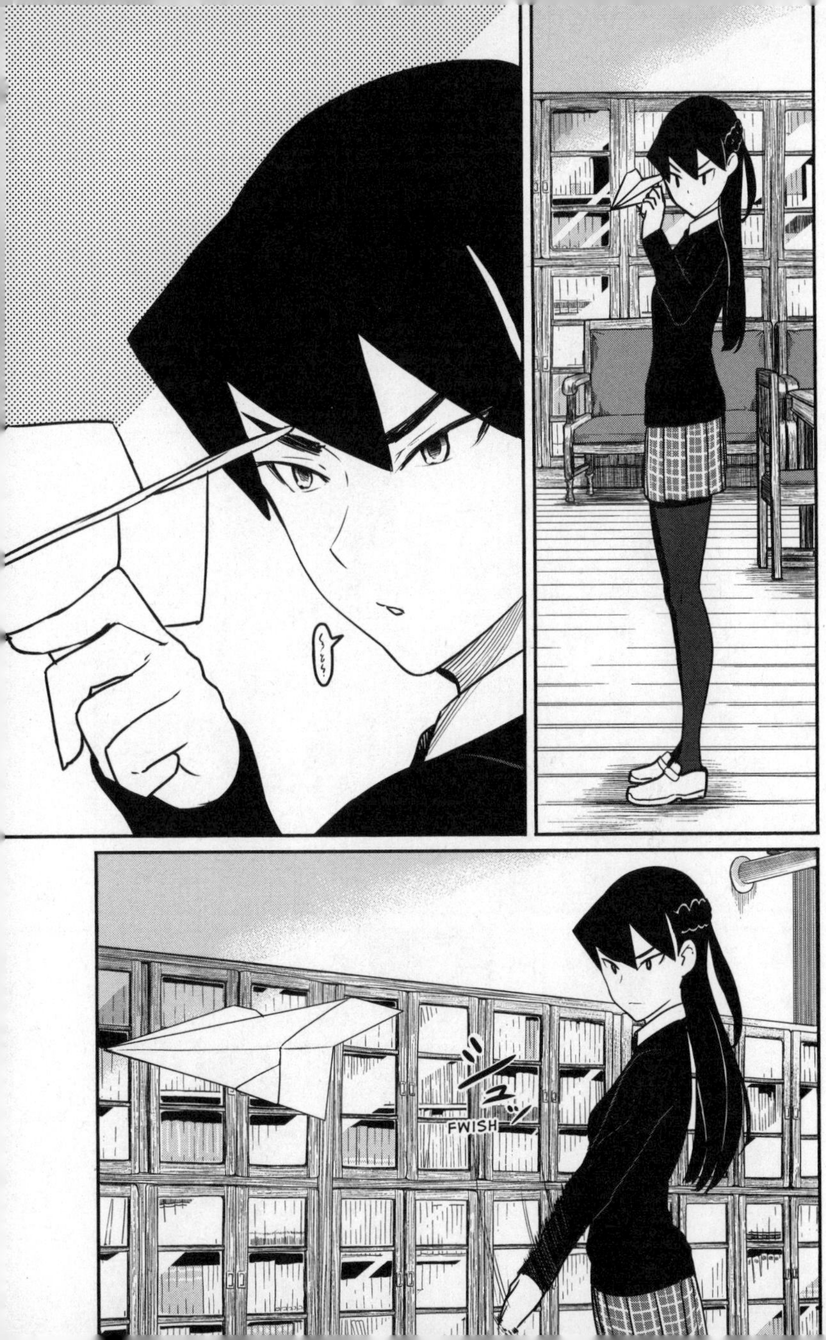
FWISH

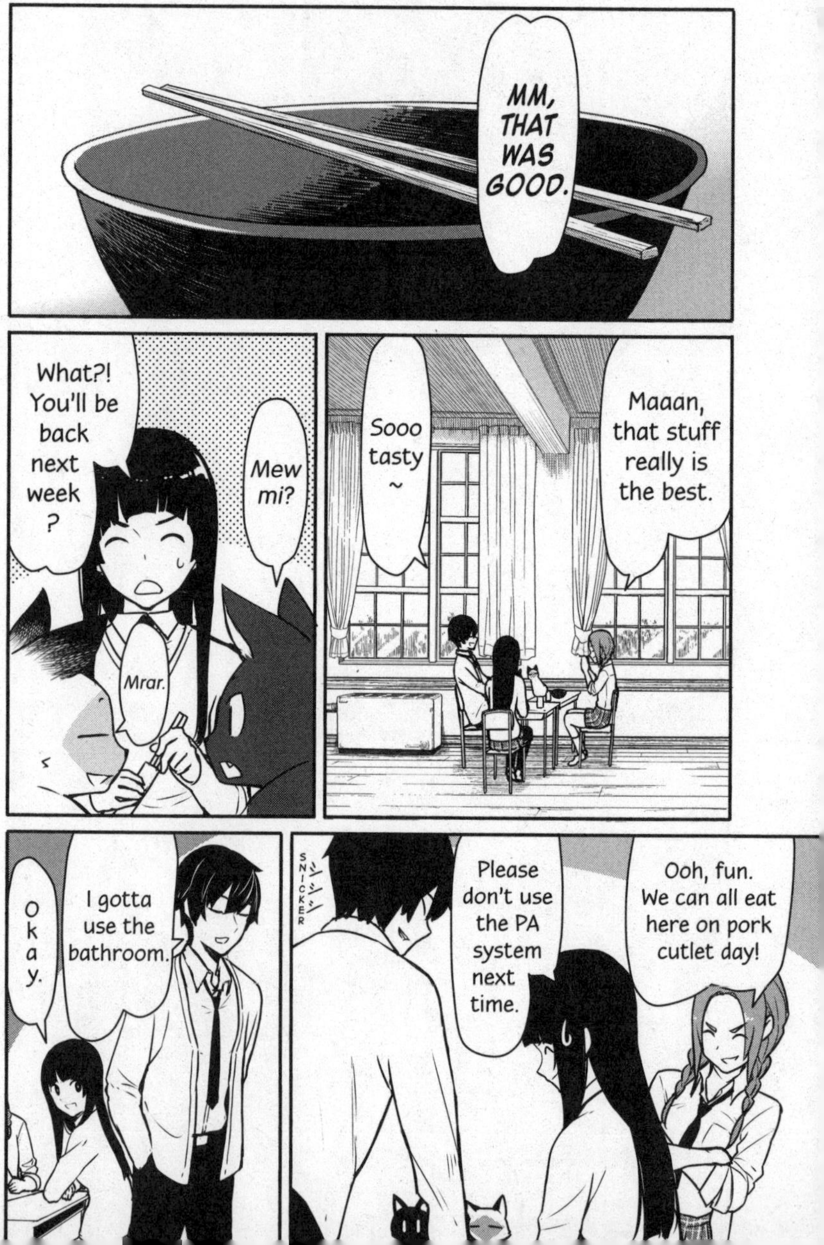
MM, THAT WAS GOOD.
Maaan, that stuff really is the best.
Sooo tasty ~
Mew mi?
What?! You'll be back next week?
Mrar.
Ooh, fun. We can all eat here on pork cutlet day!
Please don't use the PA system next time.
SNICKER
I gotta use the bathroom.
Okay.

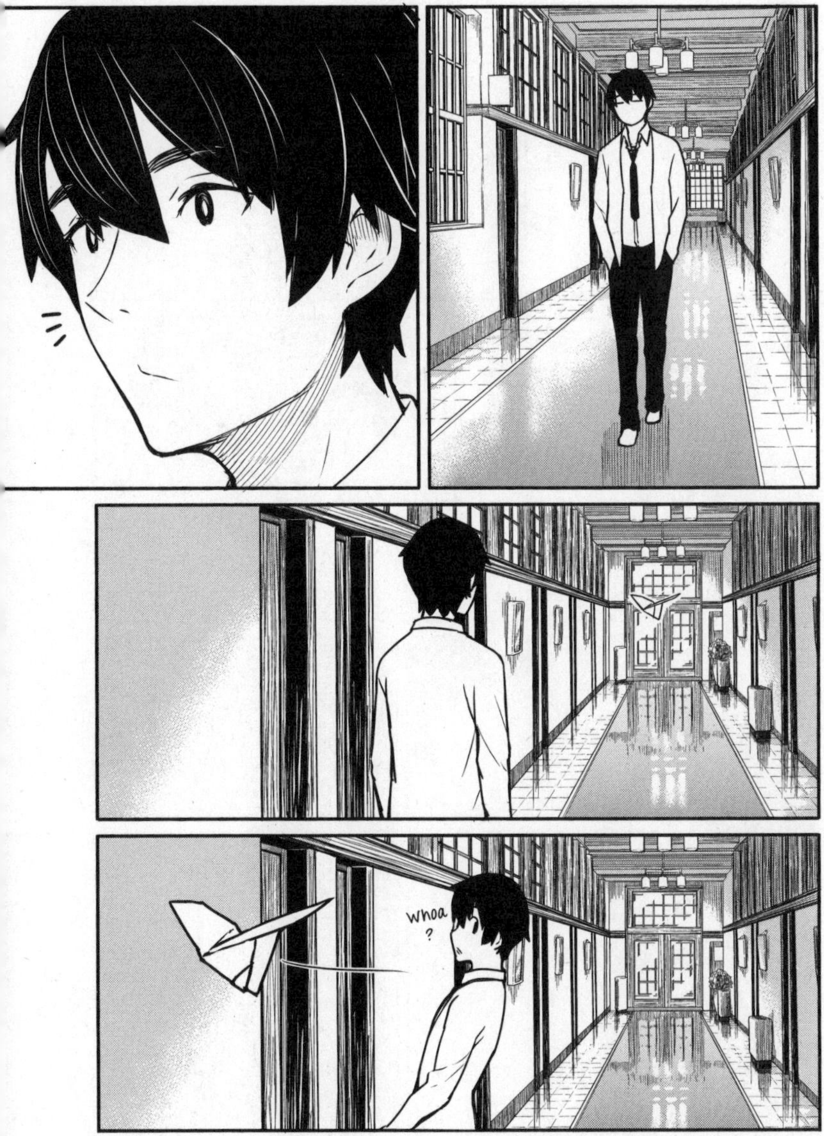
whoa
?

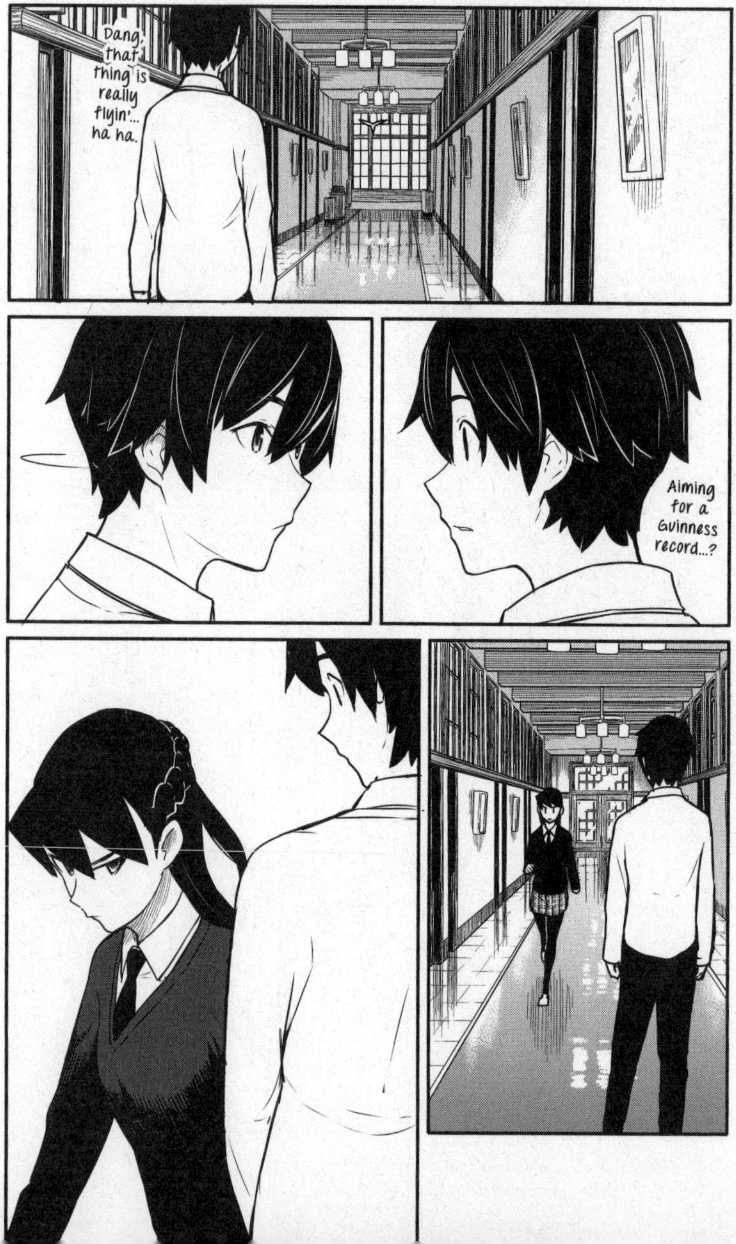
Dang, that thing is really flyin'... ha ha.
Aiming for a Guinness record...?

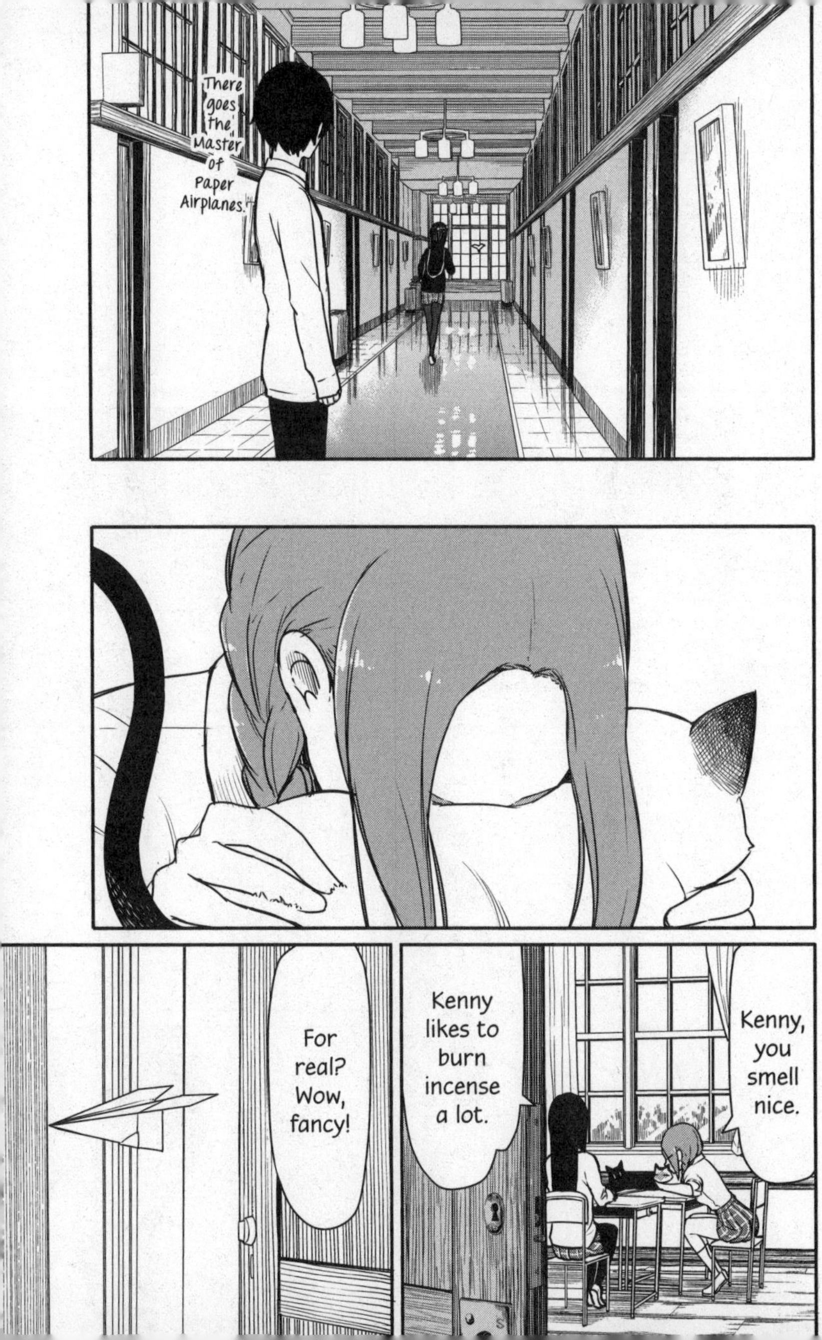
There goes the Master of Paper Airplanes.
Kenny, you smell nice.
Kenny likes to burn incense a lot.
For real? Wow, fancy!

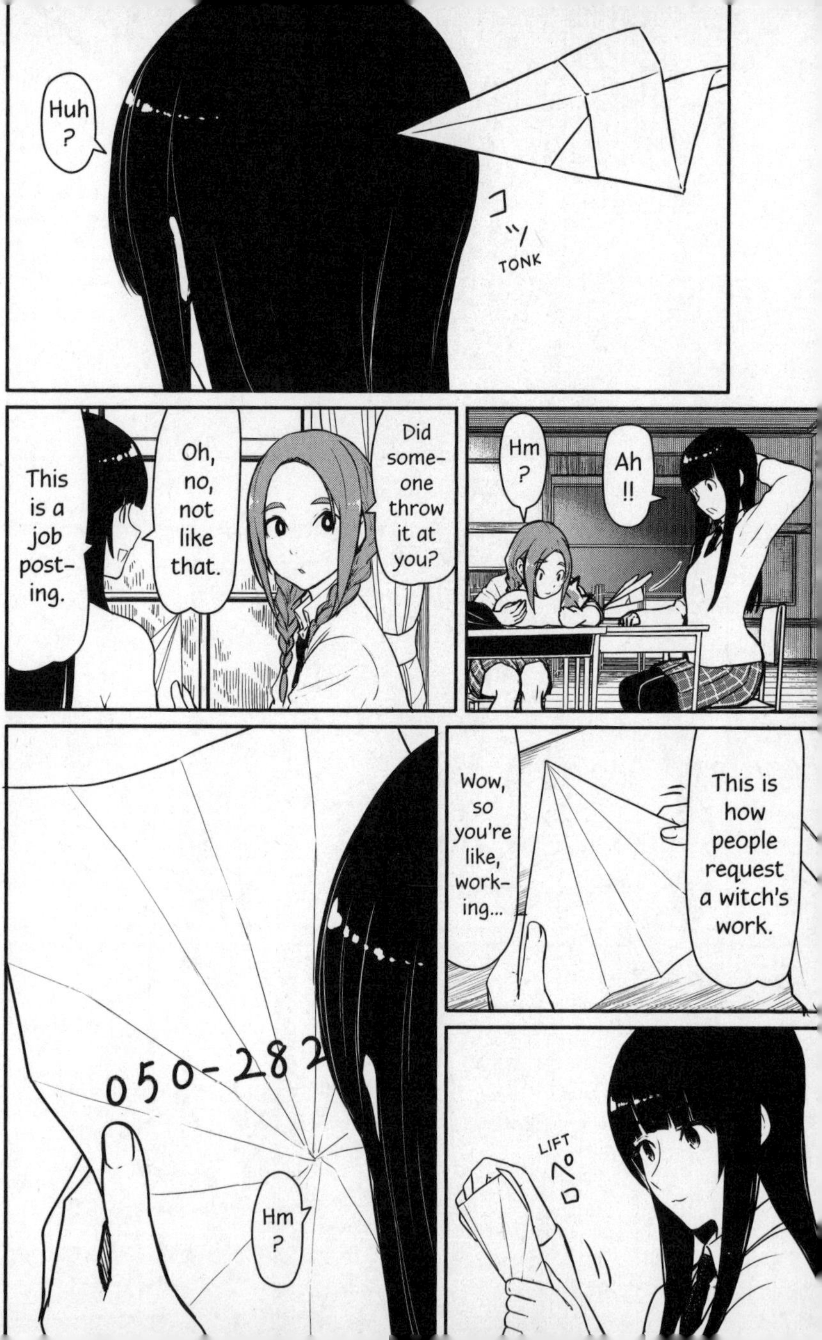

Huh ?
コッ
TONK
Ah !!
Hm ?
Did someone throw it at you?
Oh, no, not like that.
This is a job posting.
This is how people request a witch's work.
Wow, so you're like, working...
ペロ
LIFT
050-282
Hm ?

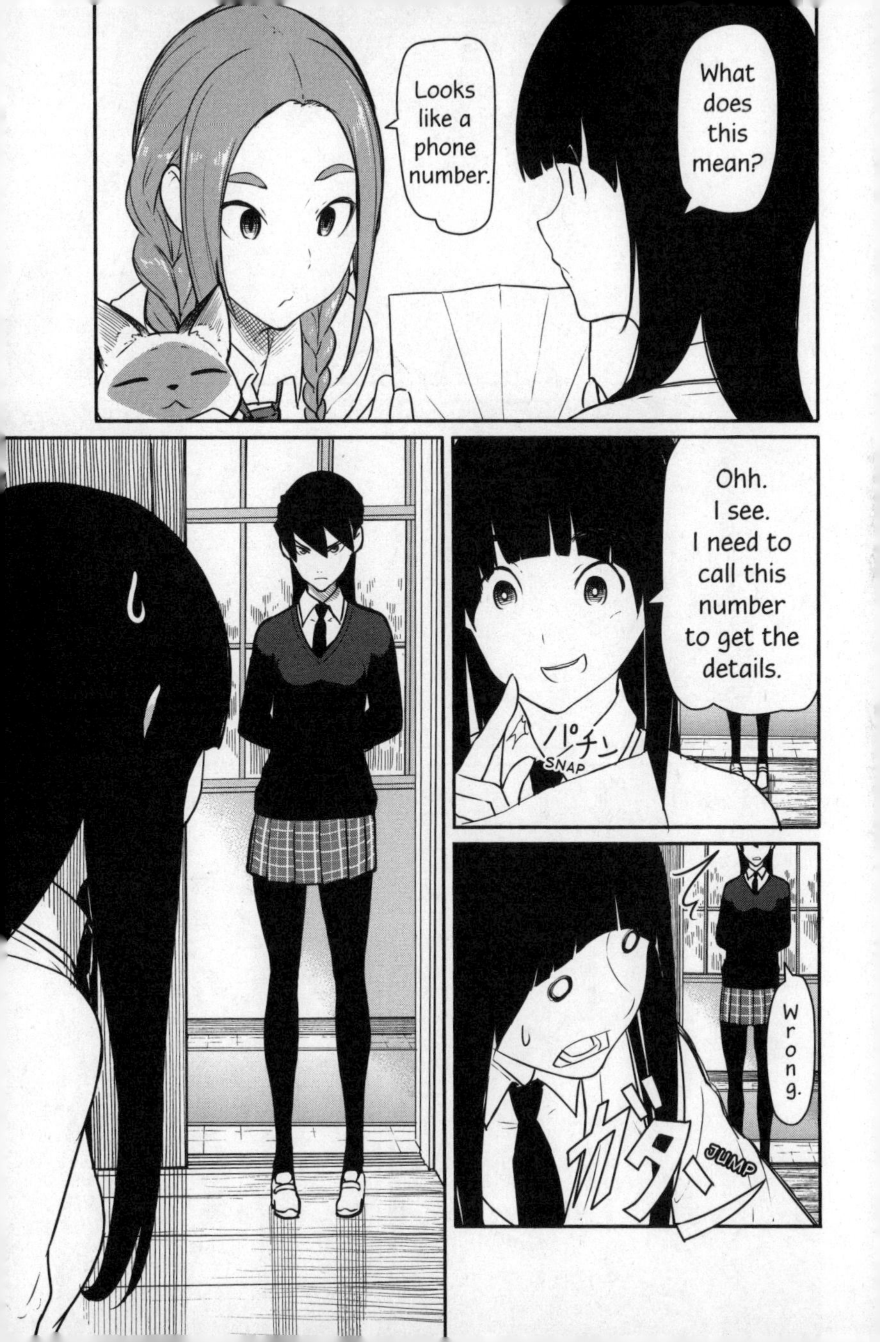
What does this mean?
Looks like a phone number.
Ohh. I see. I need to call this number to get the details.
パチン
SNAP
Wrong.
JUMP

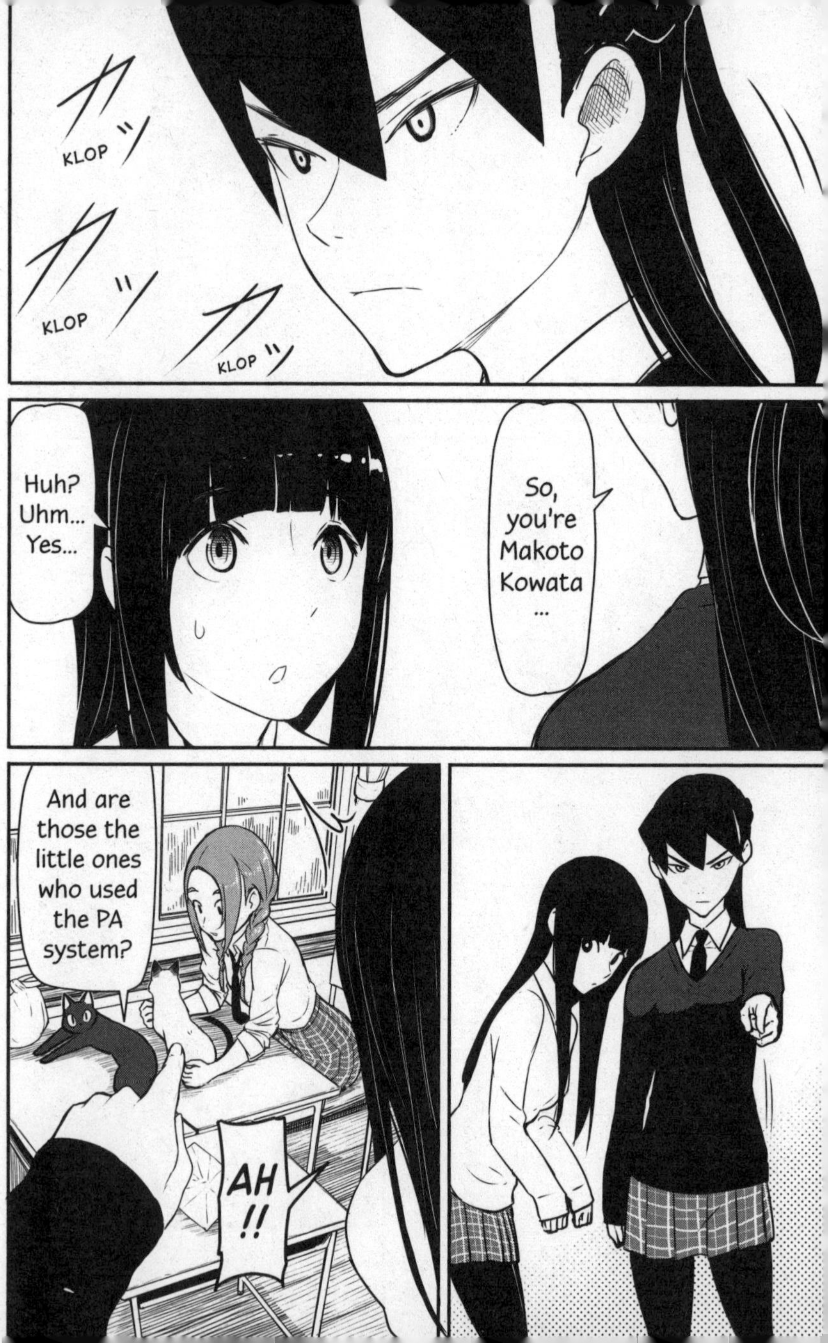
KLOP
KLOP
KLOP
So, you're Makoto Kowata ...
Huh? Uhm... Yes...
And are those the little ones who used the PA system?
AH !!

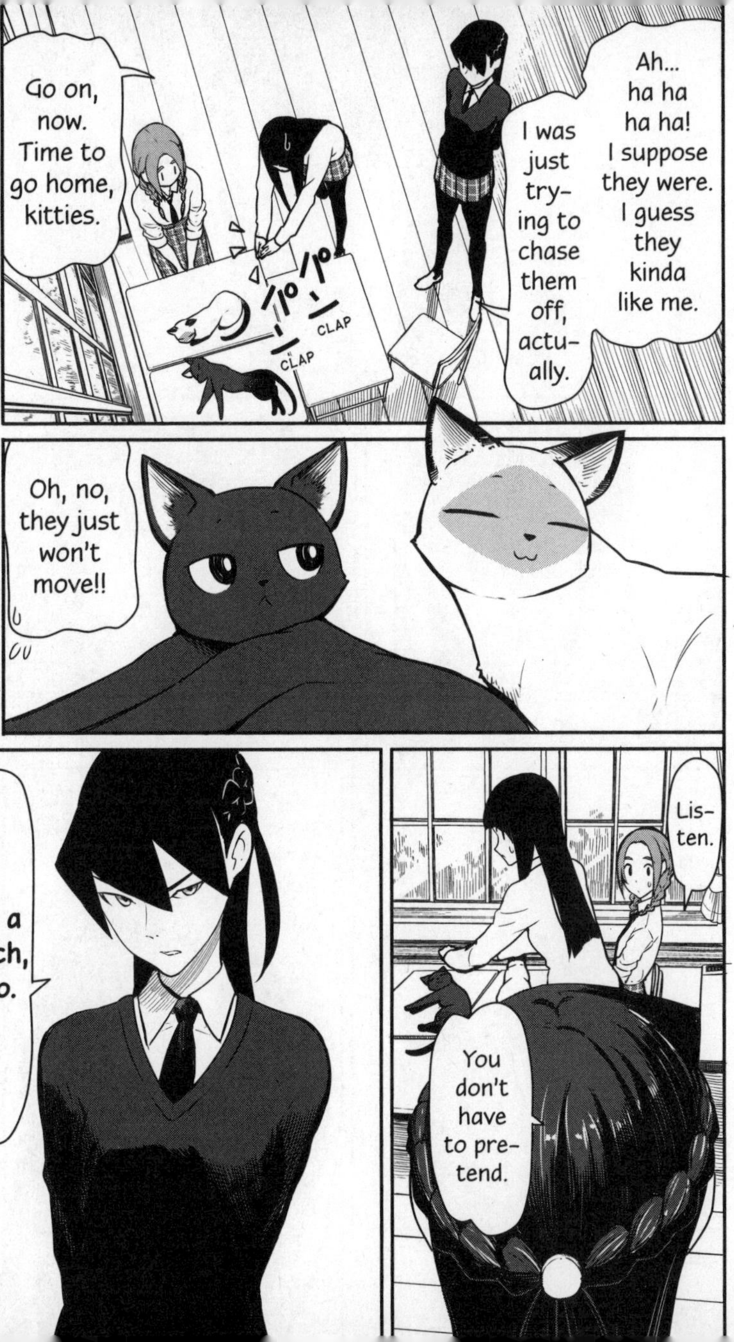
Ah... ha ha ha ha! I suppose they were. I guess they kinda like me.
I was just try-ing to chase them off, actu-ally.
Go on, now. Time to go home, kitties.
CLAP
CLAP
Oh, no, they just won't move!!
Lis-ten.
You don't have to pre-tend.
I'm a witch, too.

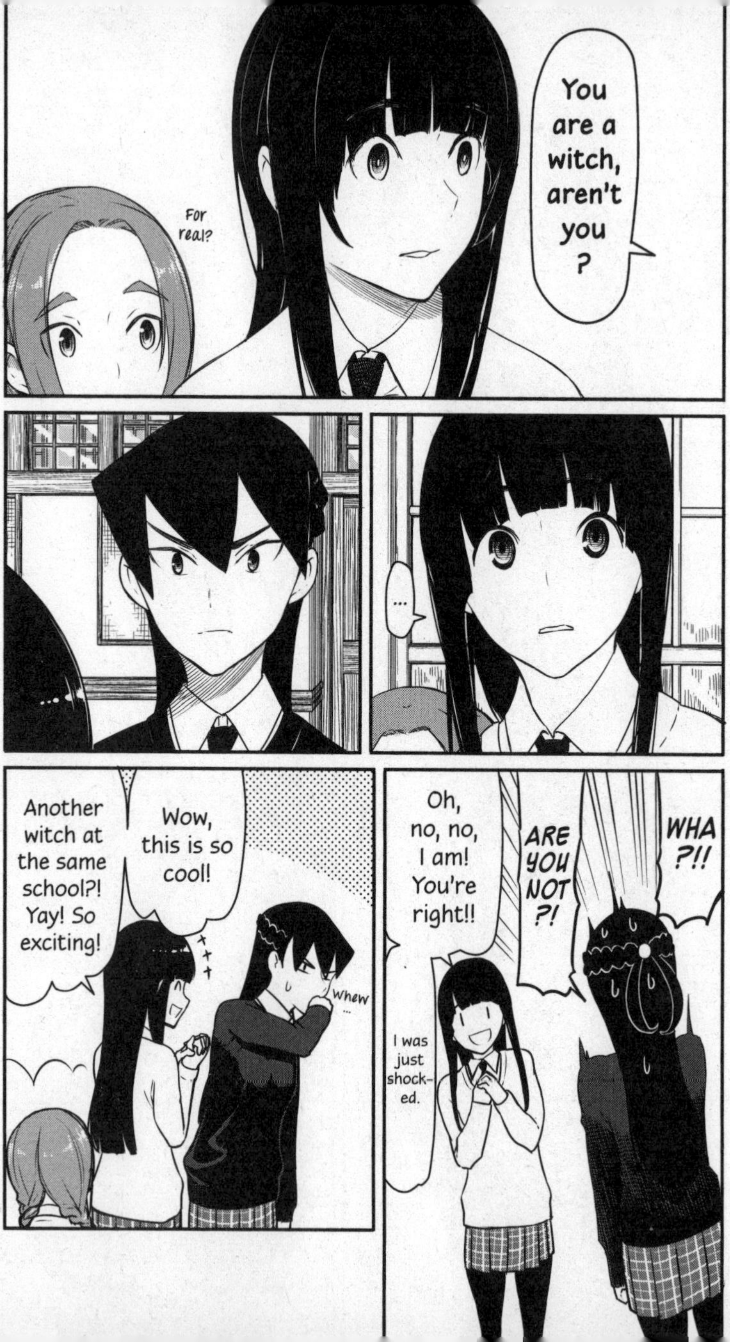
You are a witch, aren't you?
For real?
...
WHA?!!
ARE YOU NOT?!
Oh, no, no, I am! You're right!!
I was just shock-ed.
Wow, this is so cool!
Another witch at the same school?! Yay! So exciting!
Whew...

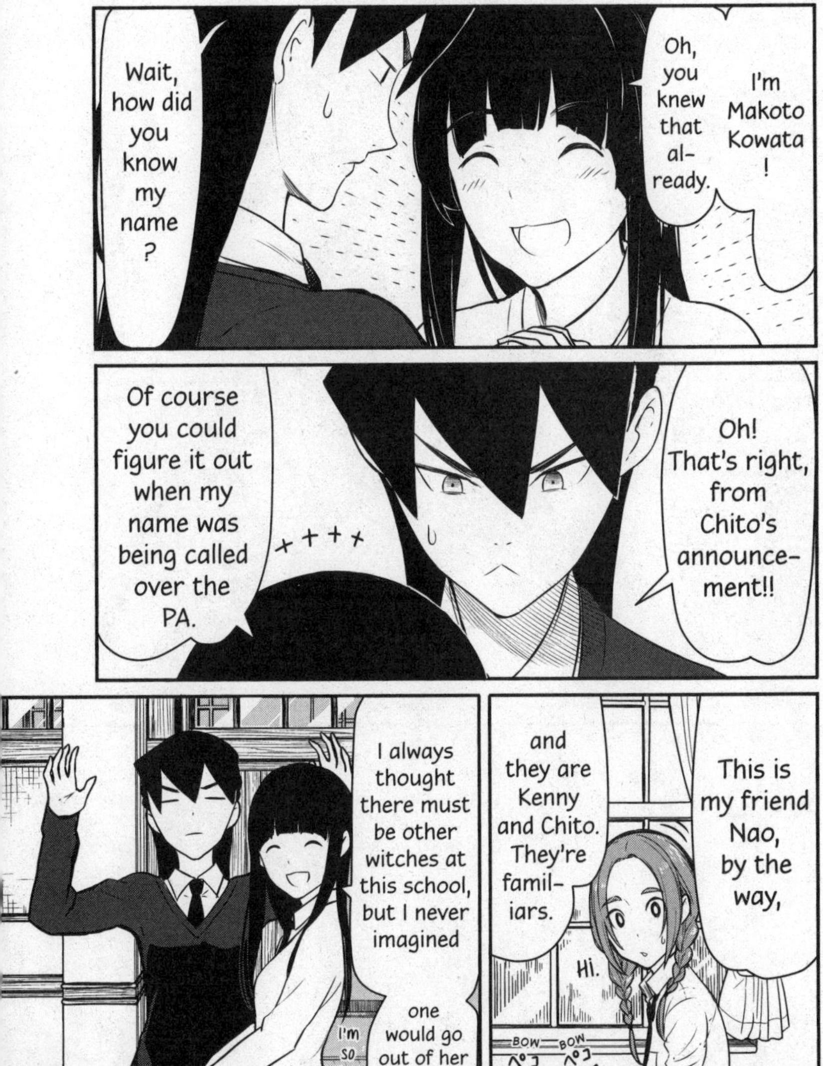
I'm Makoto Kowata!
Oh, you knew that already.
Wait, how did you know my name?
Oh! That's right, from Chito's announcement!!
Of course you could figure it out when my name was being called over the PA.
This is my friend Nao, by the way,
and they are Kenny and Chito. They're familiars.
Hi.
BOW BOW
I always thought there must be other witches at this school, but I never imagined
one would go out of her way to say hi to me.
I'm so glad.

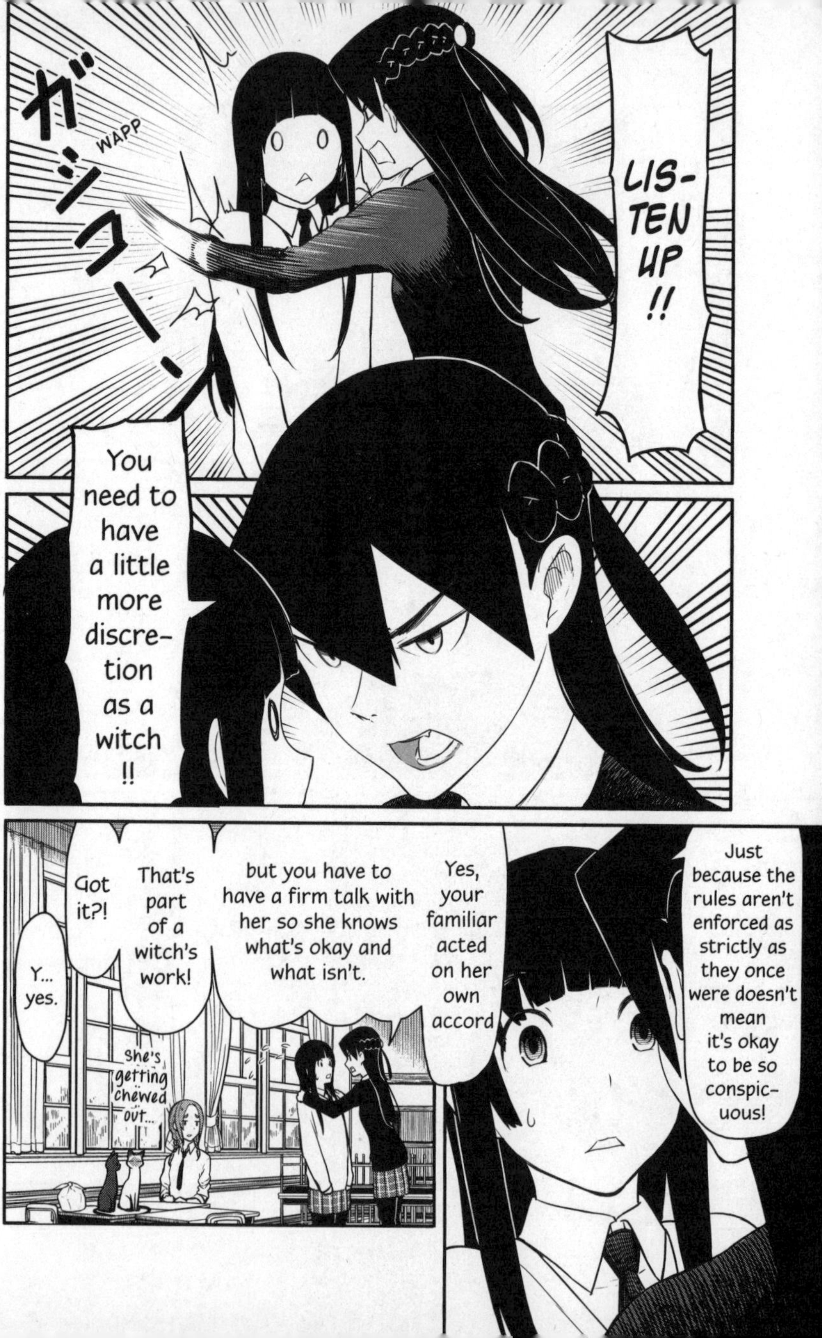
LIS-TEN UP !!
WAPP
You need to have a little more discretion as a witch !!
Just because the rules aren't enforced as strictly as they once were doesn't mean it's okay to be so conspicuous!
Yes, your familiar acted on her own accord
but you have to have a firm talk with her so she knows what's okay and what isn't.
That's part of a witch's work!
Got it?!
Y... yes.
she's getting chewed out...

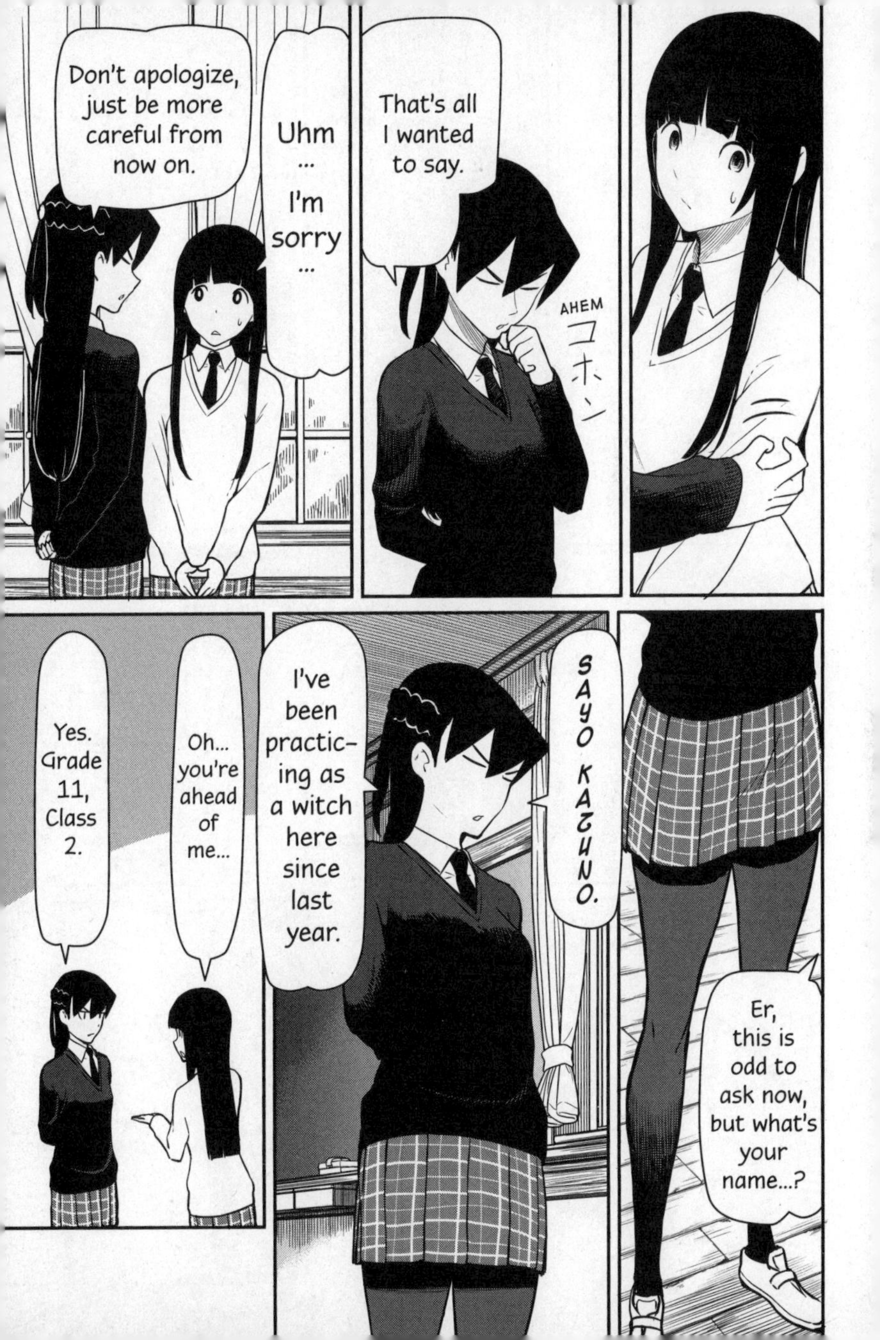
That's all I wanted to say.
AHEM
コホン
Uhm ... I'm sorry ...
Don't apologize, just be more careful from now on.
Er, this is odd to ask now, but what's your name...?
SAYO KAZUNO.
I've been practic-ing as a witch here since last year.
Oh... you're ahead of me...
Yes. Grade 11, Class 2.

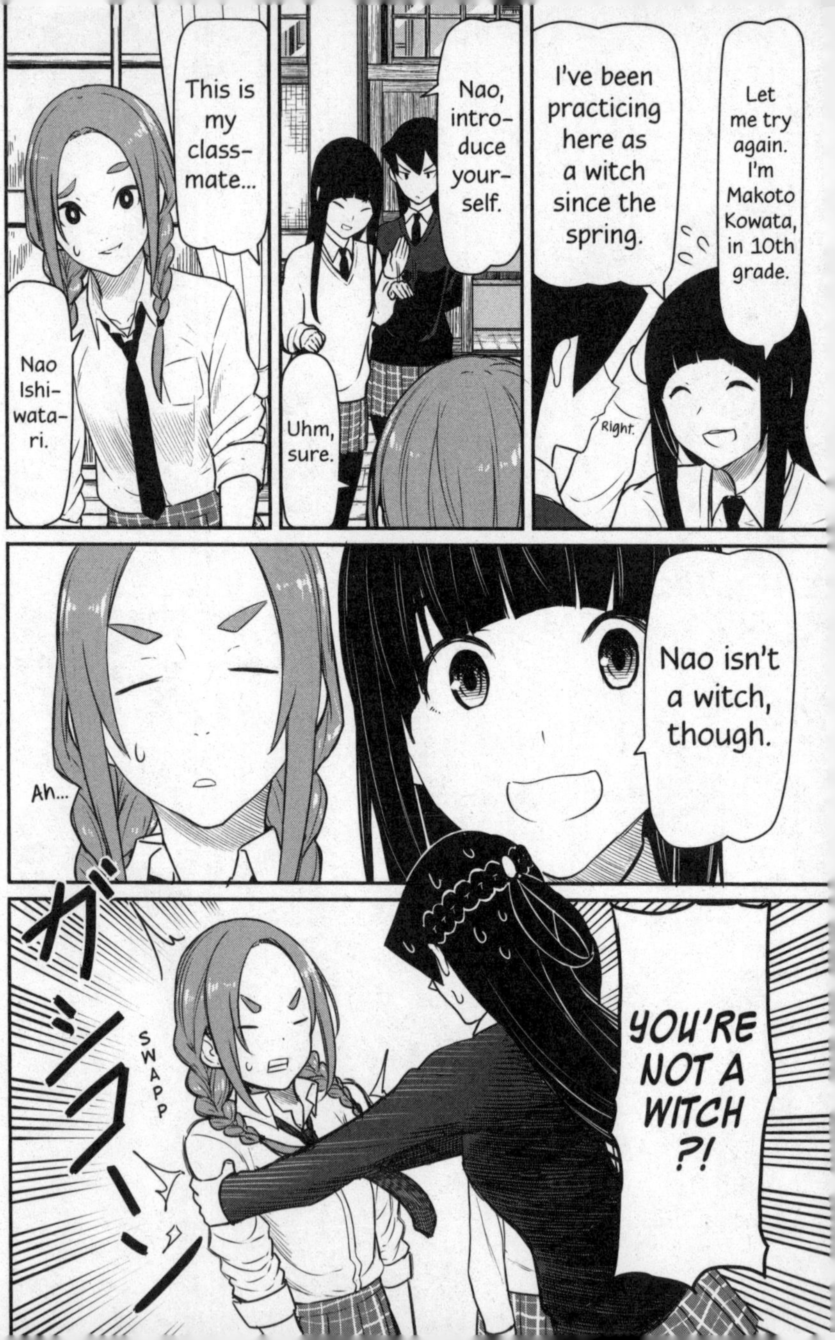
Let me try again. I'm Makoto Kowata, in 10th grade.
I've been practicing here as a witch since the spring.
Right.
Nao, introduce yourself.
Uhm, sure.
This is my classmate...
Nao Ishiwatari.
Nao isn't a witch, though.
Ah...
YOU'RE NOT A WITCH ?!
SWAPP

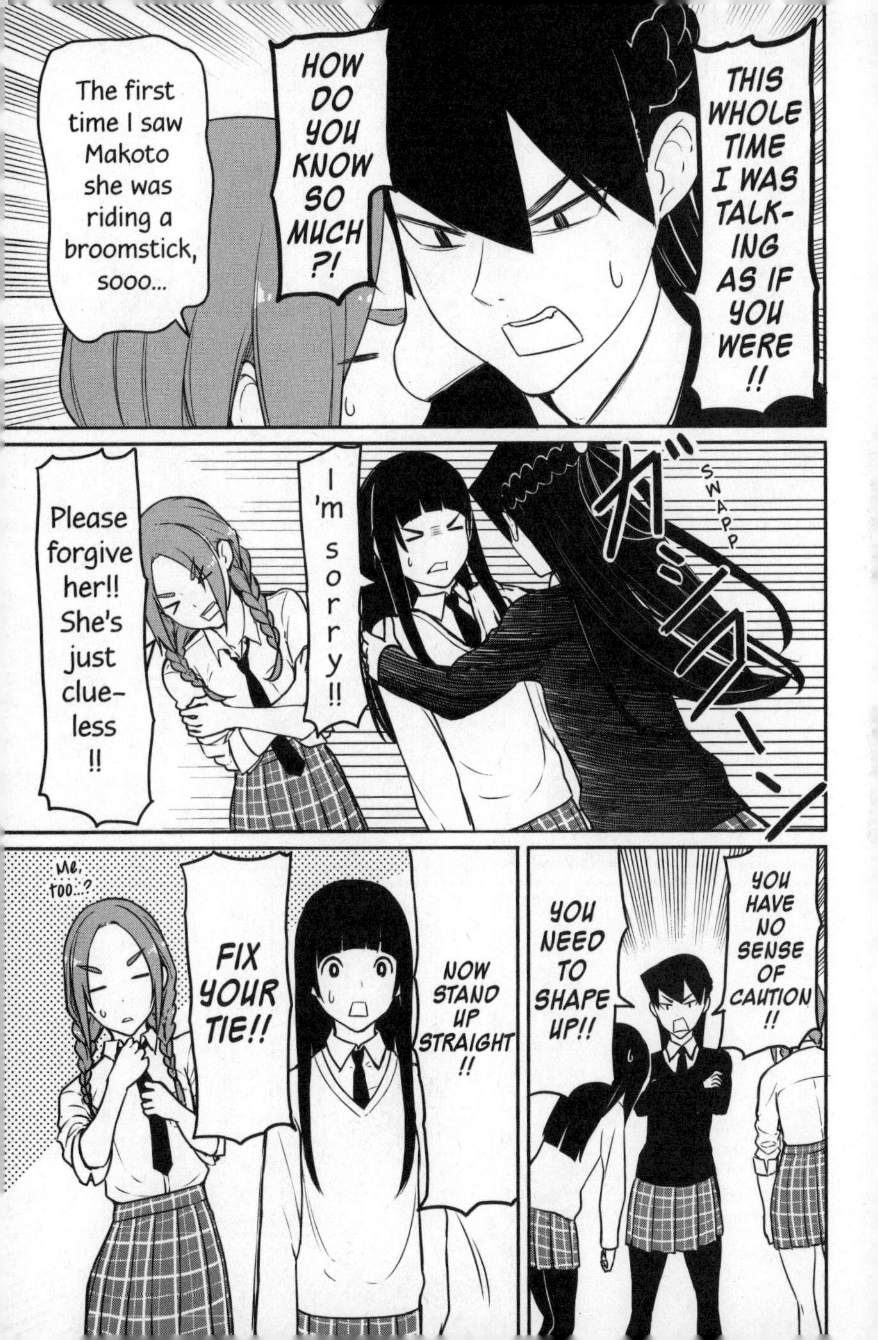
THIS WHOLE TIME I WAS TALKING AS IF YOU WERE!!
HOW DO YOU KNOW SO MUCH?!
The first time I saw Makoto she was riding a broomstick, sooo...
SWAPP
I'm sorry!!
Please forgive her!! She's just clueless!!
YOU HAVE NO SENSE OF CAUTION!!
YOU NEED TO SHAPE UP!!
NOW STAND UP STRAIGHT!!
FIX YOUR TIE!!
Me, too...?

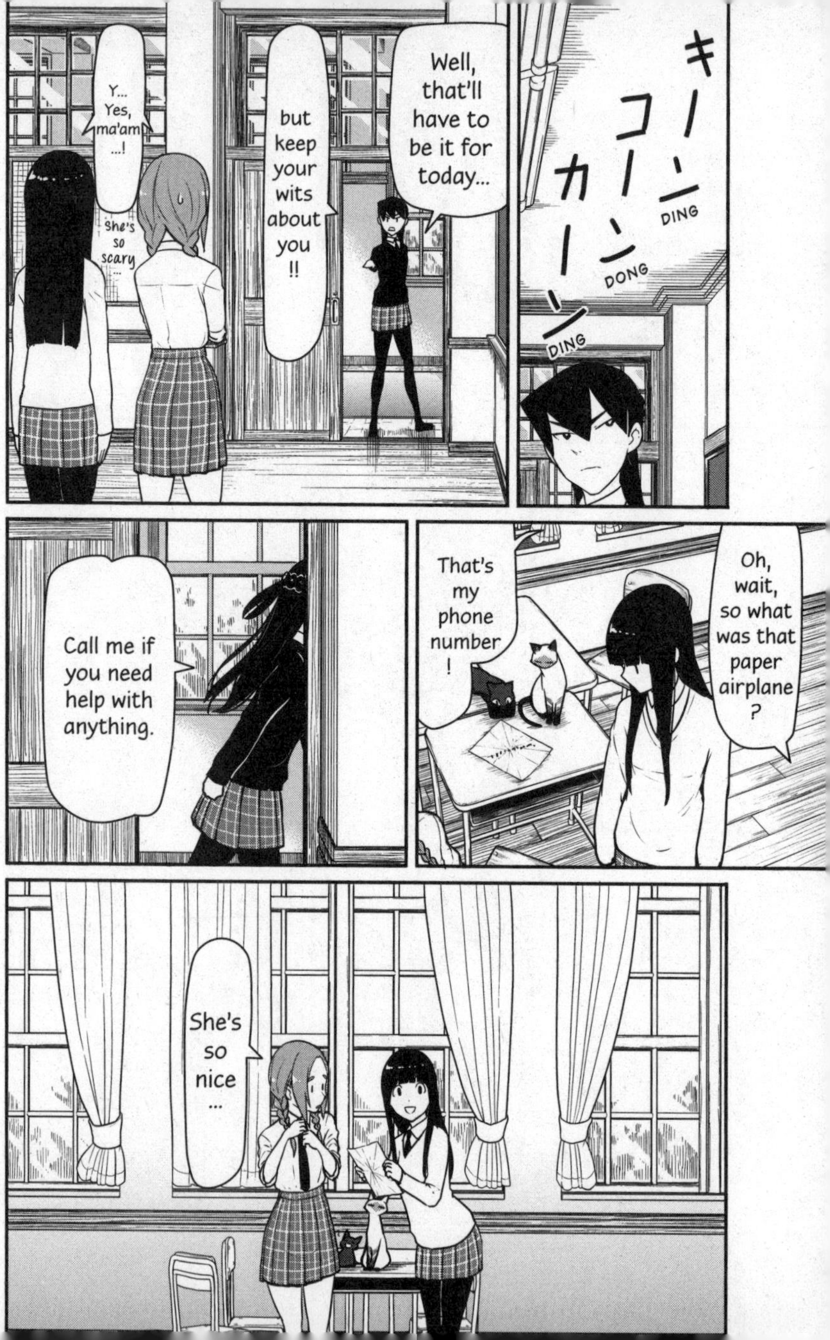

キーン
コーン
カーン
DING
DONG
DING
Well, that'll have to be it for today...
but keep your wits about you !!
Y... Yes, ma'am ...!
She's so scary ...
Oh, wait, so what was that paper airplane ?
That's my phone number !
Call me if you need help with anything.
She's so nice ...

Flying
Witch

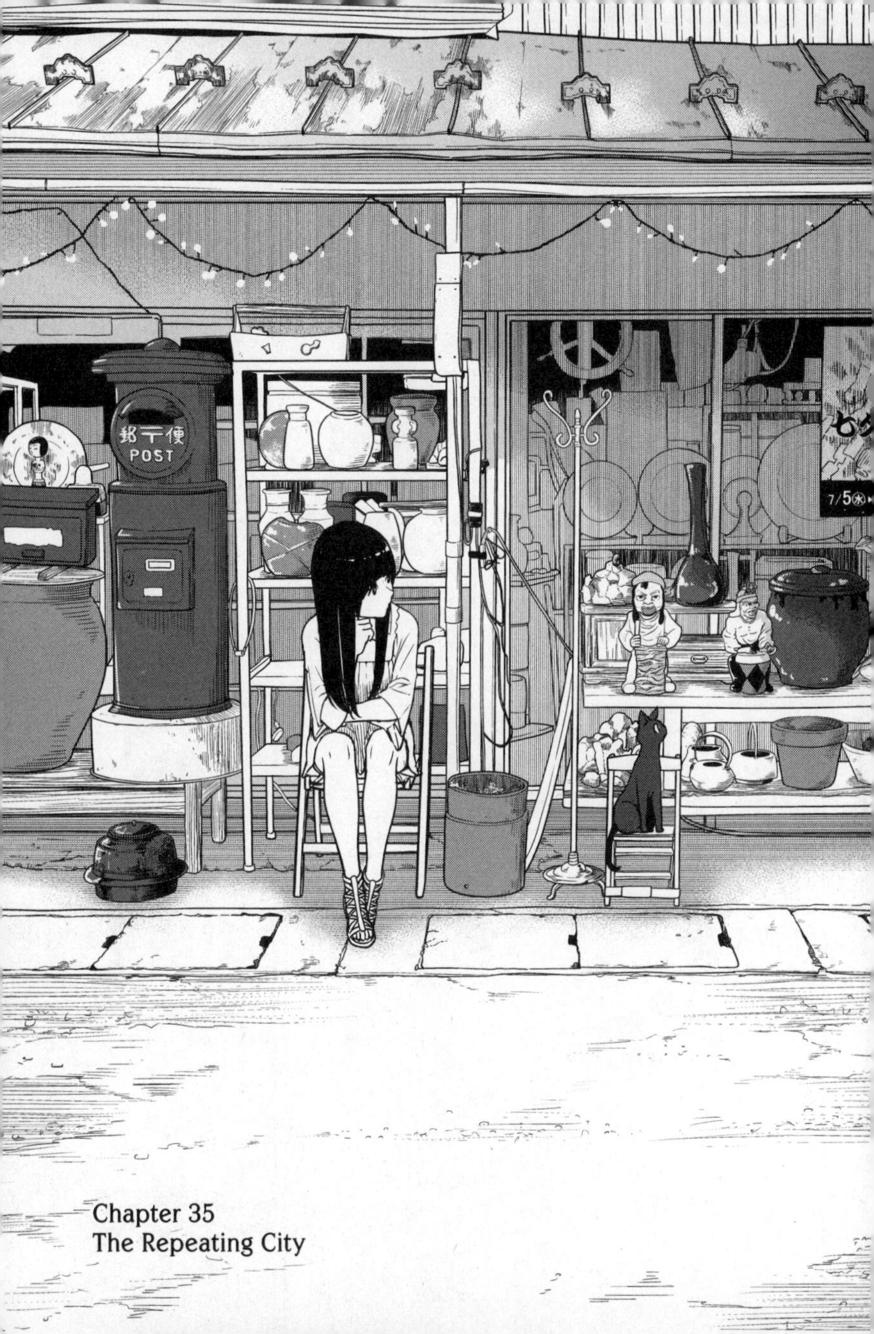
郵〒便
POST
7/5水

Chapter 35
The Repeating City

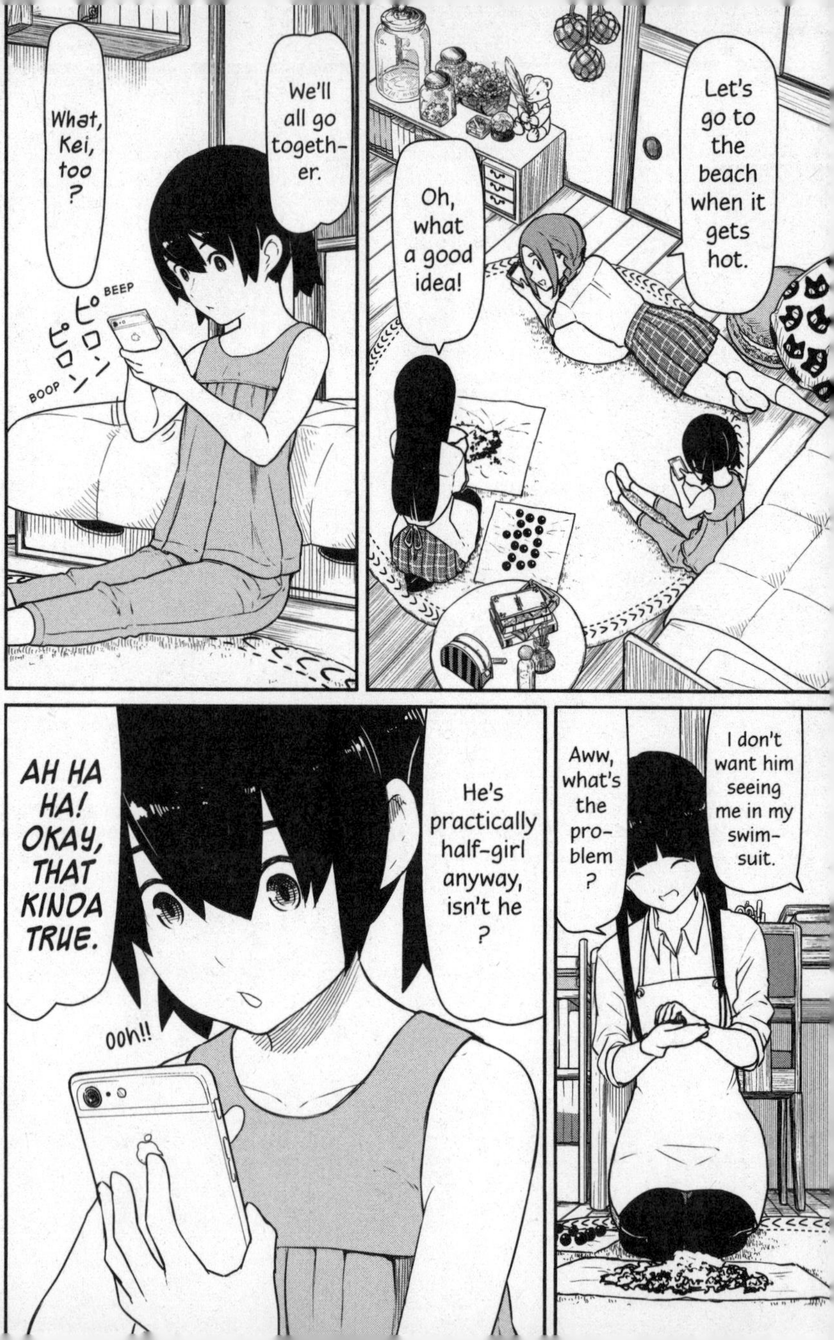
Let's go to the beach when it gets hot.
Oh, what a good idea!
We'll all go togeth-er.
What, Kei, too?
ピロン BEEP
ピロン BOOP
I don't want him seeing me in my swim-suit.
Aww, what's the pro-blem?
He's practically half-girl anyway, isn't he?
AH HA HA! OKAY, THAT KINDA TRUE.
ooh!!

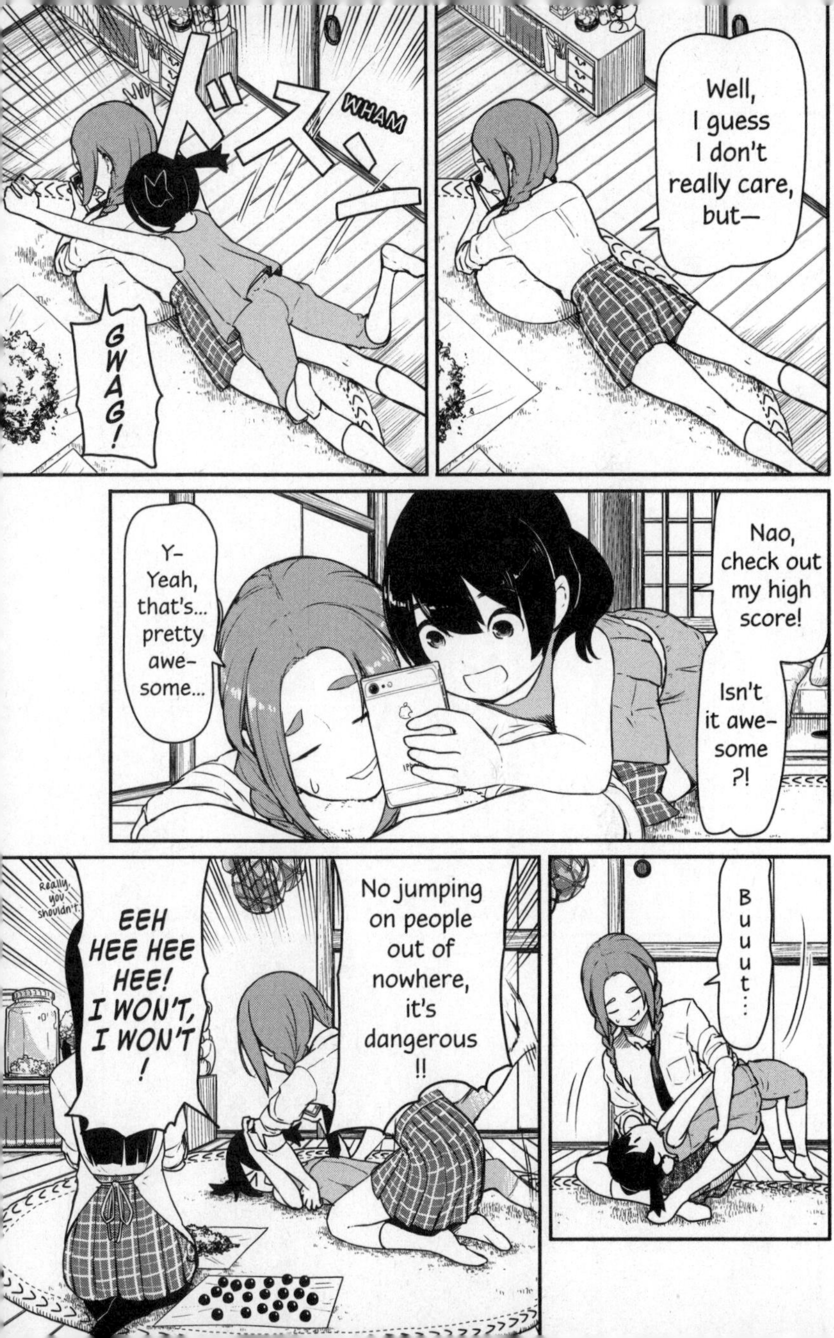
Well, I guess I don't really care, but—
WHAM
GWAG!
Nao, check out my high score!
Isn't it awe-some?!
Y-Yeah, that's... pretty awe-some...
Buuut...
No jumping on people out of nowhere, it's dangerous!!
EEH HEE HEE HEE! I WON'T, I WON'T!
Really, you shouldn't.

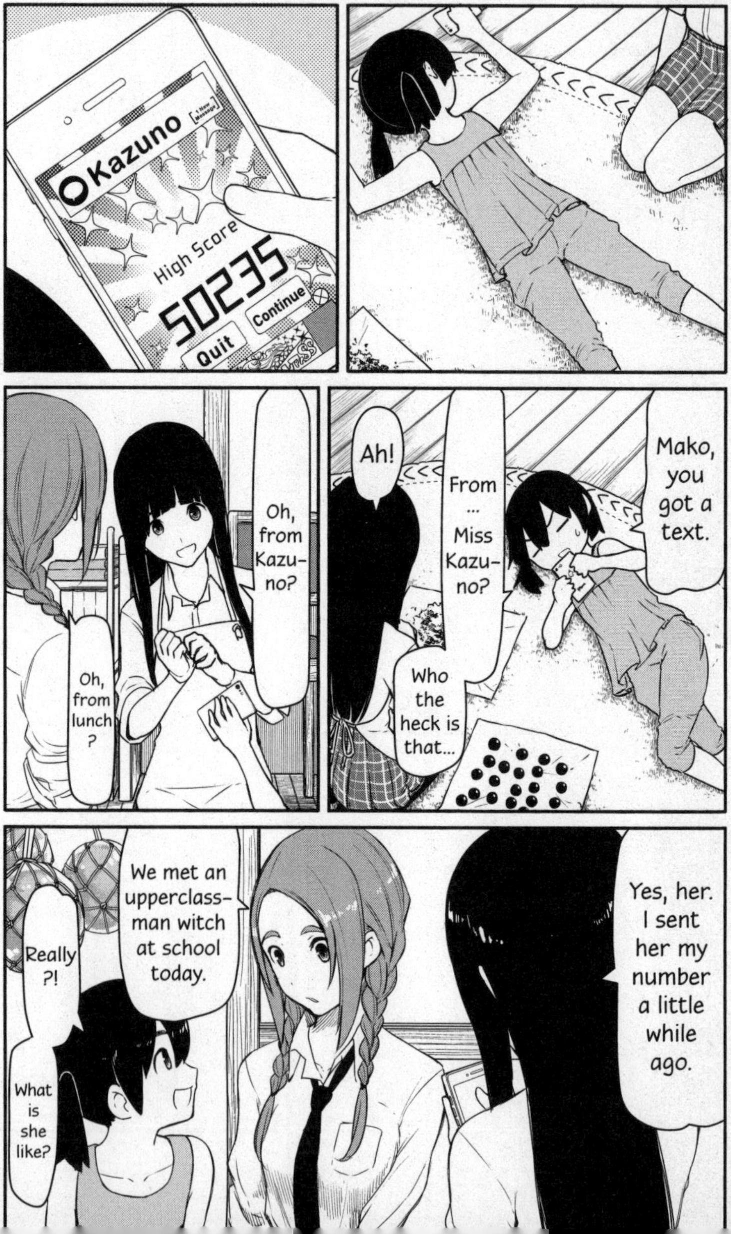
Kazuno
1 New Message
High Score
50235
Continue
Quit
Mako, you got a text.
From ... Miss Kazuno?
Ah!
Who the heck is that...
Oh, from Kazuno?
Oh, from lunch?
Yes, her. I sent her my number a little while ago.
We met an upperclassman witch at school today.
Really?!
What is she like?

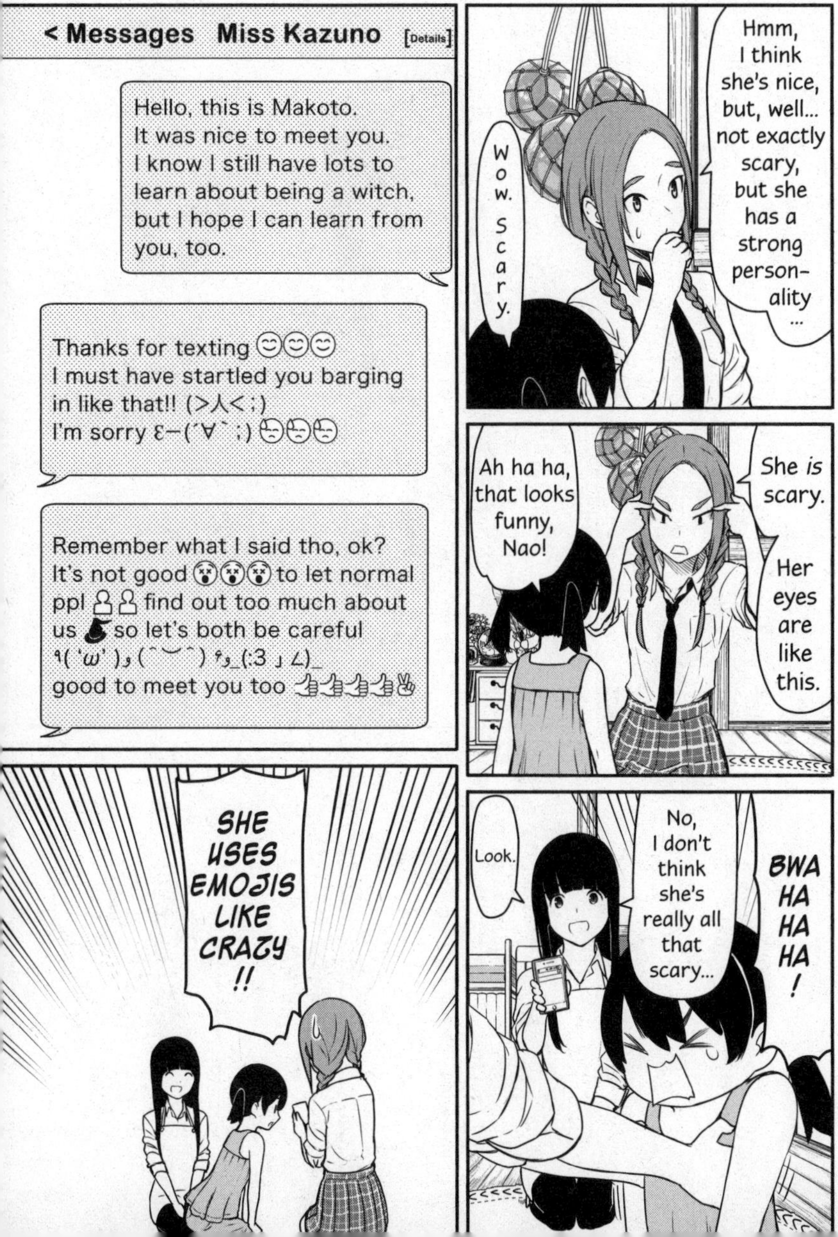
Hmm, I think she's nice, but, well... not exactly scary, but she has a strong person-ality...
Wow. Scary.
She *is* scary.
Her eyes are like this.
Ah ha ha, that looks funny, Nao!
No, I don't think she's really all that scary...
Look.
BWA HA HA HA!
< Messages Miss Kazuno [Details]
Hello, this is Makoto. It was nice to meet you. I know I still have lots to learn about being a witch, but I hope I can learn from you, too.
Thanks for texting I must have startled you barging in like that!! (>人<;) I'm sorry ε-(´∀`;)
Remember what I said tho, ok? It's not good to let normal ppl find out too much about us so let's both be careful ٩('ω')و (^‿^) ٩و_(:3 」∠)_ good to meet you too
SHE USES EMOJIS LIKE CRAZY!!

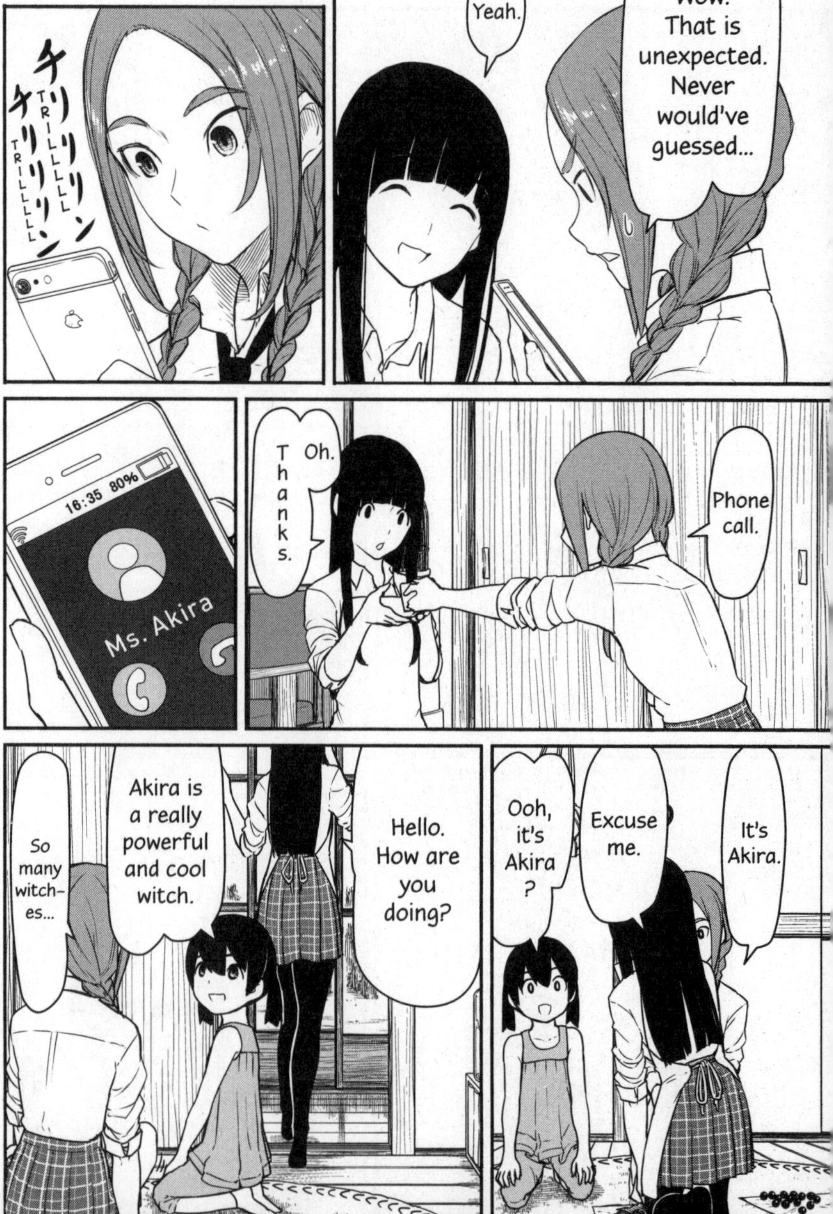
Wow. That is unexpected. Never would've guessed...
Yeah.
チリリリン
TRILLLLL
チリリリン
TRILLLLL
Phone call.
Oh.
Thanks.
16:35 80%
Ms. Akira
It's Akira.
Excuse me.
Ooh, it's Akira?
Hello. How are you doing?
Akira is a really powerful and cool witch.
So many witch-es...

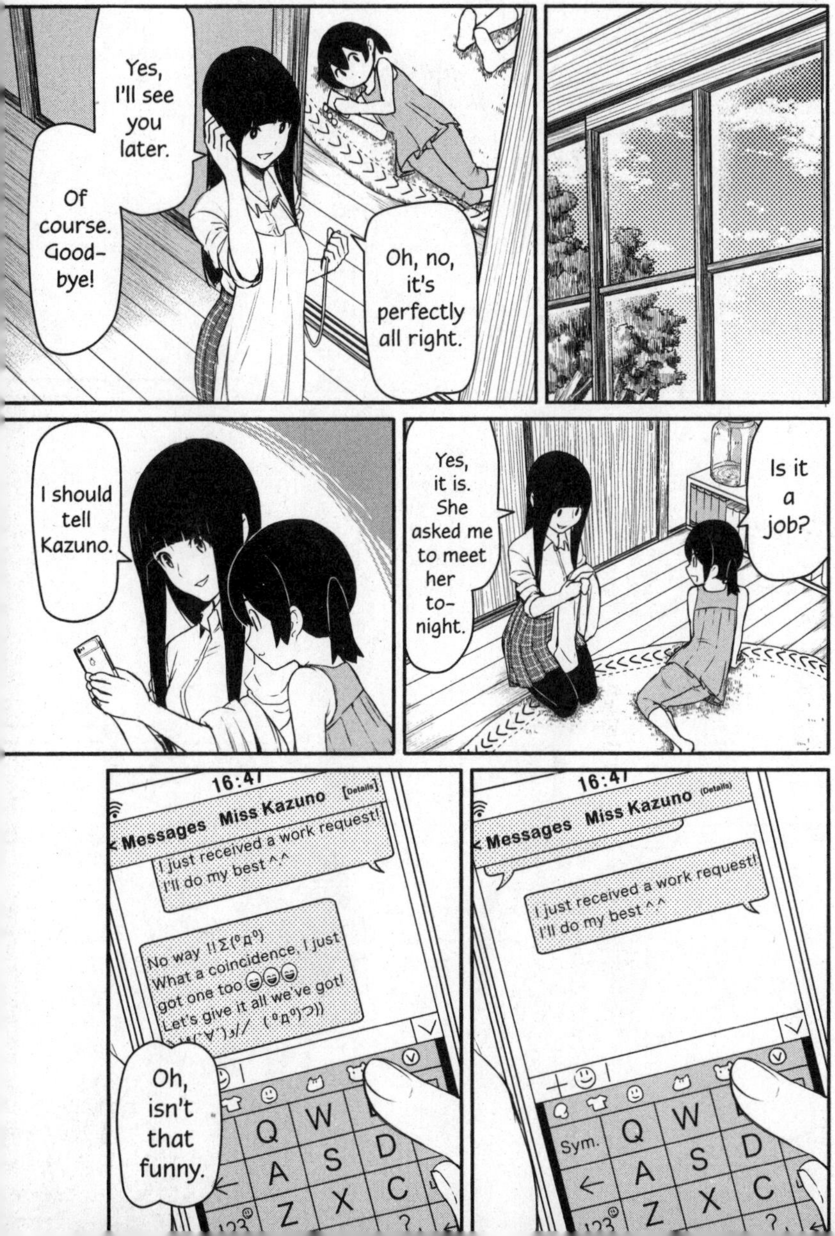
Oh, no, it's perfectly all right.
Yes, I'll see you later.
Of course. Good-bye!
Is it a job?
Yes, it is. She asked me to meet her to-night.
I should tell Kazuno.
16:47
Messages Miss Kazuno Details
I just received a work request! I'll do my best ^.^
16:47
Messages Miss Kazuno Details
I just received a work request! I'll do my best ^.^
No way !!Σ(ﾟДﾟ) What a coincidence, I just got one too
Let's give it all we've got!
Oh, isn't that funny.

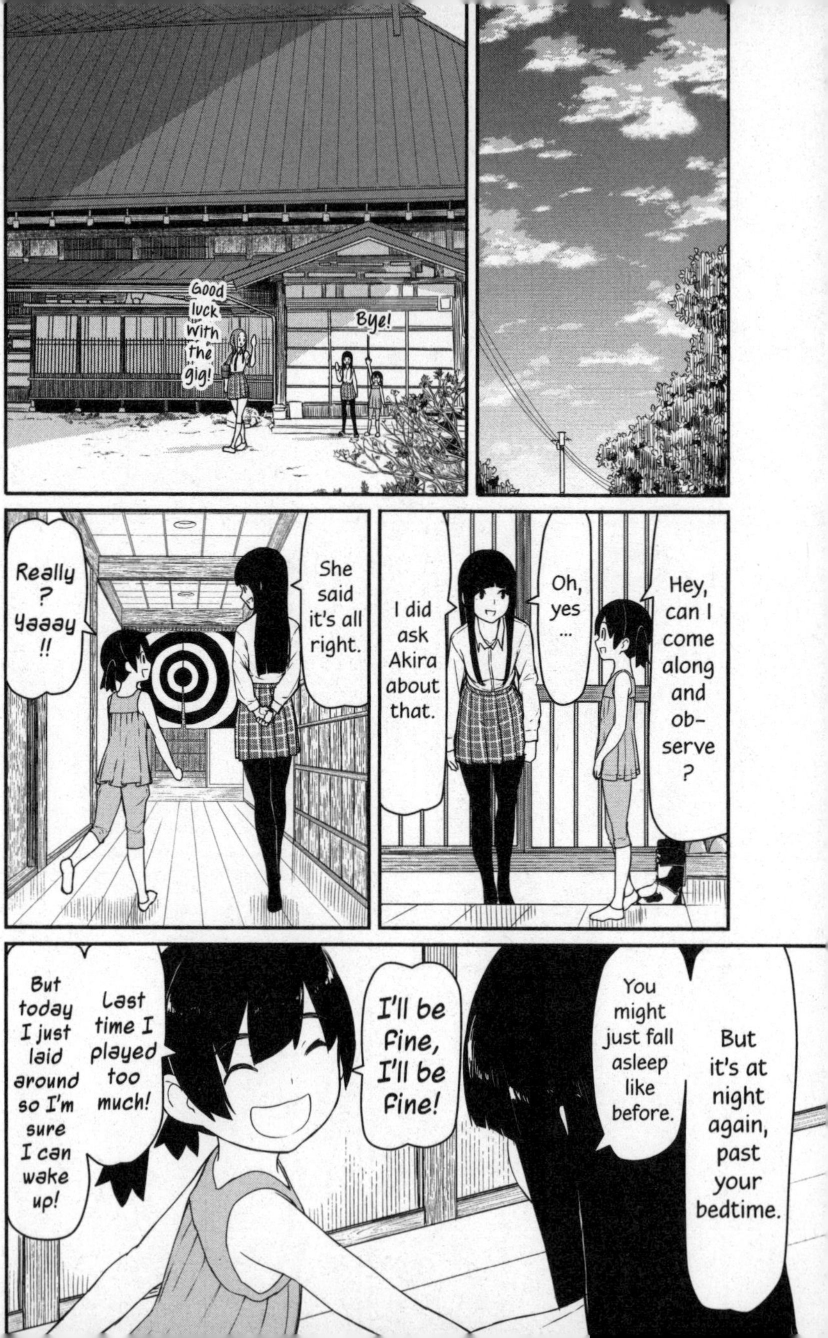

Good luck with the gig!
Bye!
Hey, can I come along and ob-serve?
Oh, yes ...
I did ask Akira about that.
She said it's all right.
Really? Yaaay!!
But it's at night again, past your bedtime.
You might just fall asleep like before.
I'll be fine, I'll be fine!
Last time I played too much!
But today I just laid around so I'm sure I can wake up!

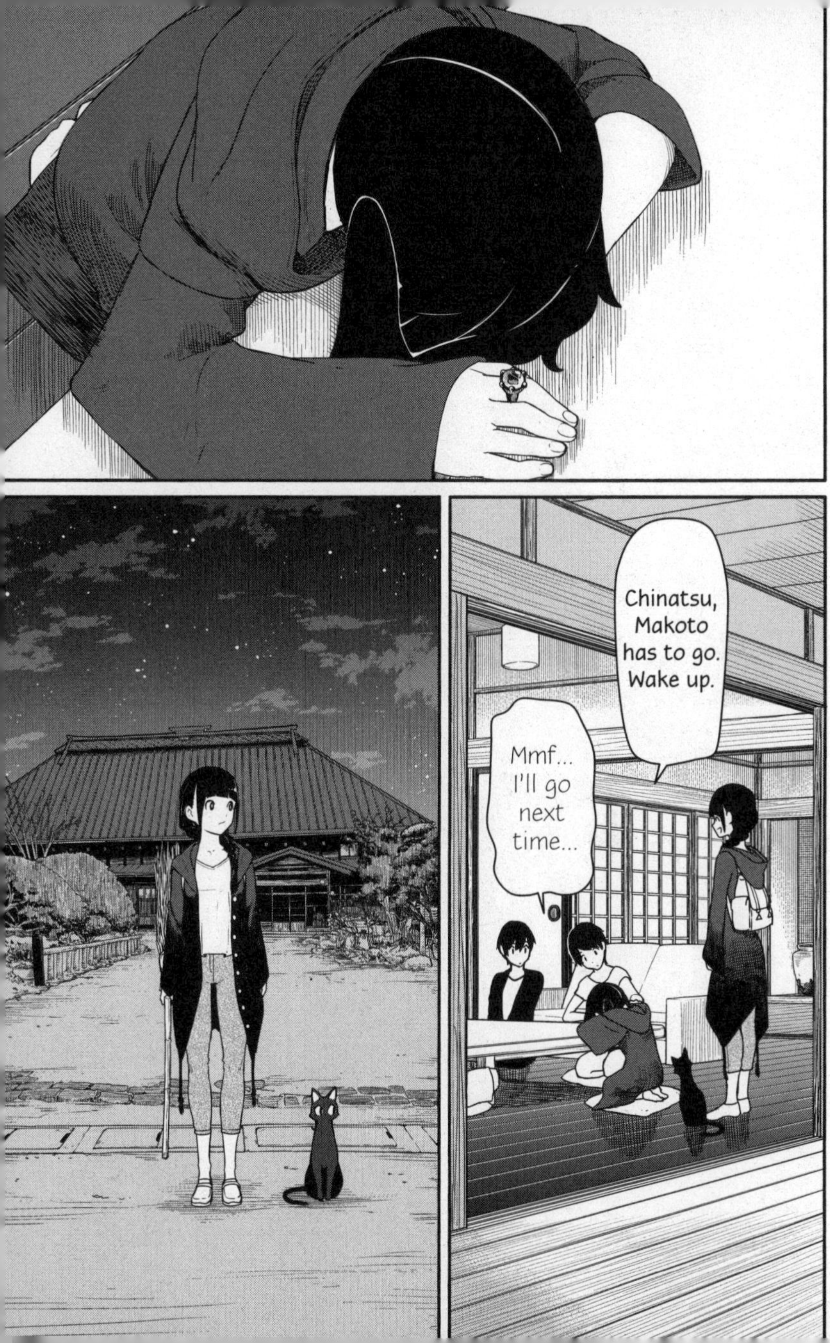
Chinatsu, Makoto has to go. Wake up.
Mmf... I'll go next time...

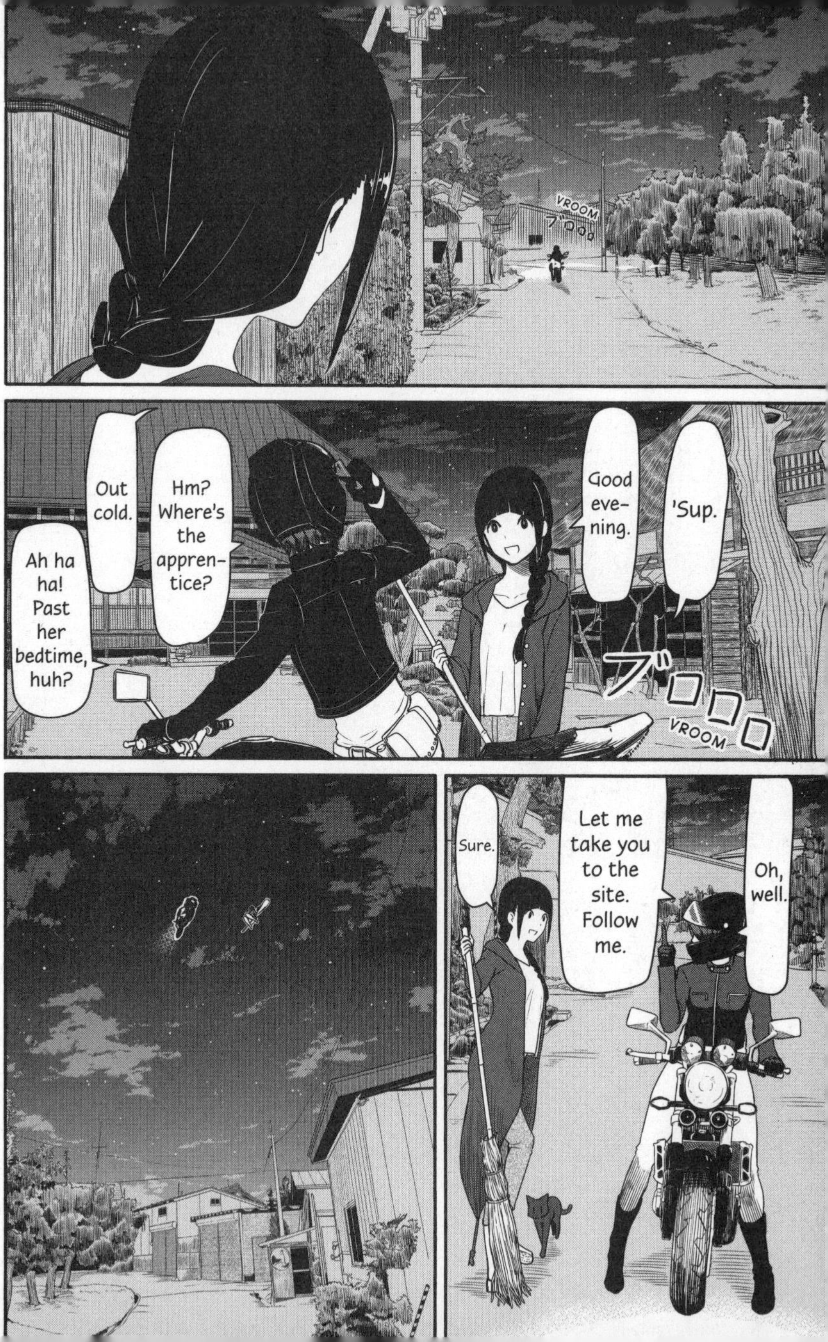
VROOM
ブロロロ
'Sup.
Good evening.
Hm? Where's the apprentice?
Out cold.
Ah ha ha! Past her bedtime, huh?
ブロロロ
VROOM
Oh, well.
Let me take you to the site. Follow me.
Sure.

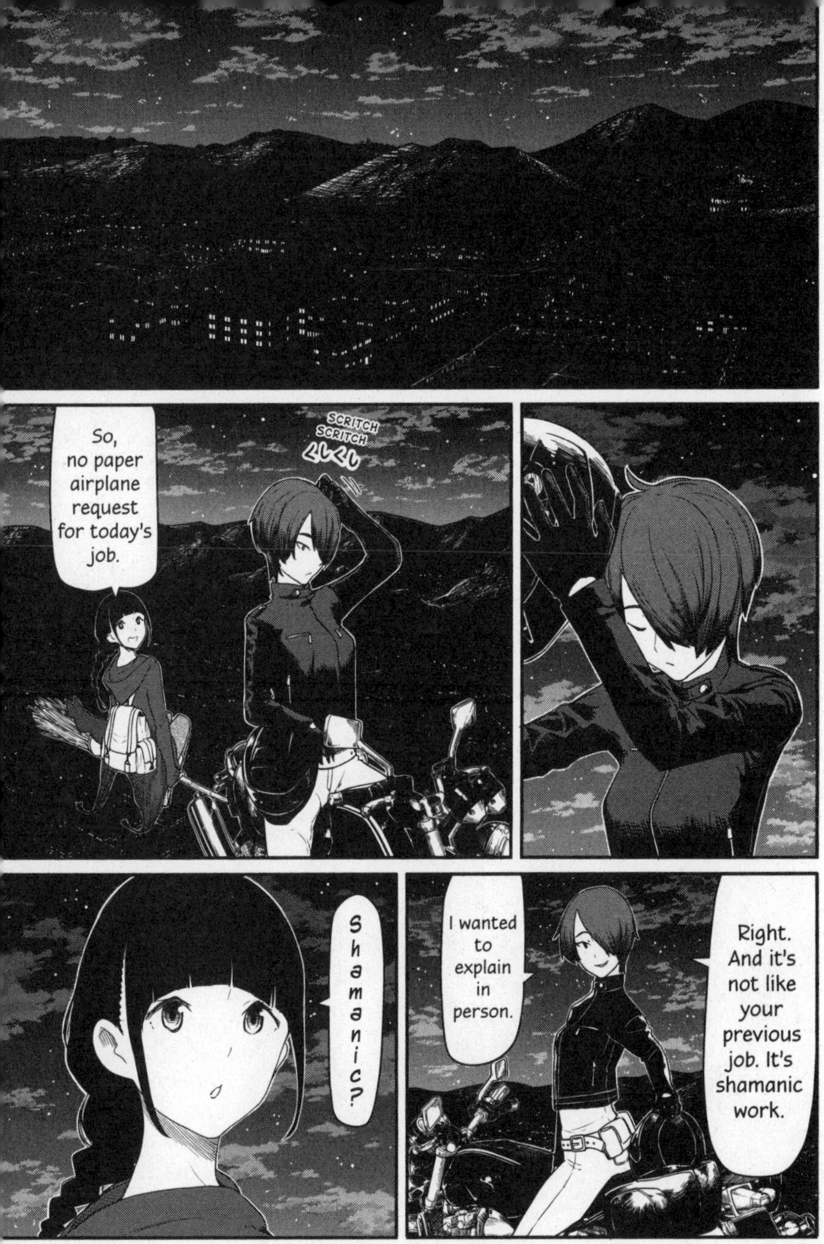
SCRITCH SCRITCH
くしくし
So, no paper airplane request for today's job.
Right. And it's not like your previous job. It's shamanic work.
I wanted to explain in person.
Shamanic?

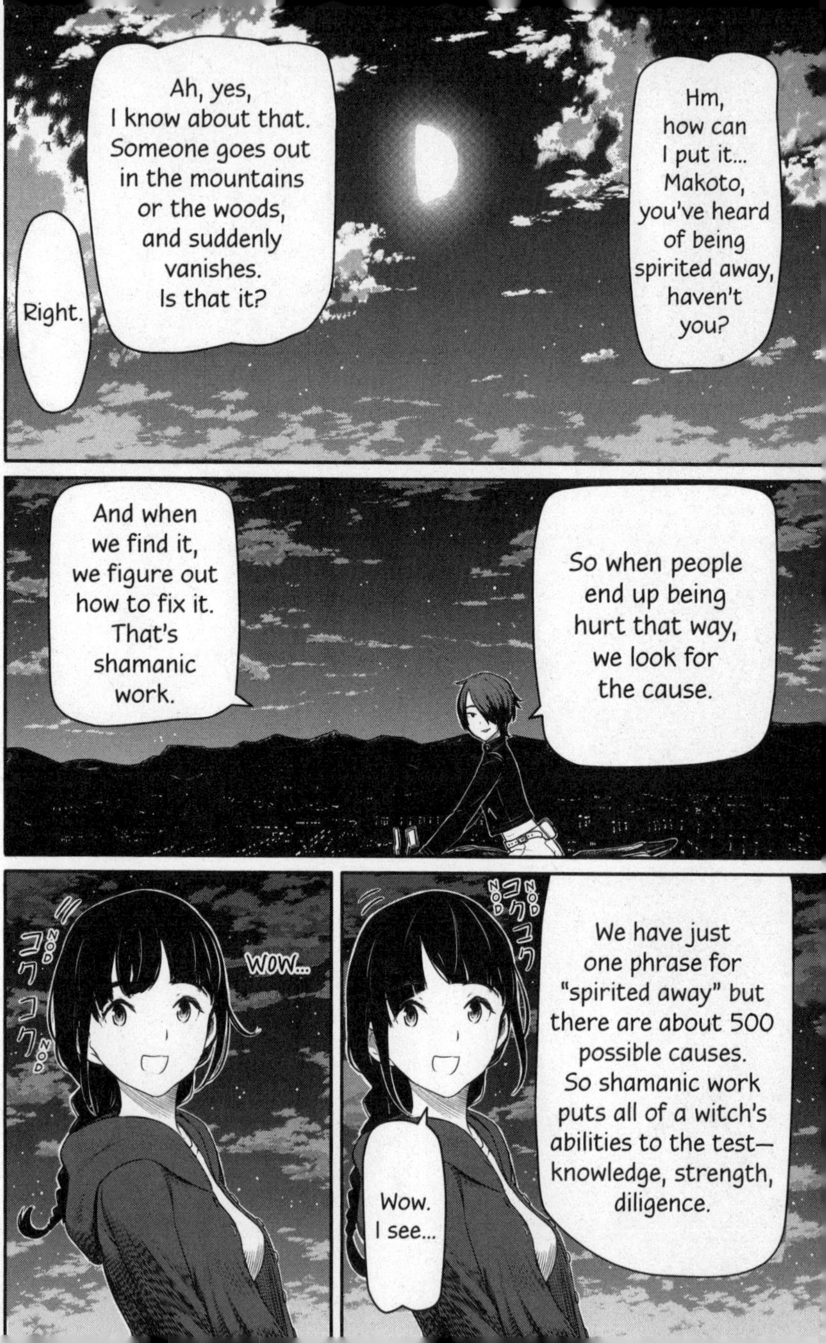
Hm, how can I put it... Makoto, you've heard of being spirited away, haven't you?
Ah, yes, I know about that. Someone goes out in the mountains or the woods, and suddenly vanishes. Is that it?
Right.
So when people end up being hurt that way, we look for the cause.
And when we find it, we figure out how to fix it. That's shamanic work.
コクコク NOD NOD
We have just one phrase for "spirited away" but there are about 500 possible causes. So shamanic work puts all of a witch's abilities to the test—knowledge, strength, diligence.
Wow. I see...
WOW...
コクコク NOD NOD

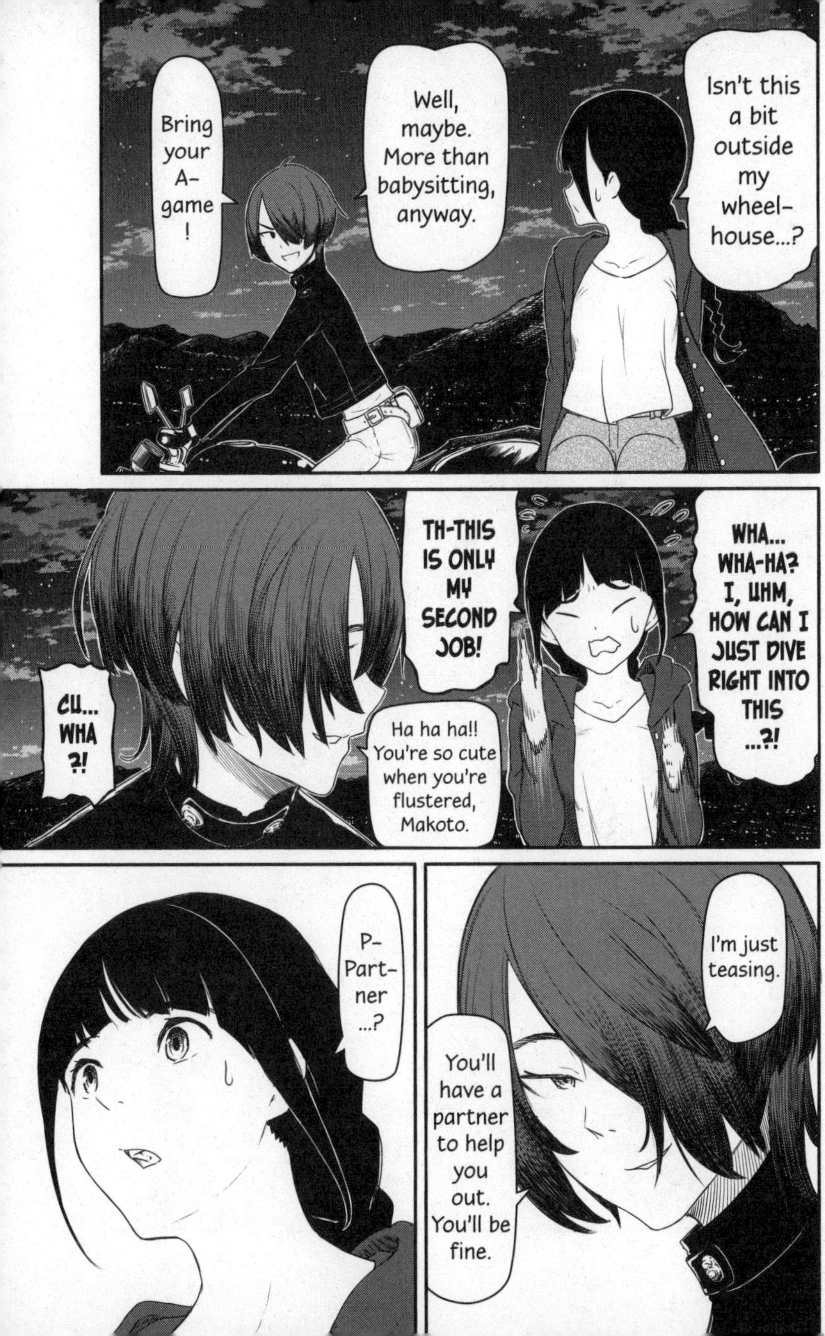
Isn't this a bit outside my wheelhouse...?
Well, maybe. More than babysitting, anyway.
Bring your A-game!
WHA... WHA-HA? I, UHM, HOW CAN I JUST DIVE RIGHT INTO THIS ...?!
TH-THIS IS ONLY MY SECOND JOB!
Ha ha ha!! You're so cute when you're flustered, Makoto.
CU... WHA ?!
I'm just teasing.
You'll have a partner to help you out. You'll be fine.
P-Partner...?

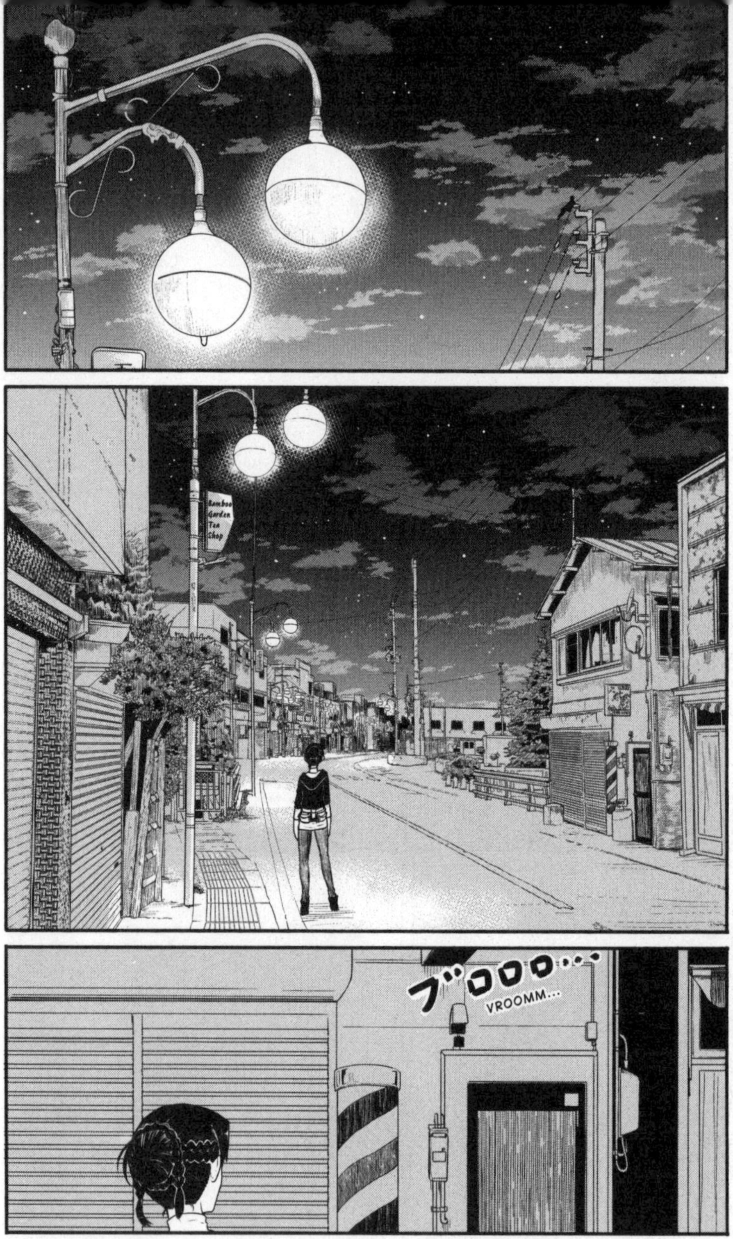
Bamboo Garden Tea Shop
ブロロロ...
VROOMM...

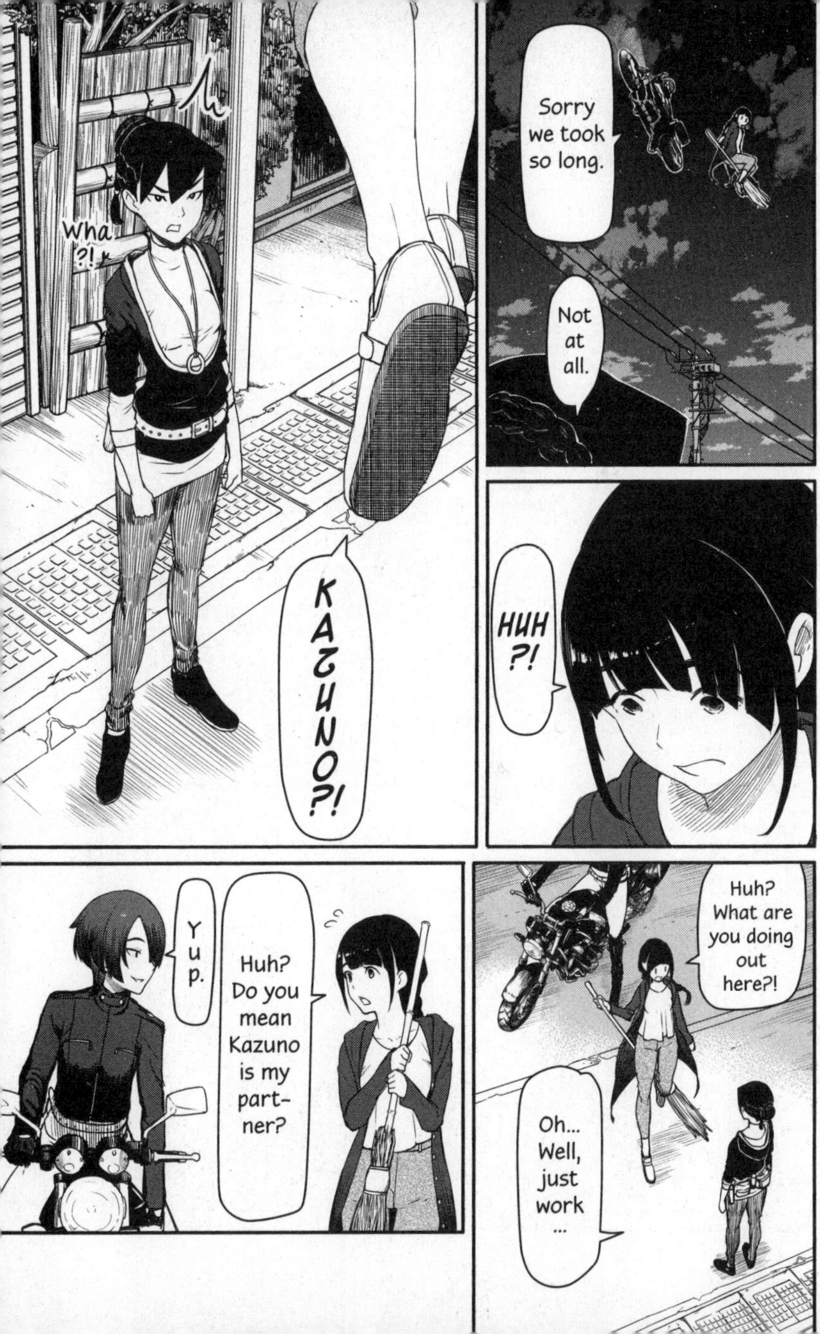
Sorry we took so long.
Not at all.
HUH?!
Wha?!
KAZUNO?!
Huh? What are you doing out here?!
Oh... Well, just work ...
Huh? Do you mean Kazuno is my partner?
Yup.

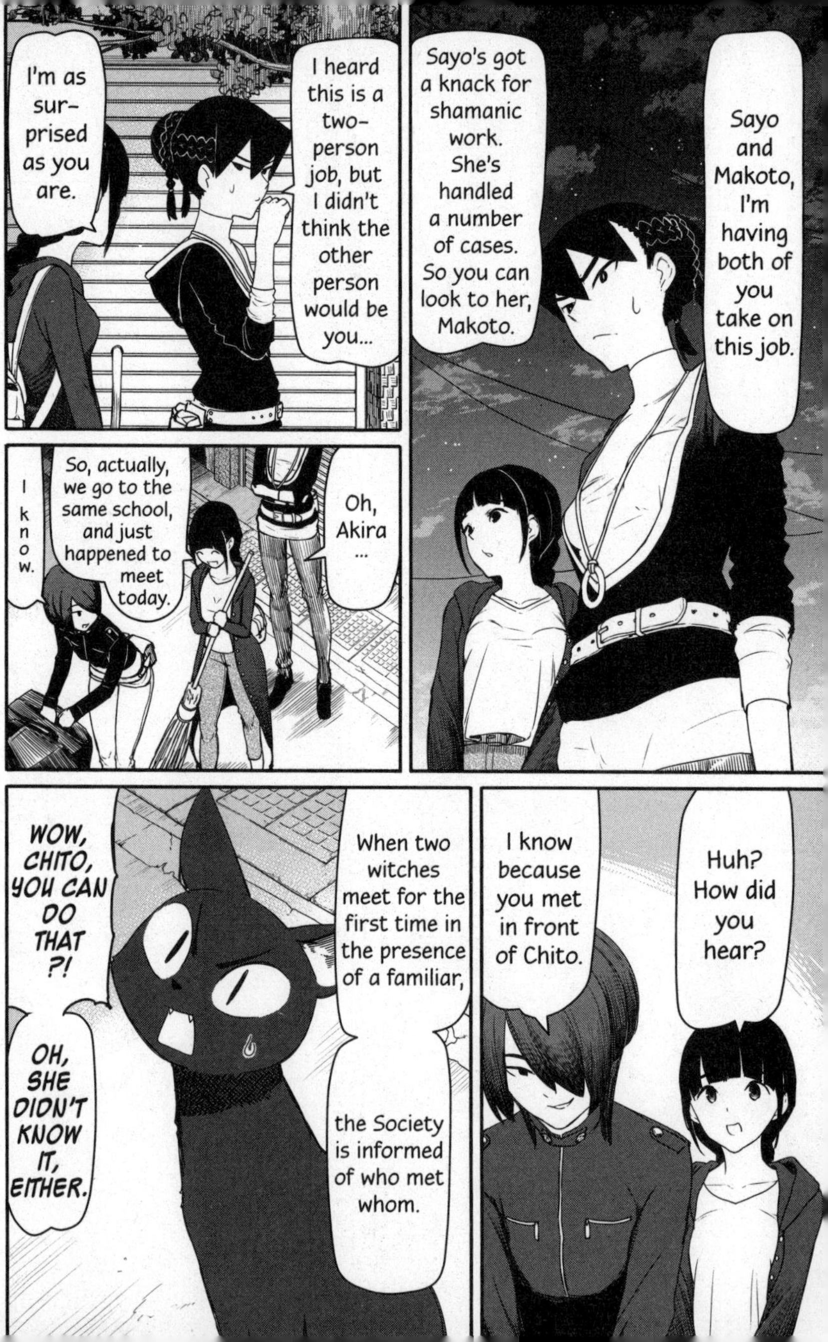
Sayo and Makoto, I'm having both of you take on this job.
Sayo's got a knack for shamanic work. She's handled a number of cases. So you can look to her, Makoto.
I heard this is a two-person job, but I didn't think the other person would be you...
I'm as sur-prised as you are.
Oh, Akira...
So, actually, we go to the same school, and just happened to meet today.
I know.
Huh? How did you hear?
I know because you met in front of Chito.
When two witches meet for the first time in the presence of a familiar,
the Society is informed of who met whom.
WOW, CHITO, YOU CAN DO THAT?!
OH, SHE DIDN'T KNOW IT, EITHER.

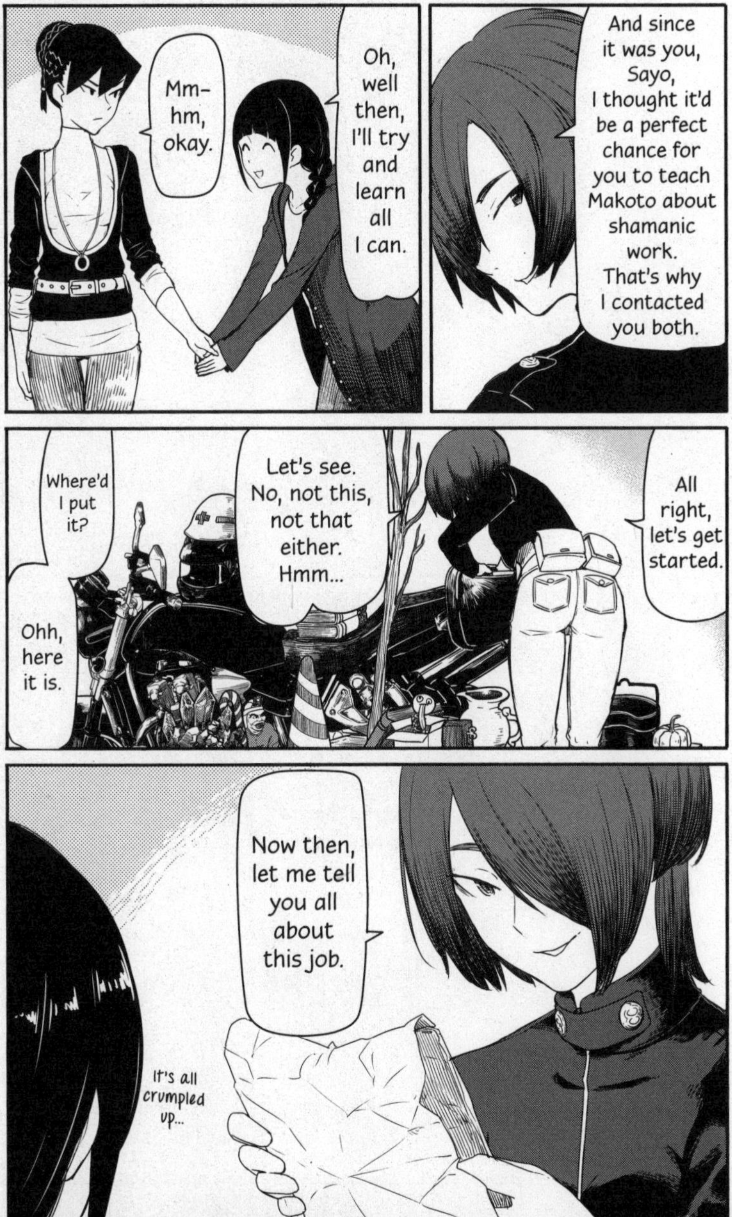
And since it was you, Sayo, I thought it'd be a perfect chance for you to teach Makoto about shamanic work. That's why I contacted you both.
Oh, well then, I'll try and learn all I can.
Mm-hm, okay.
All right, let's get started.
Let's see. No, not this, not that either. Hmm...
Where'd I put it?
Ohh, here it is.
Now then, let me tell you all about this job.
It's all crumpled up...

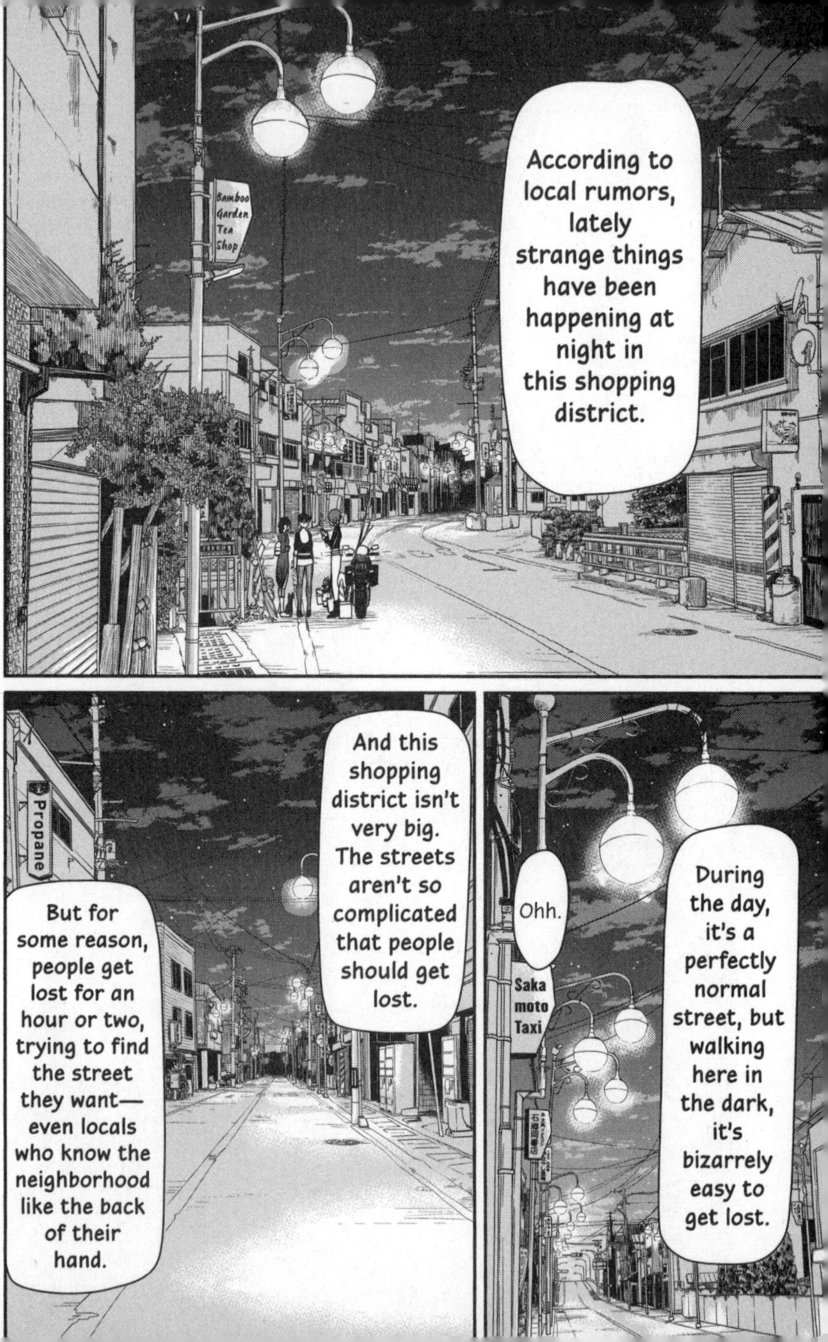
Bamboo Garden Tea Shop
According to local rumors, lately strange things have been happening at night in this shopping district.
Saka moto Taxi
During the day, it's a perfectly normal street, but walking here in the dark, it's bizarrely easy to get lost.
Ohh.
Propane
And this shopping district isn't very big. The streets aren't so complicated that people should get lost.
But for some reason, people get lost for an hour or two, trying to find the street they want—even locals who know the neighborhood like the back of their hand.

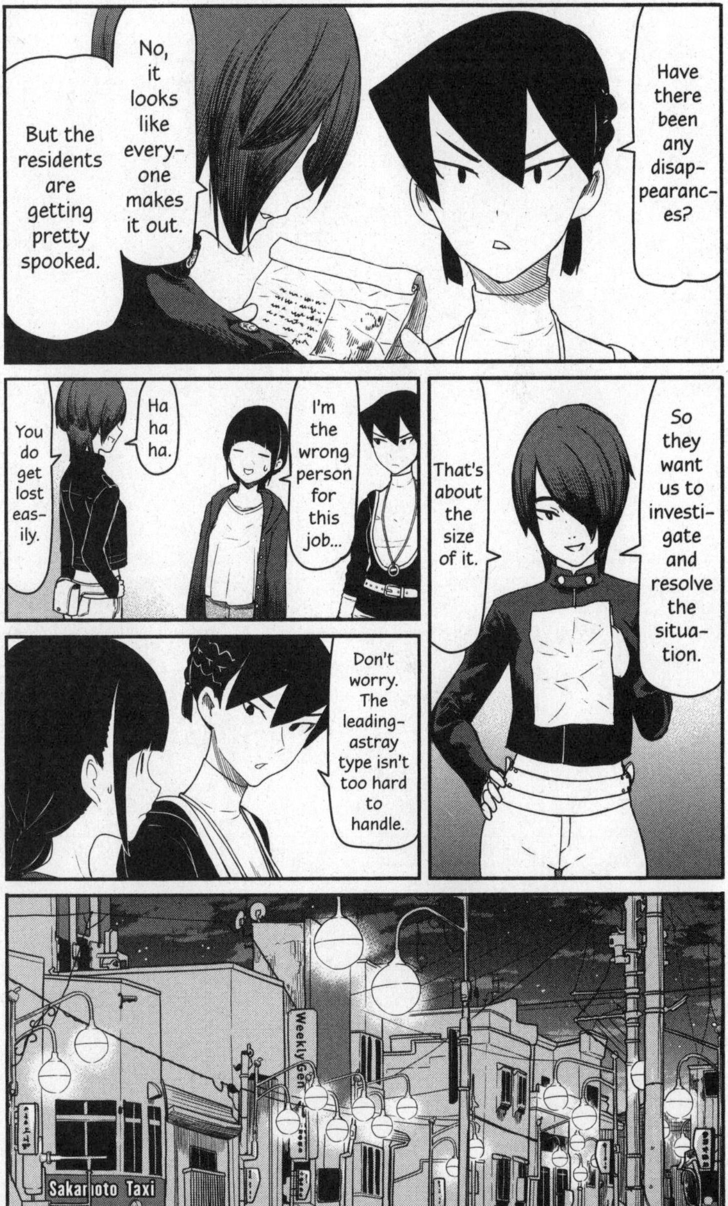
Have there been any disappearances?
No, it looks like everyone makes it out.
But the residents are getting pretty spooked.
So they want us to investigate and resolve the situation.
That's about the size of it.
I'm the wrong person for this job...
Ha ha ha.
You do get lost easily.
Don't worry. The leading-astray type isn't too hard to handle.
Weekly Gen
Sakamoto Taxi

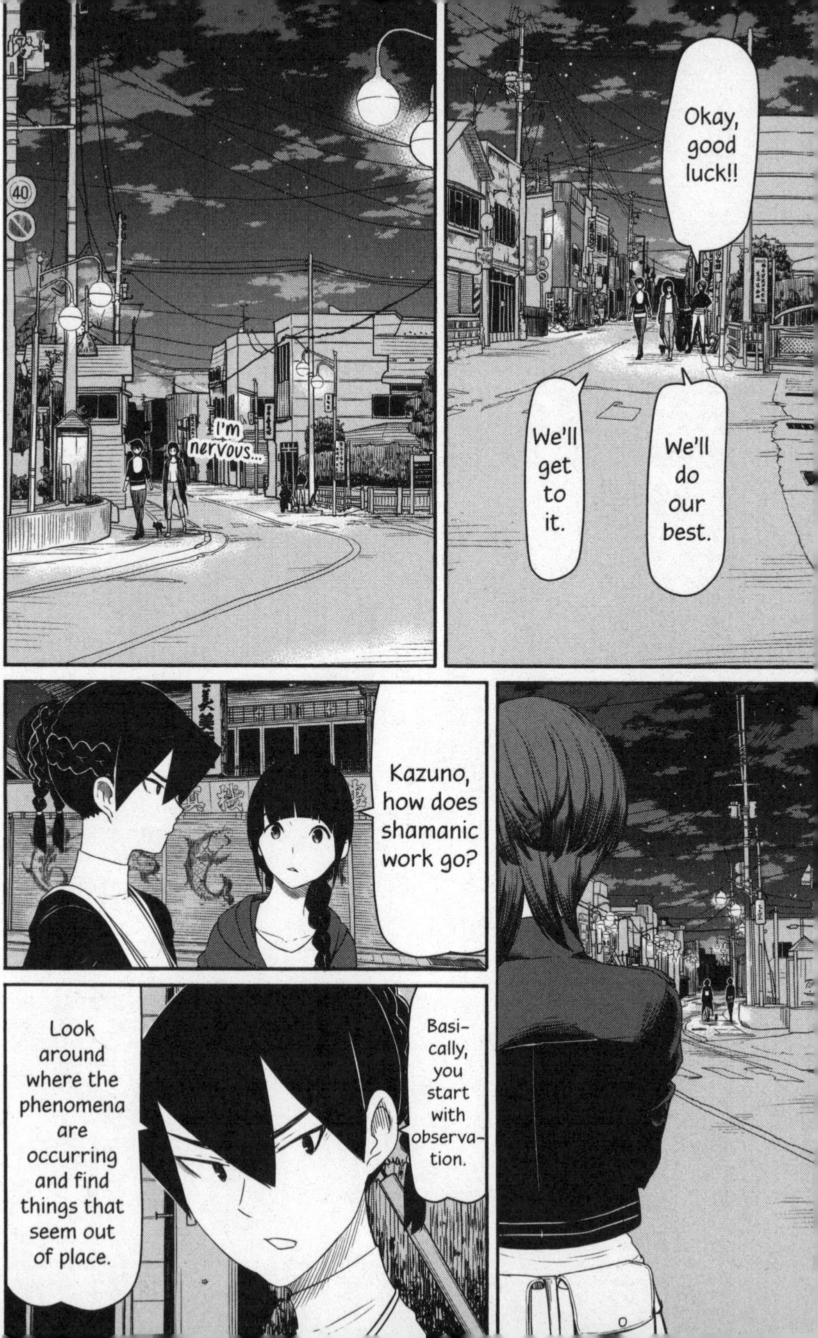
Okay, good luck!!
We'll do our best.
We'll get to it.
I'm nervous...
Kazuno, how does shamanic work go?
Basically, you start with observation.
Look around where the phenomena are occurring and find things that seem out of place.

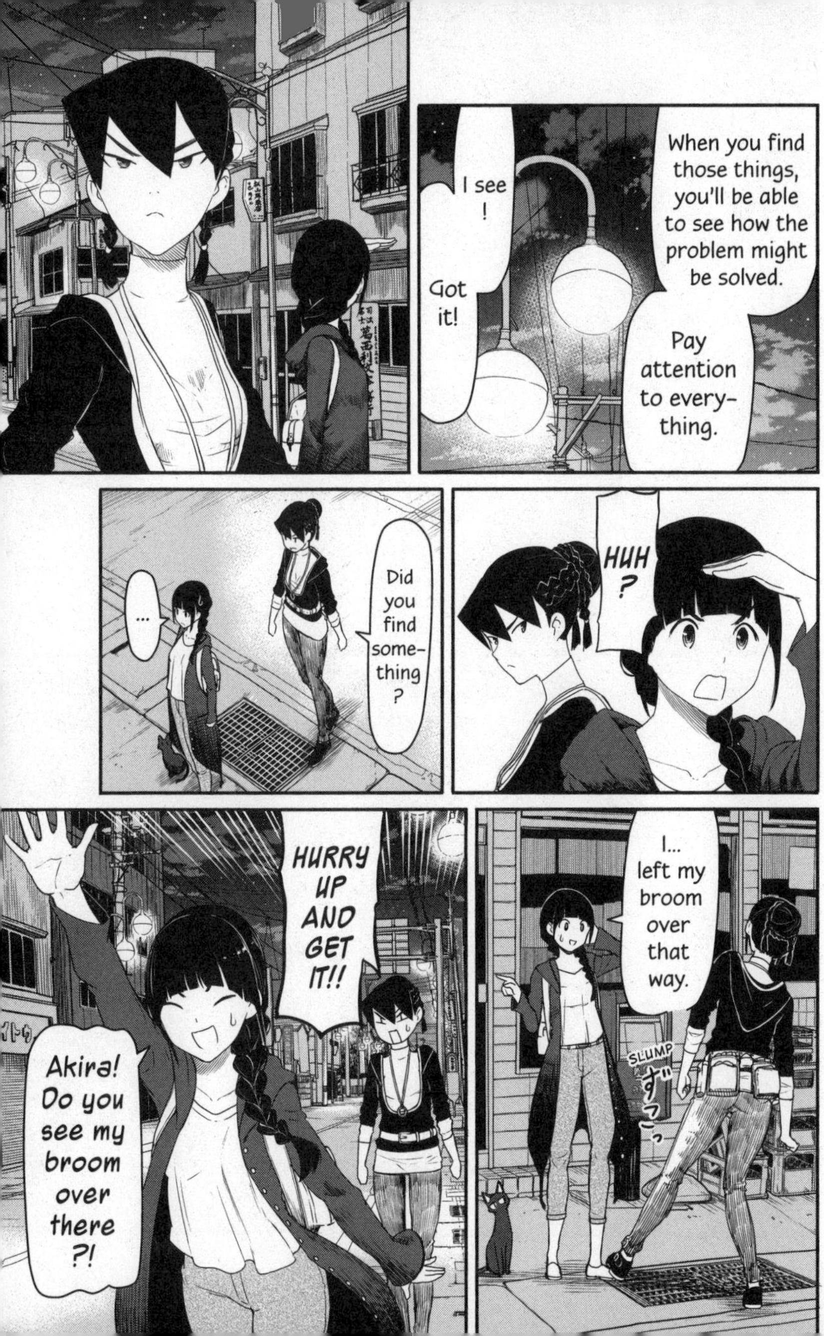
When you find those things, you'll be able to see how the problem might be solved.
Pay attention to every-thing.
I see!
Got it!
HUH?
Did you find some-thing?
...
I... left my broom over that way.
SLUMP
HURRY UP AND GET IT!!
Akira! Do you see my broom over there?!

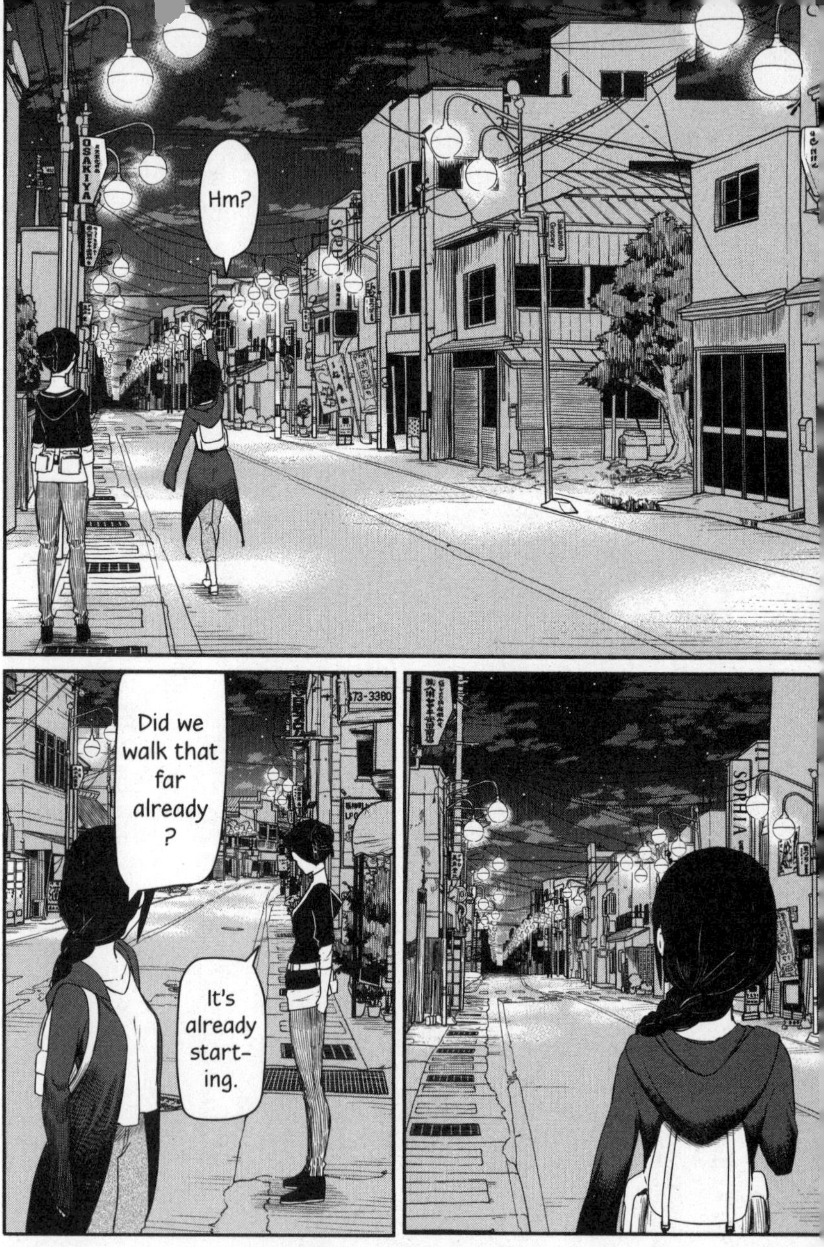
OSAKIYA
Hm?
SOPHIA
Did we walk that far already?
It's already start-ing.

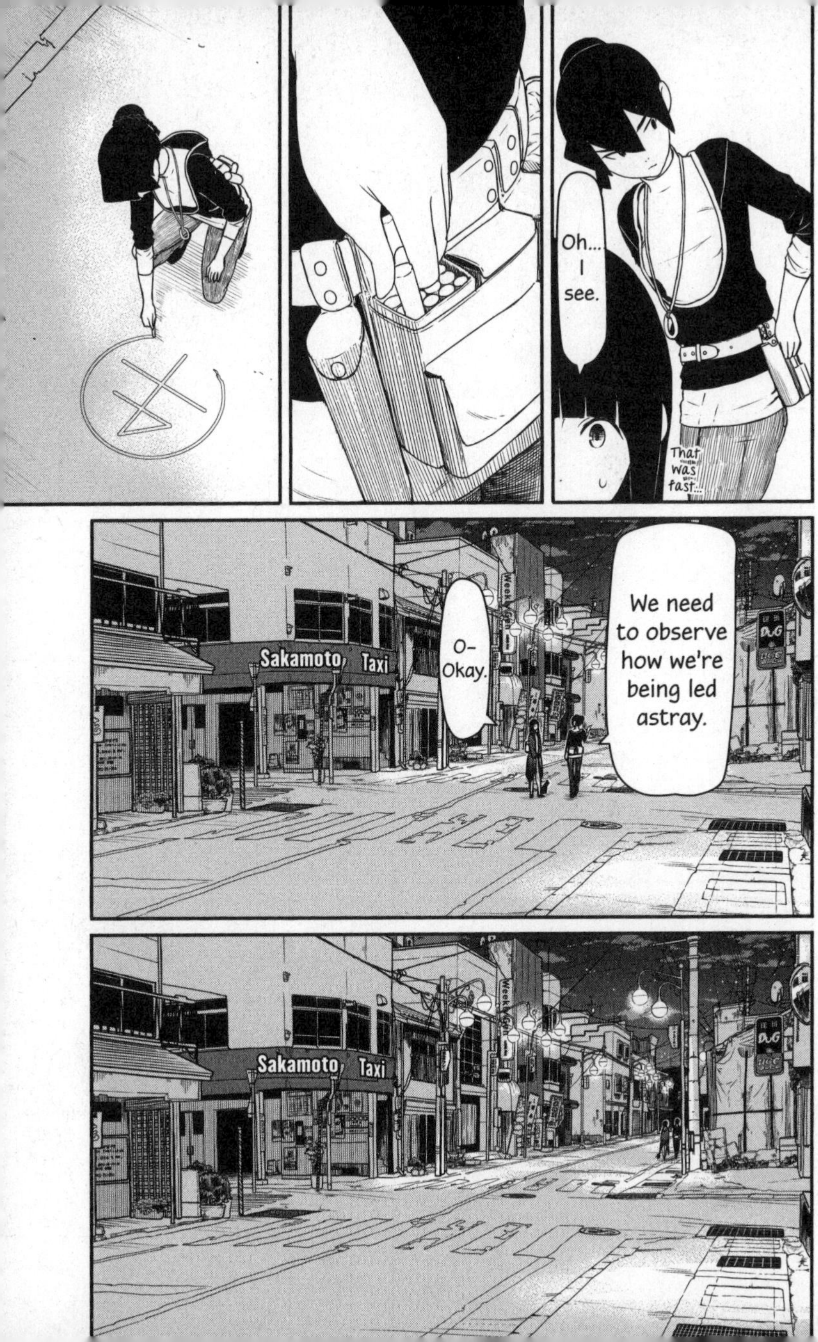
Oh... I see.
That was fast...
We need to observe how we're being led astray.
O-Okay.
Sakamoto Taxi
Sakamoto Taxi

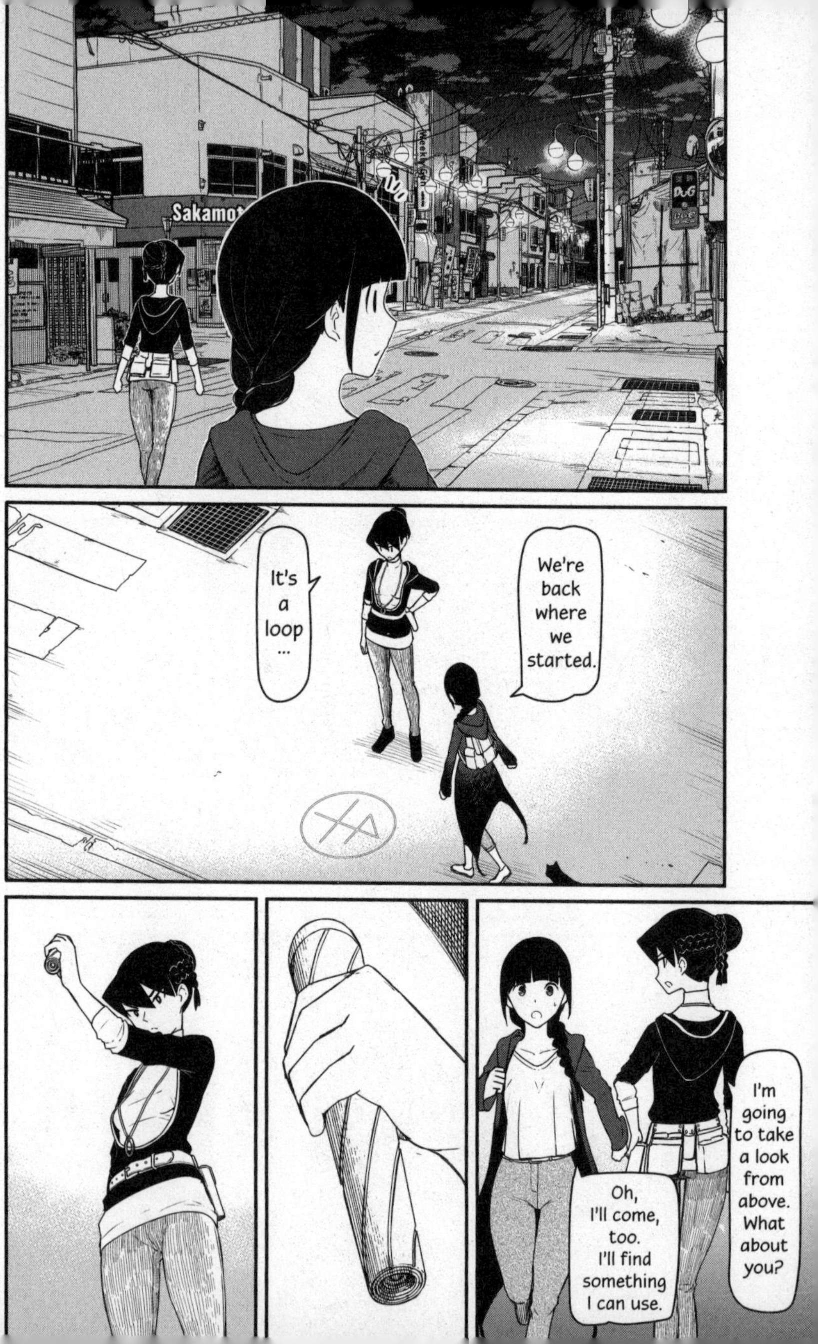
Sakamot
We're back where we started.
It's a loop ...
I'm going to take a look from above. What about you?
Oh, I'll come, too. I'll find something I can use.

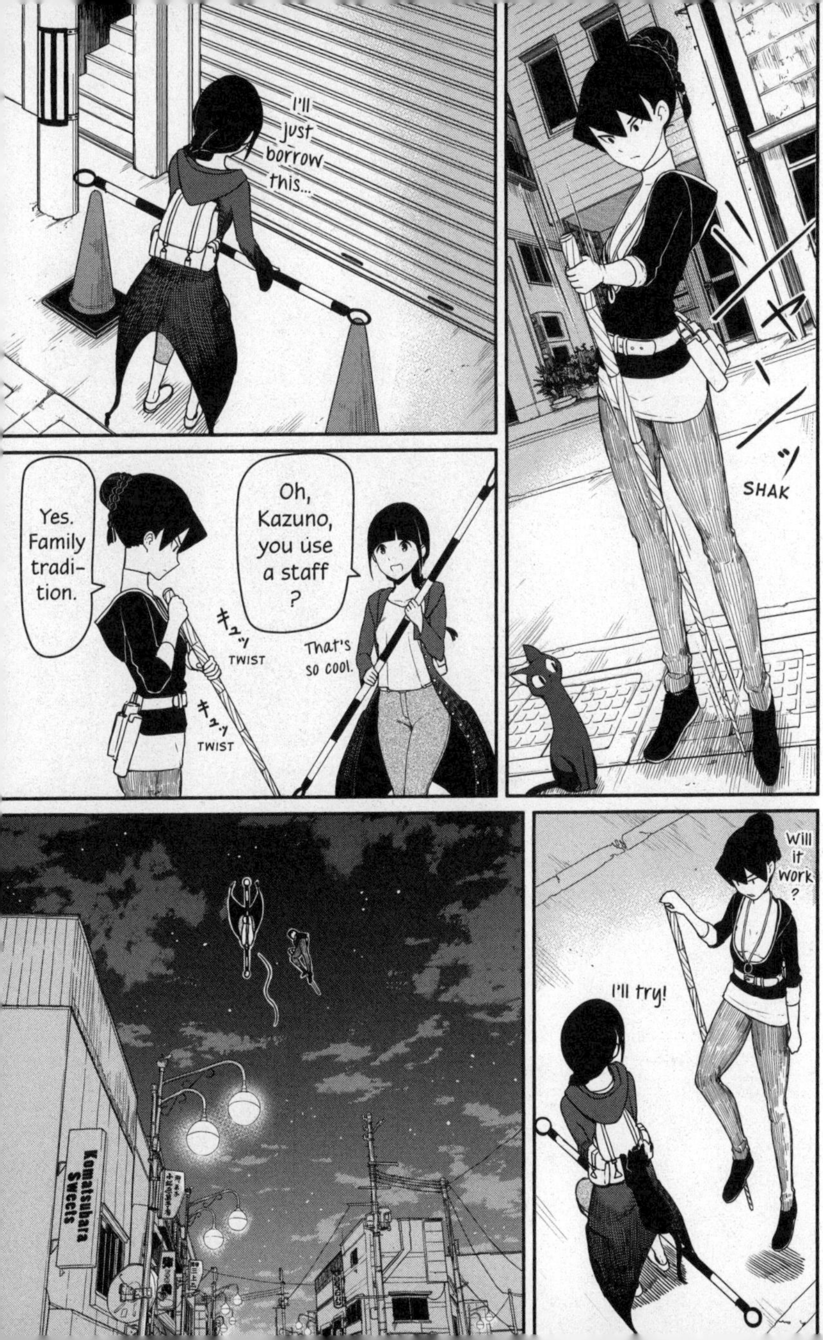
シャッ
SHAK
I'll just borrow this...
Oh, Kazuno, you use a staff?
That's so cool.
Yes. Family tradi-tion.
キュッ
TWIST
キュッ
TWIST
Will it work?
I'll try!
Komatsubara Sweets

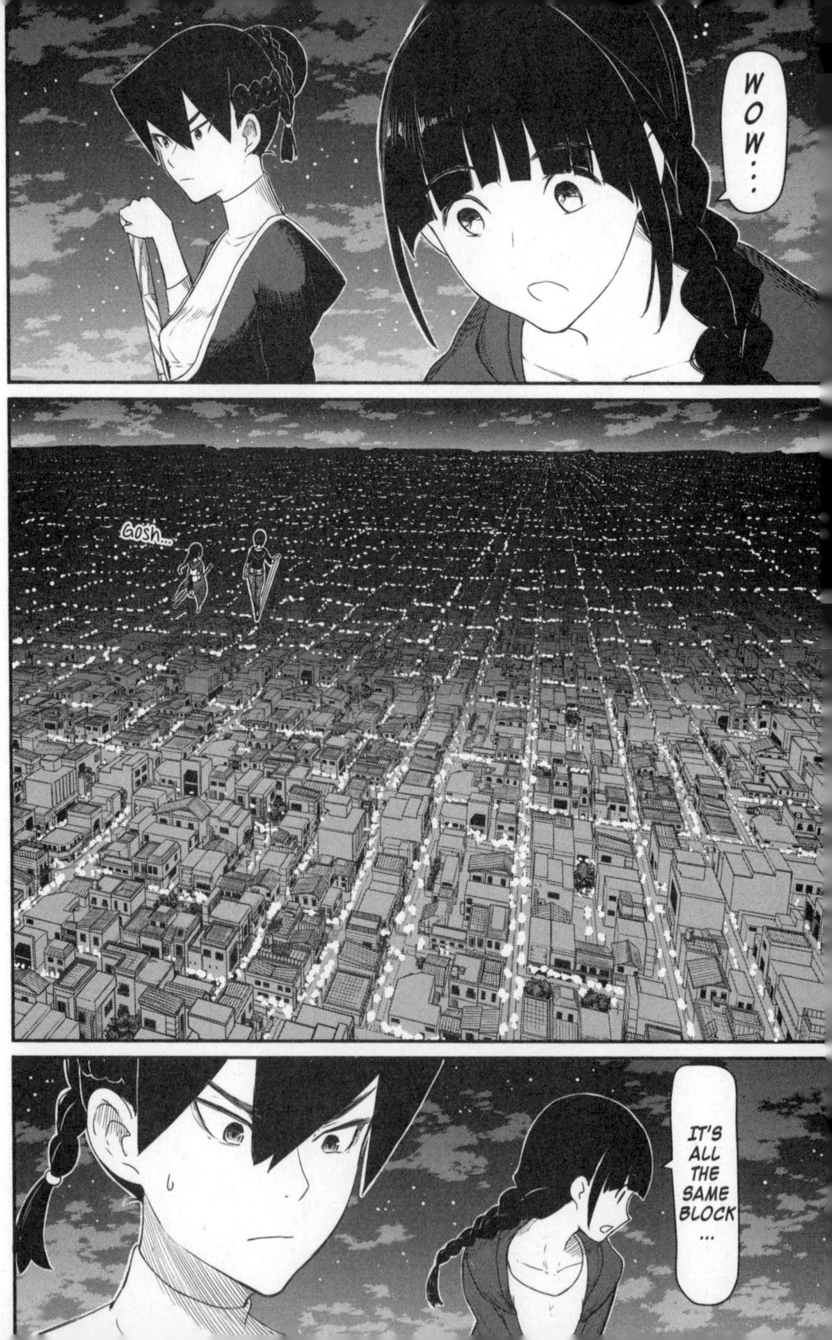
WOW...
Gosh...
IT'S ALL THE SAME BLOCK...

Flying
Witch

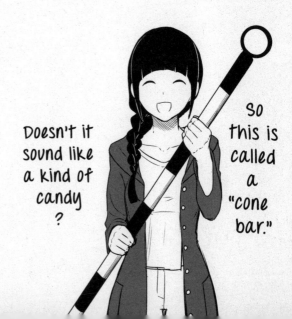

So this is called a "cone bar."
Doesn't it sound like a kind of candy?

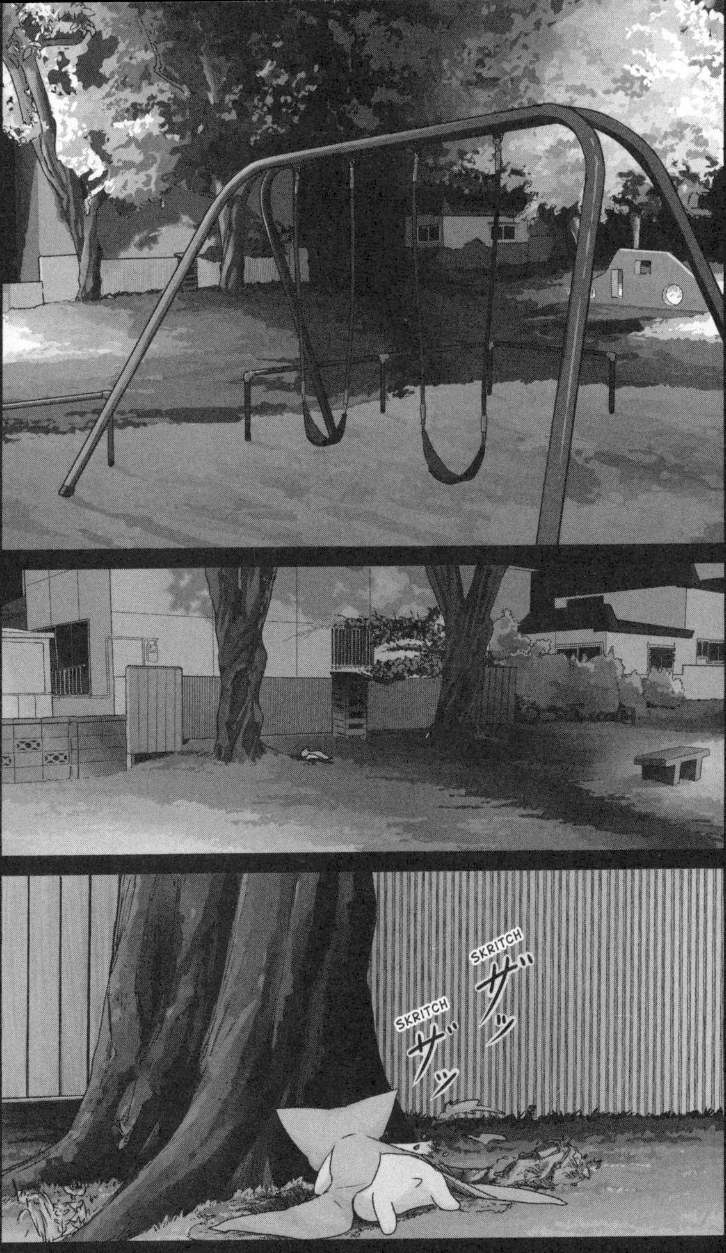
SKRITCH
ザッ
SKRITCH
ザッ

Chapter 36
The Narunaru: How to Observe and Catch It

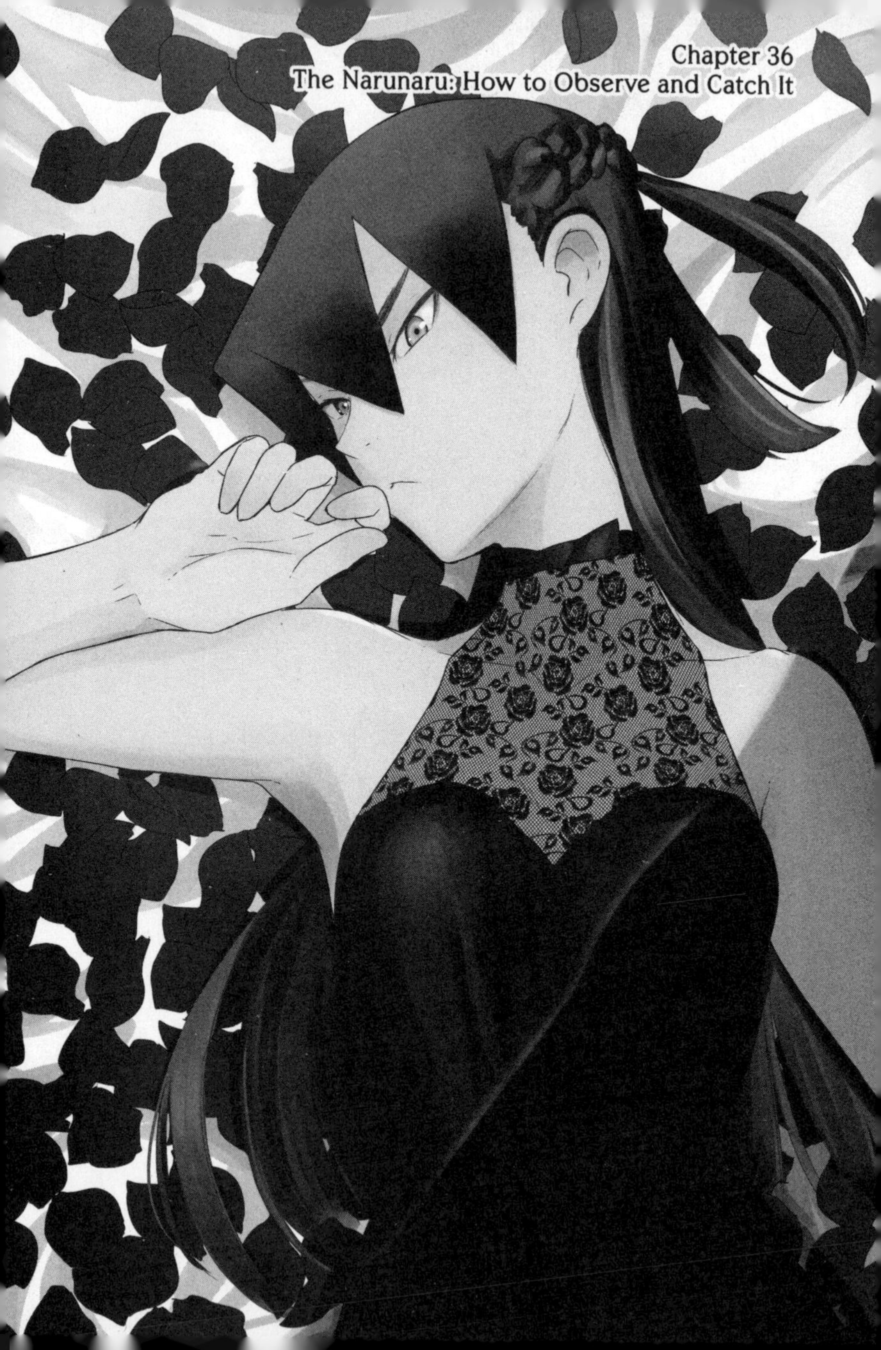

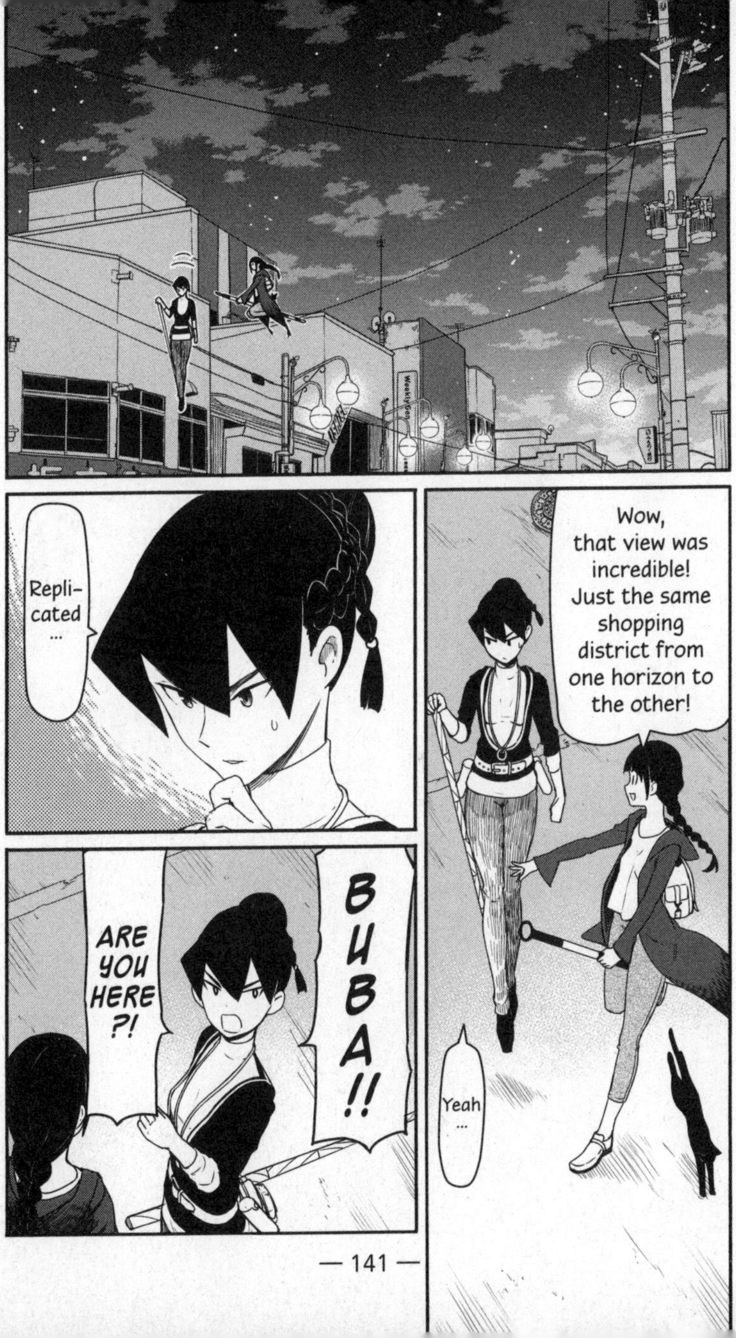
Wow, that view was incredible! Just the same shopping district from one horizon to the other!
Yeah ...
Repli-cated ...
BUBA!!
ARE YOU HERE?!

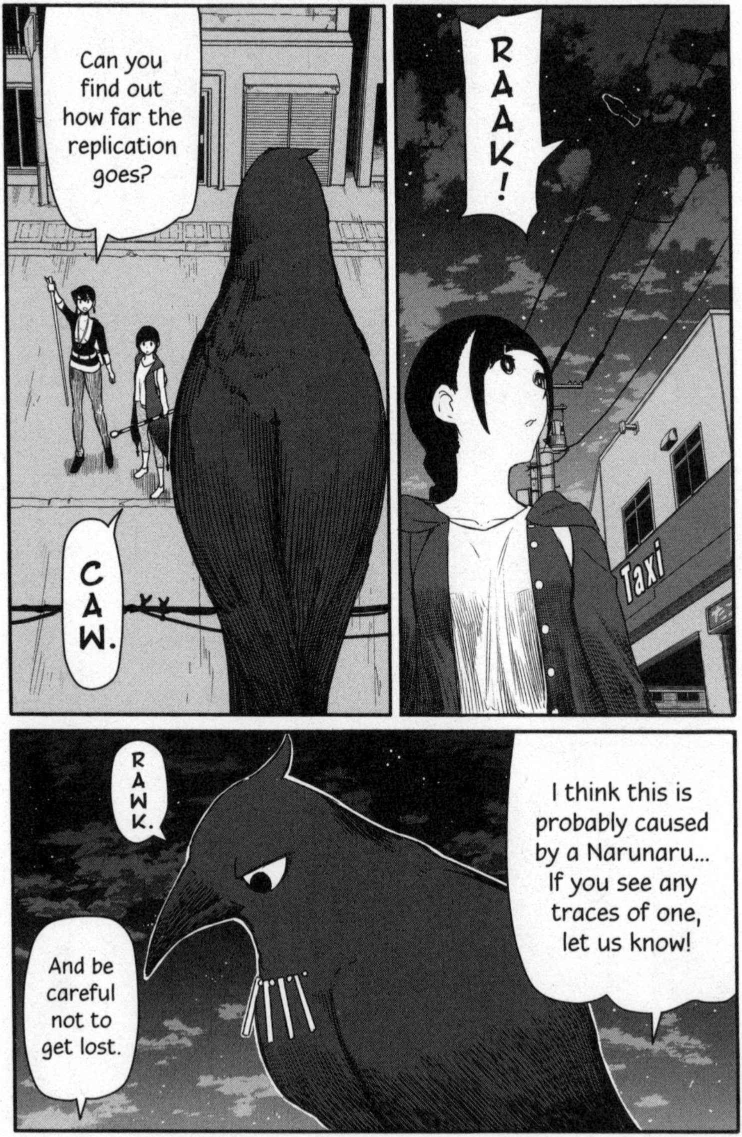
RAAK!
Taxi
Can you find out how far the replication goes?
CAW.
I think this is probably caused by a Narunaru... If you see any traces of one, let us know!
RAWK.
And be careful not to get lost.

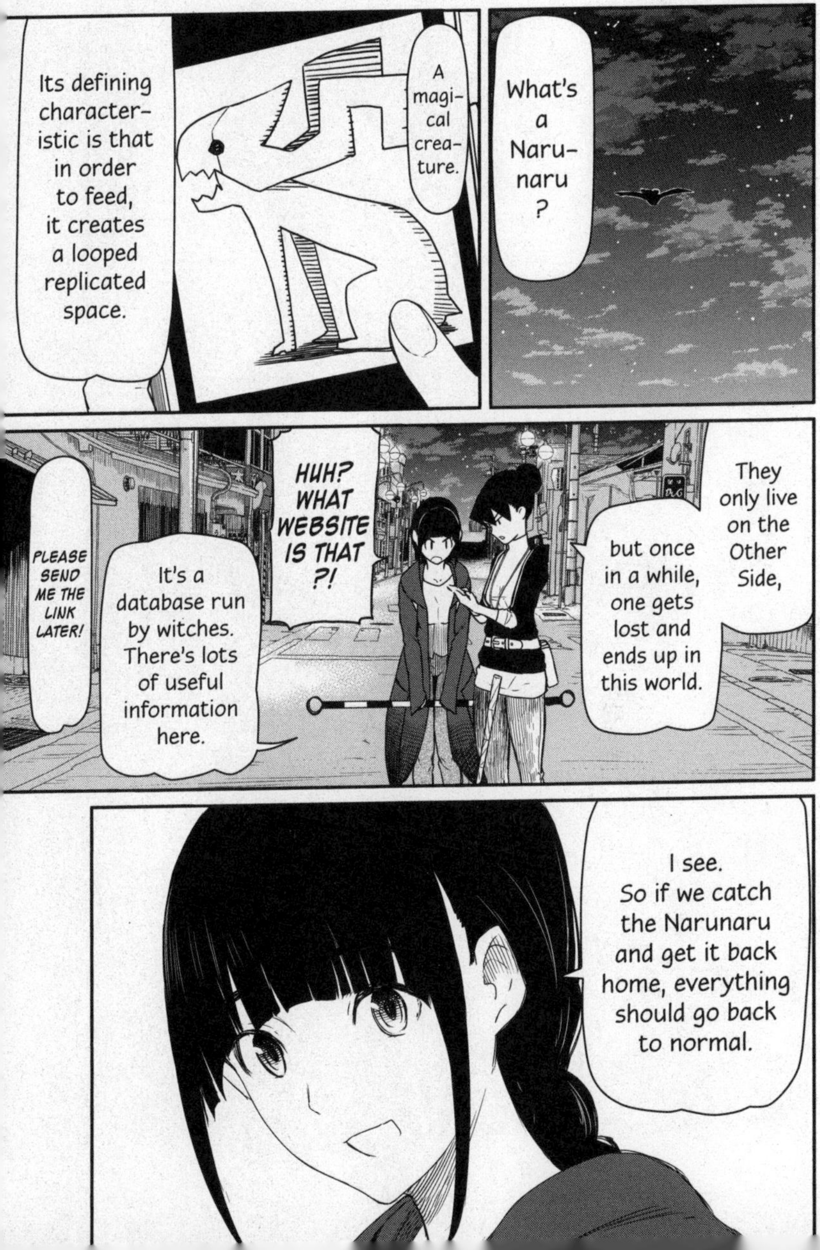
What's a Narunaru?
A magical creature.
Its defining characteristic is that in order to feed, it creates a looped replicated space.
They only live on the Other Side,
but once in a while, one gets lost and ends up in this world.
HUH? WHAT WEBSITE IS THAT?!
It's a database run by witches. There's lots of useful information here.
PLEASE SEND ME THE LINK LATER!
I see. So if we catch the Narunaru and get it back home, everything should go back to normal.

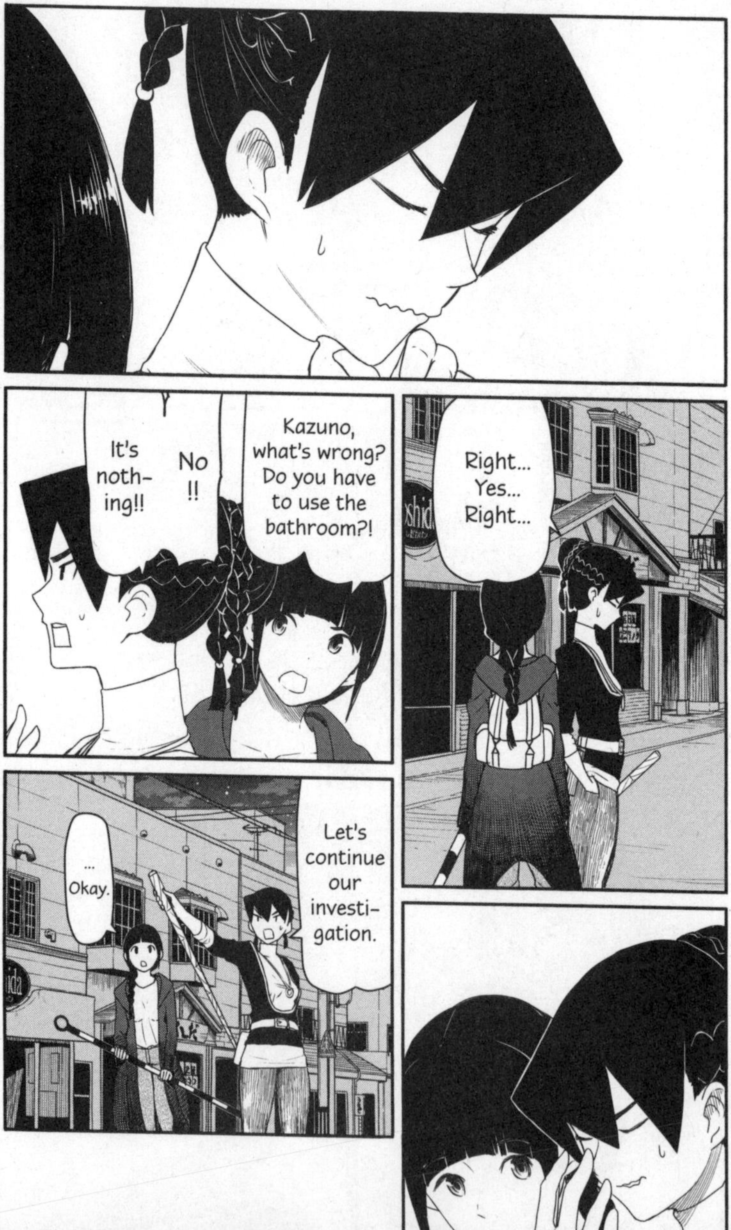
Right... Yes... Right...
Kazuno, what's wrong? Do you have to use the bathroom?!
No !!
It's noth-ing!!
Let's continue our investi-gation.
... Okay.

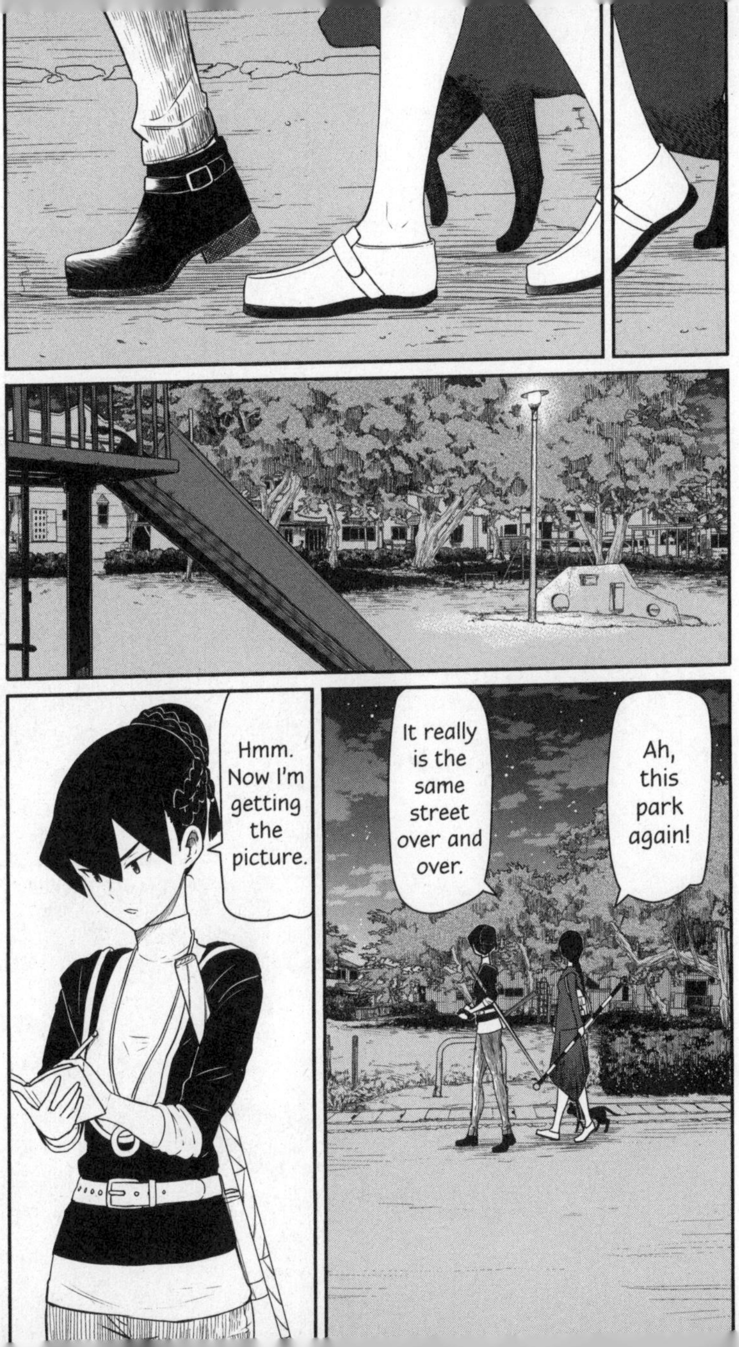
Ah, this park again!
It really is the same street over and over.
Hmm. Now I'm getting the picture.

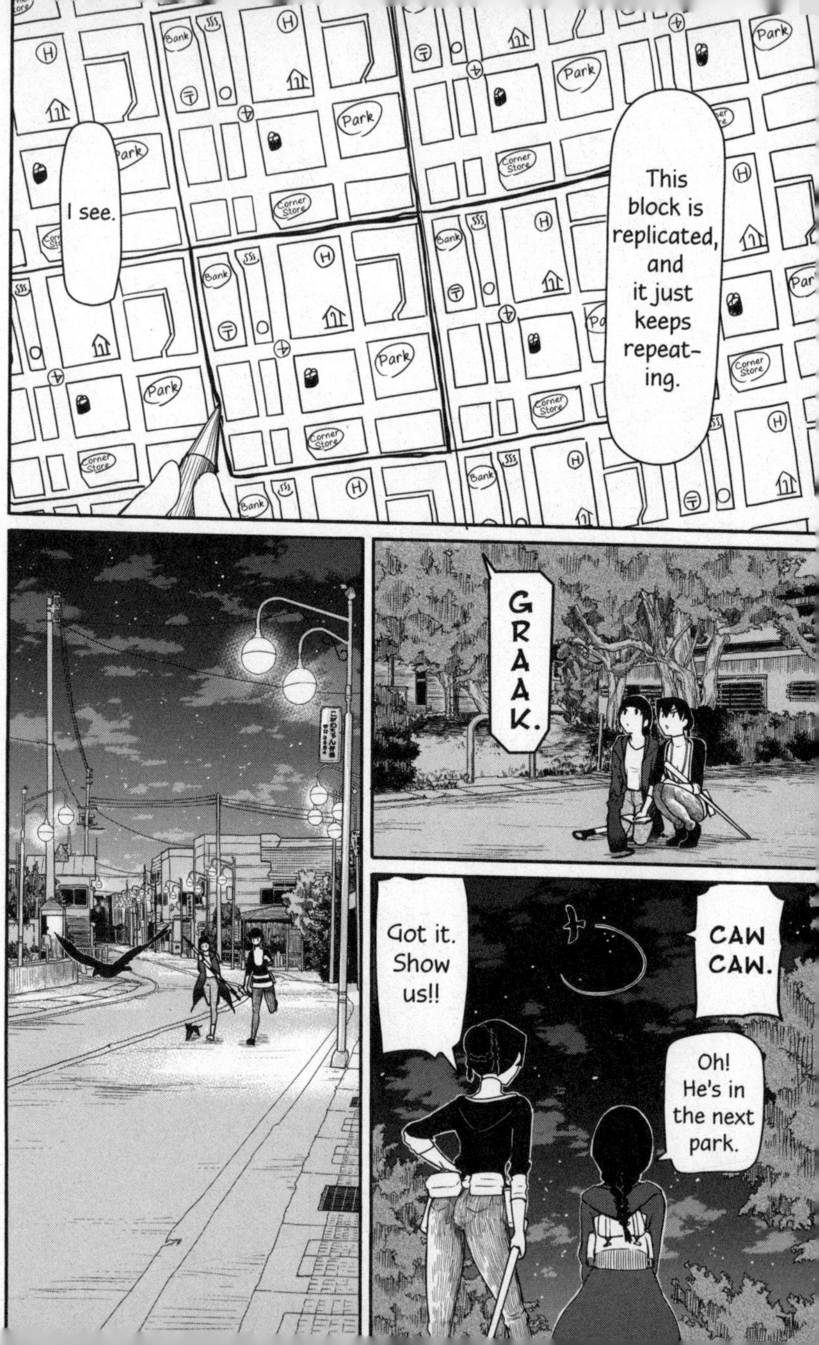
This block is replicated, and it just keeps repeating.
I see.
GRAAK.
CAW CAW.
Got it. Show us!!
Oh! He's in the next park.

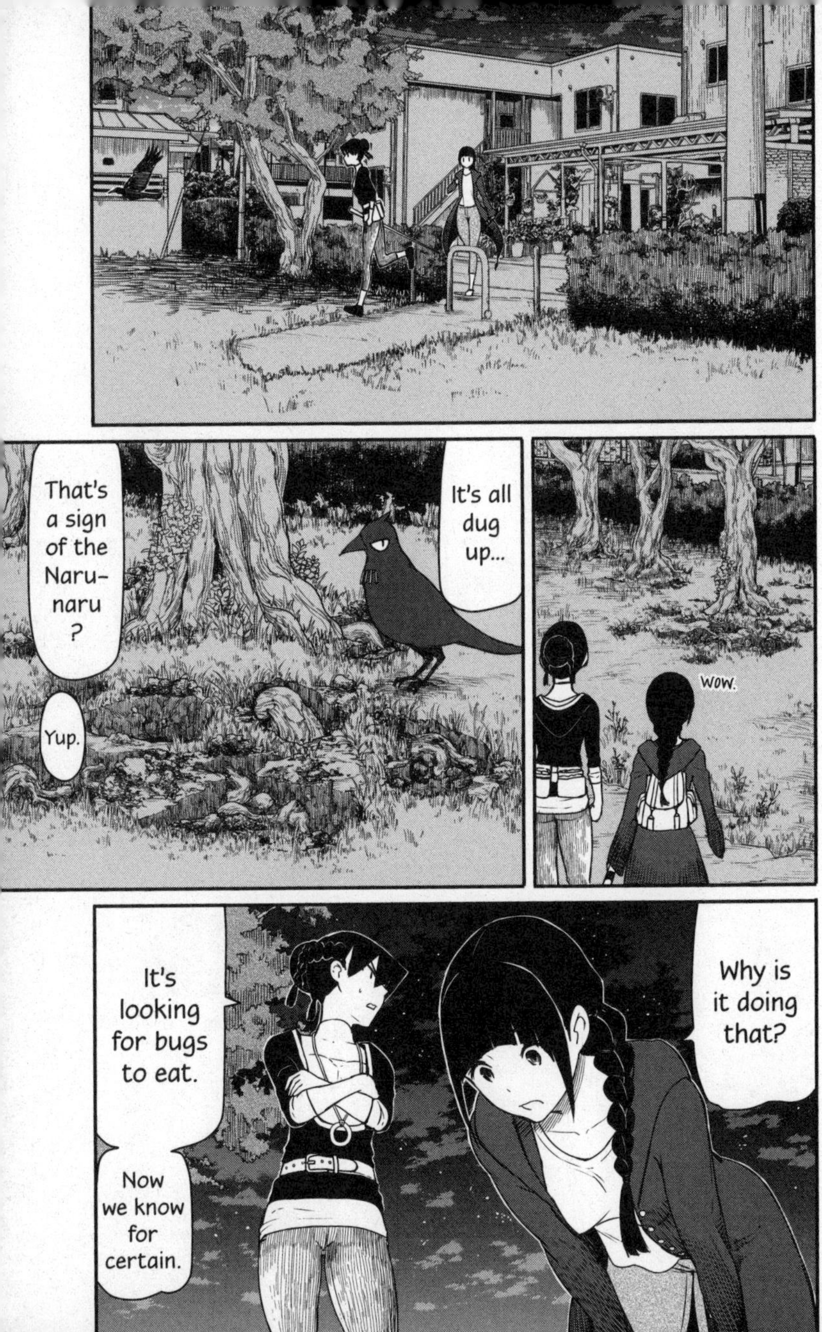
wow.
It's all dug up...
That's a sign of the Naru-naru?
Yup.
Why is it doing that?
It's looking for bugs to eat.
Now we know for certain.

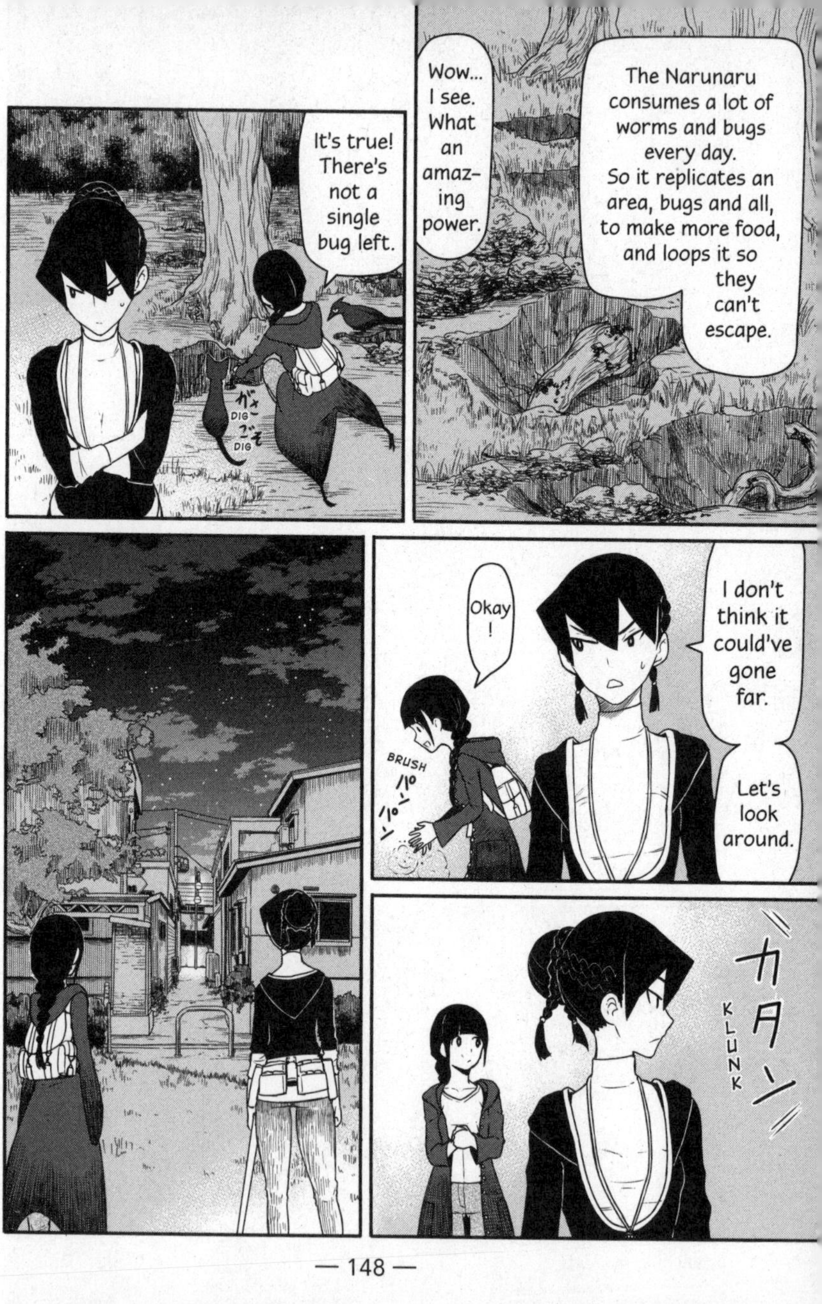

The Narunaru consumes a lot of worms and bugs every day.
So it replicates an area, bugs and all, to make more food, and loops it so they can't escape.
Wow... I see. What an amaz-ing power.
It's true! There's not a single bug left.
DIG
DIG
I don't think it could've gone far.
Let's look around.
Okay!
BRUSH
パン
パン
カタン
KLUNK

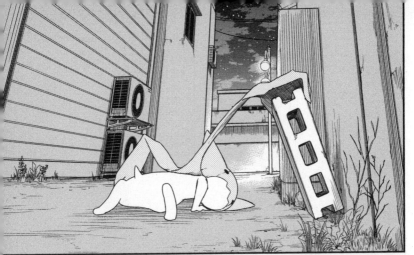

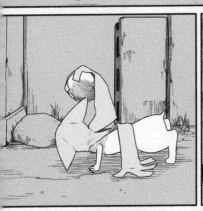

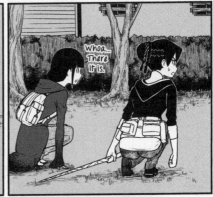

Whoa... There it is.
Ah-ha! Luck's on our side...
How do we catch it?
I won't have to do *that*...

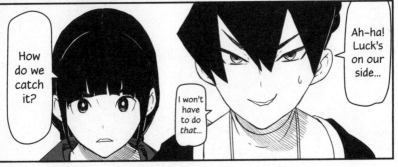

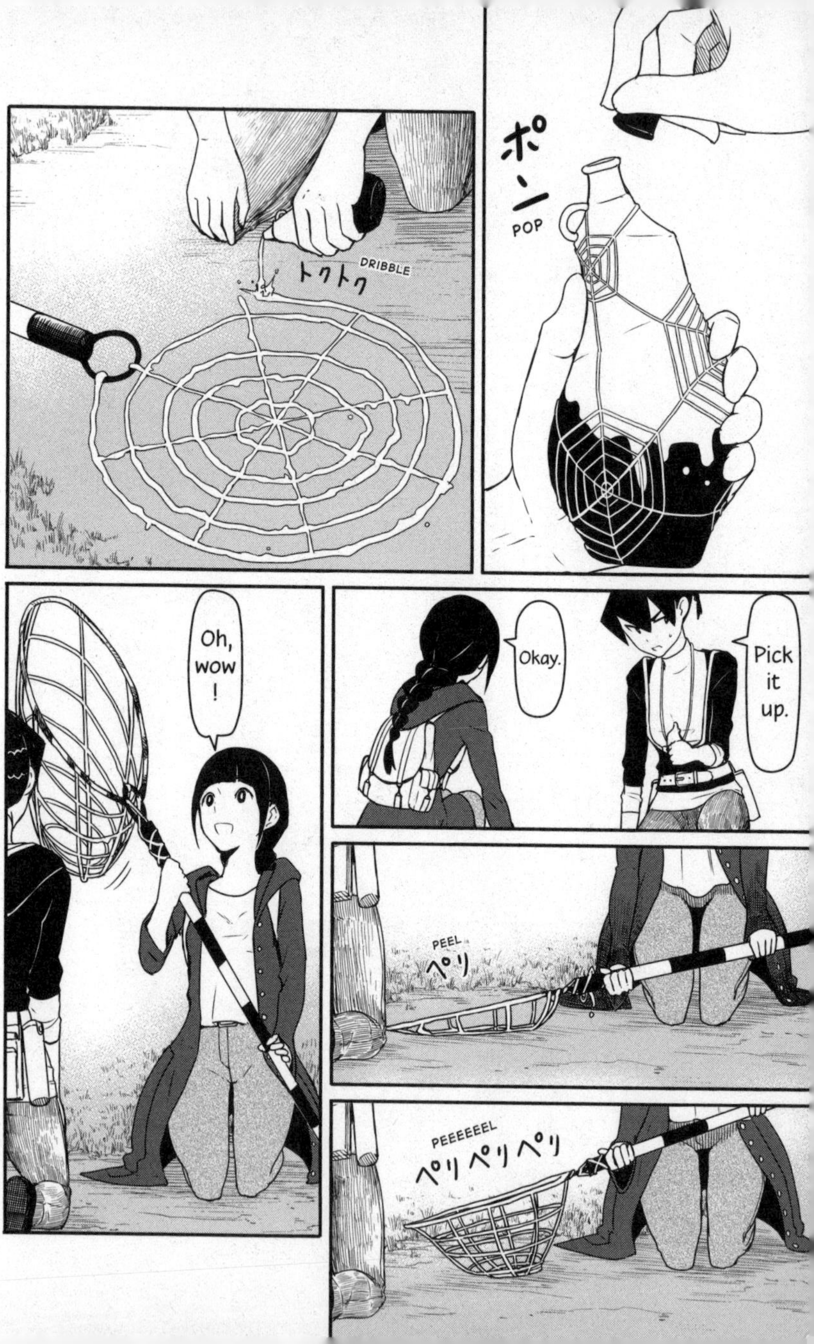
ポン
POP
トクトク
DRIBBLE
Pick it up.
Okay.
PEEL
ペリ
PEEEEEEL
ペリペリペリ
Oh, wow!

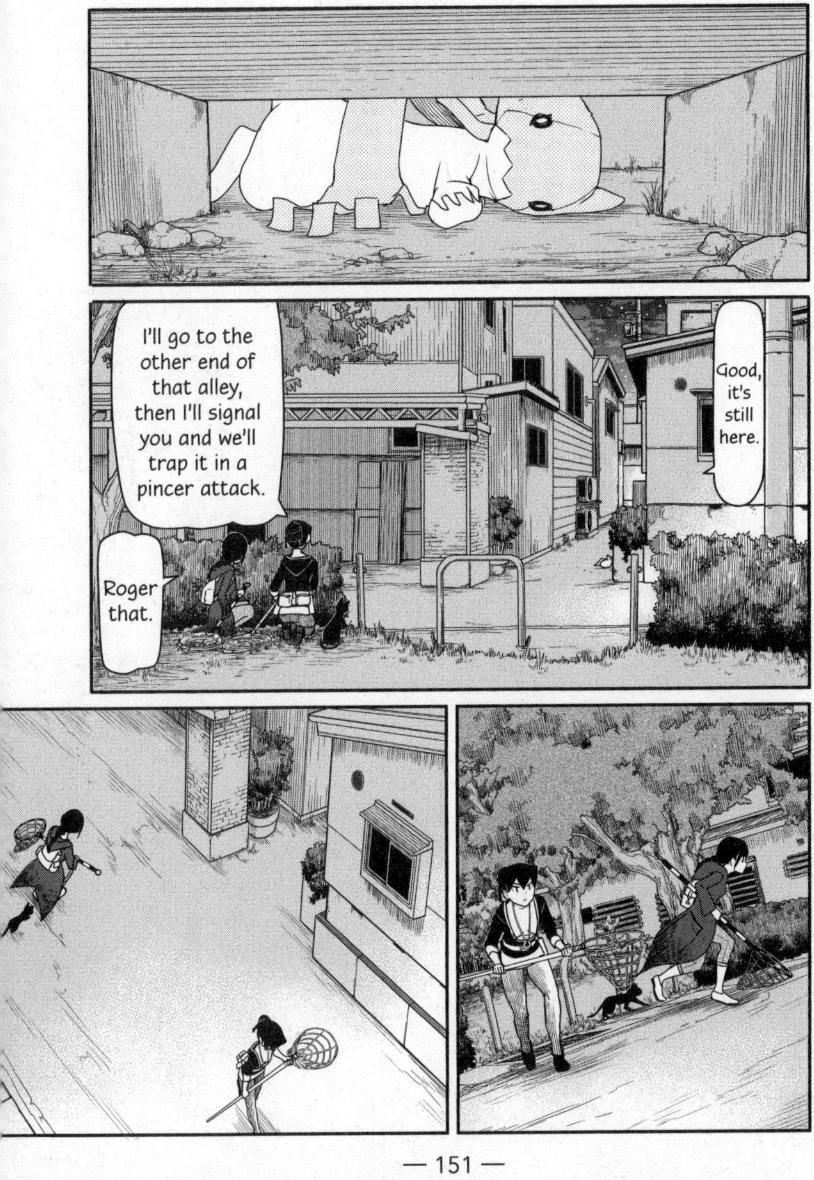
Good, it's still here.
I'll go to the other end of that alley, then I'll signal you and we'll trap it in a pincer attack.
Roger that.

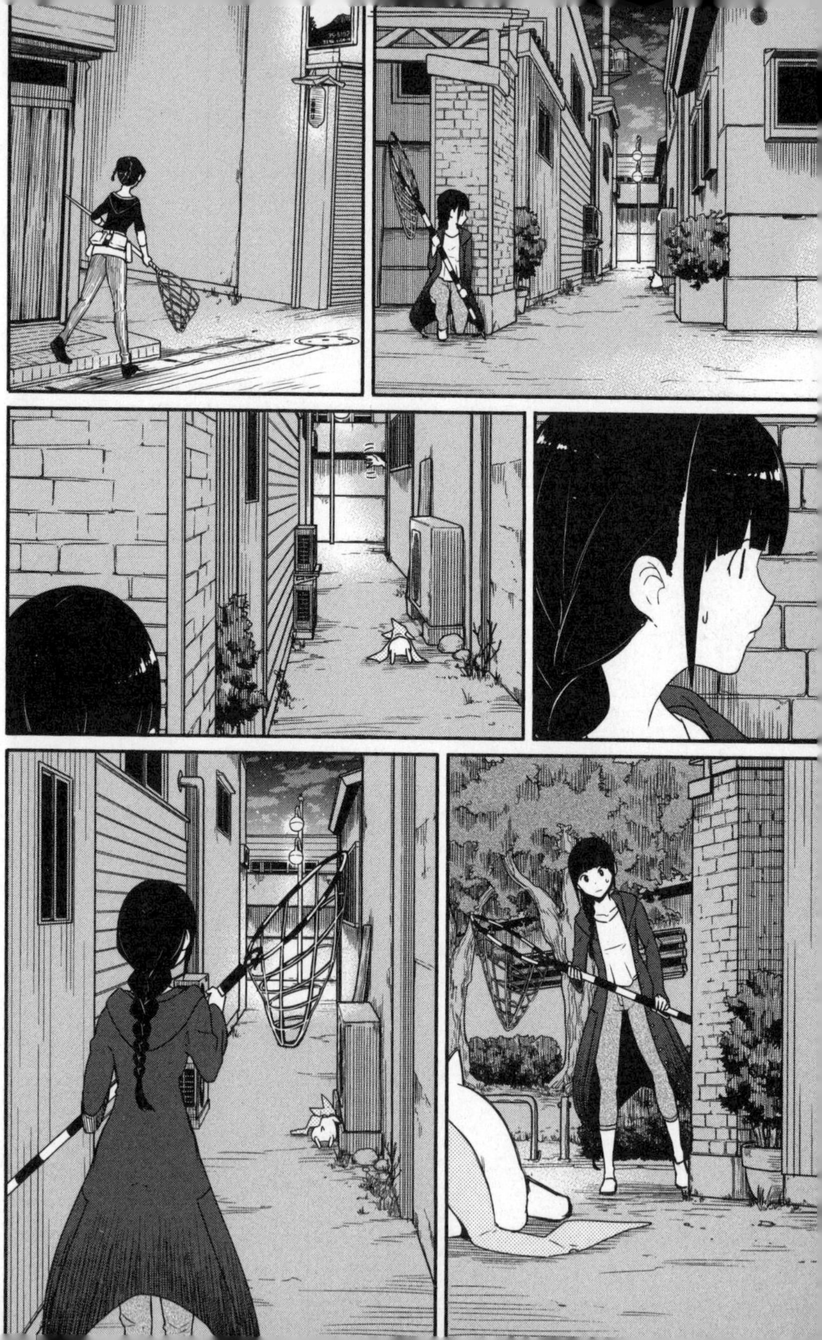

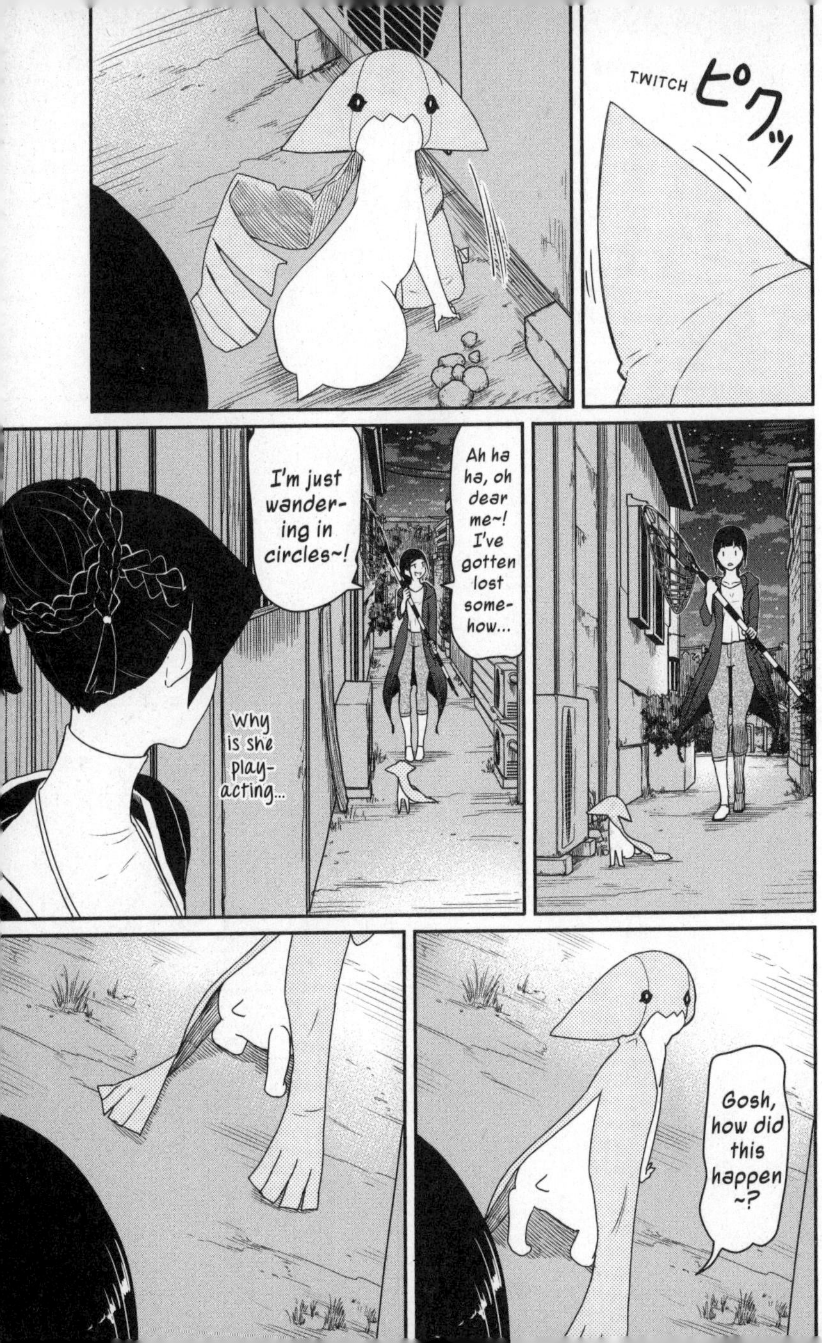
T.WITCH ピクッ
Ah ha ha, oh dear me~! I've gotten lost some-how...
I'm just wander-ing in circles~!
why is she play-acting...
Gosh, how did this happen ~?

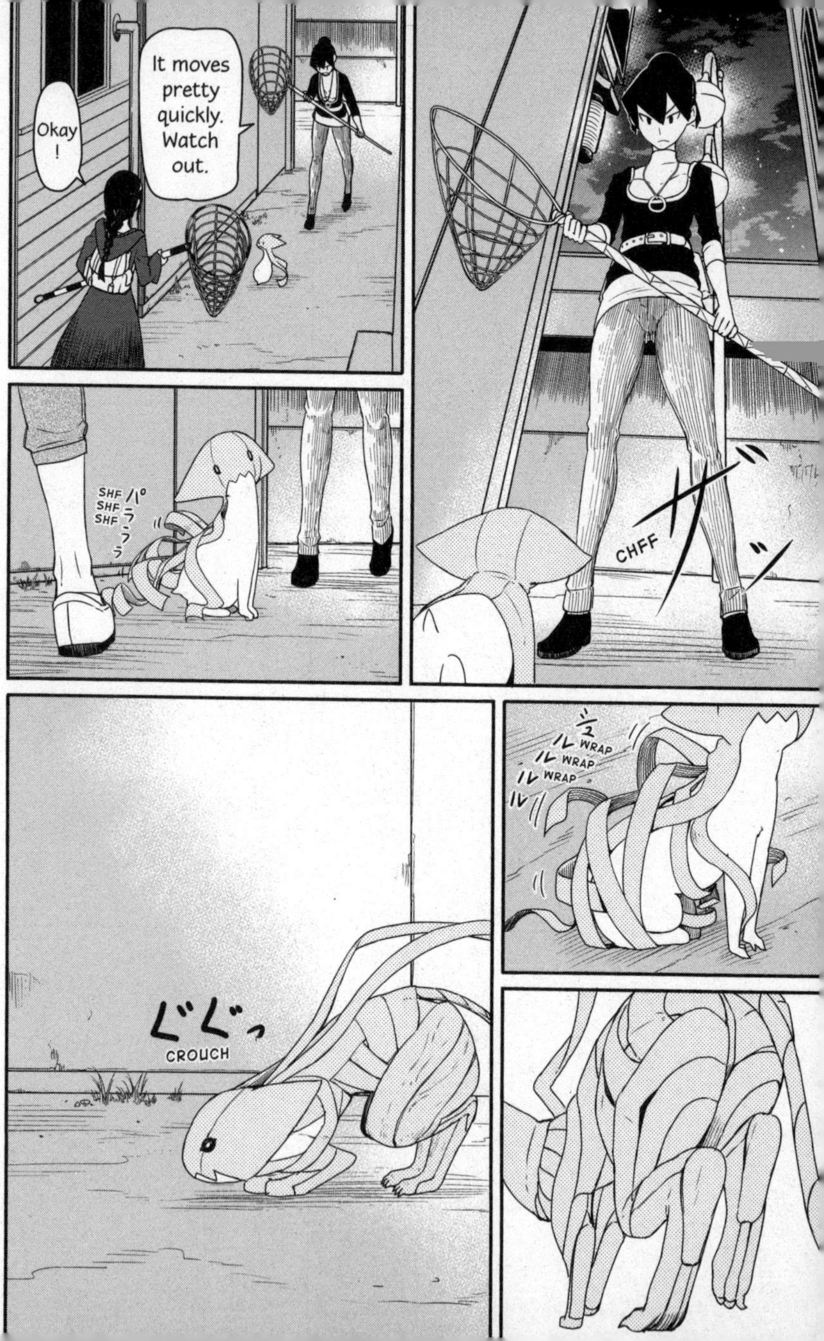
CHFF
It moves pretty quickly. Watch out.
Okay!
SHF SHF SHF
パラララ
シュルルル
WRAP WRAP WRAP
ぐぐっ
CROUCH

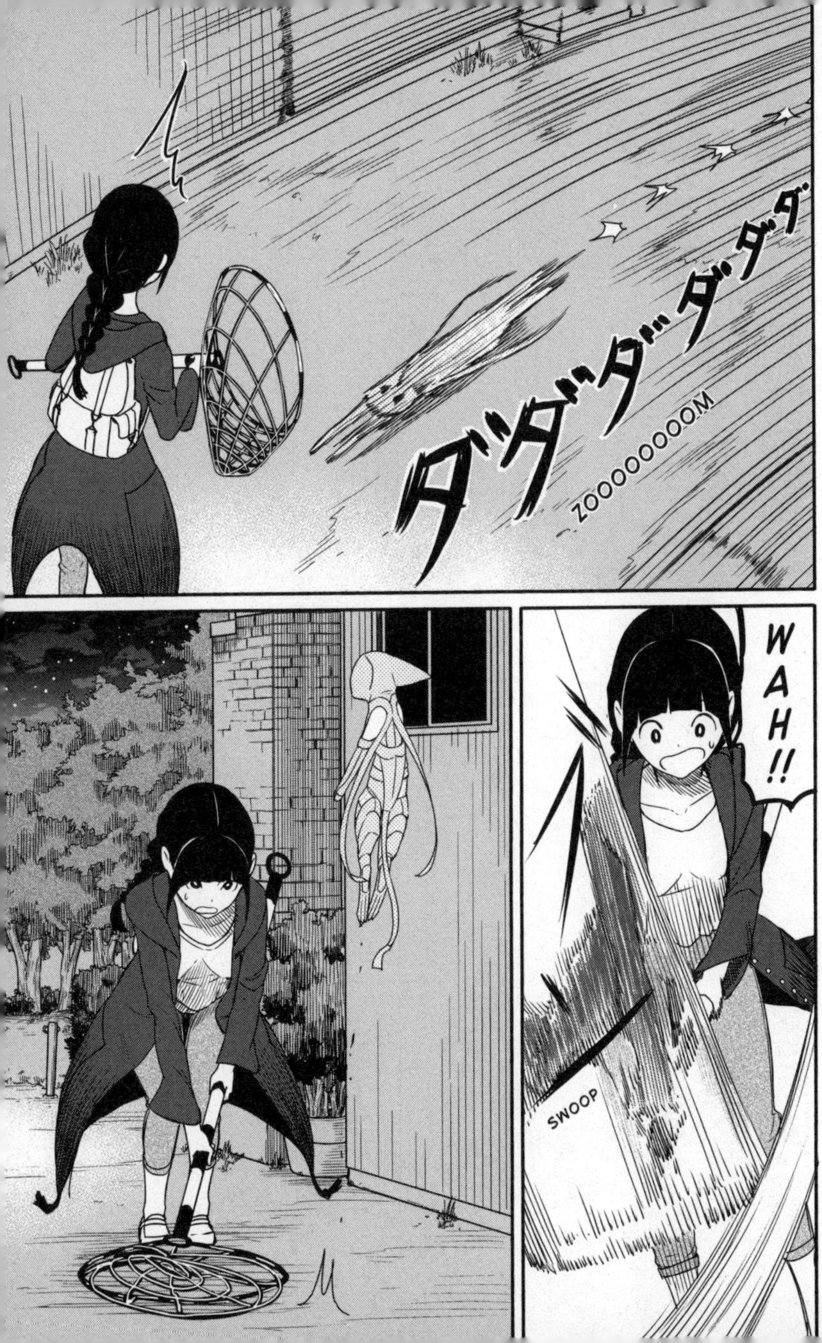
ダダダダダダ
ZOOOOOOOOM
WAH!!
SWOOP

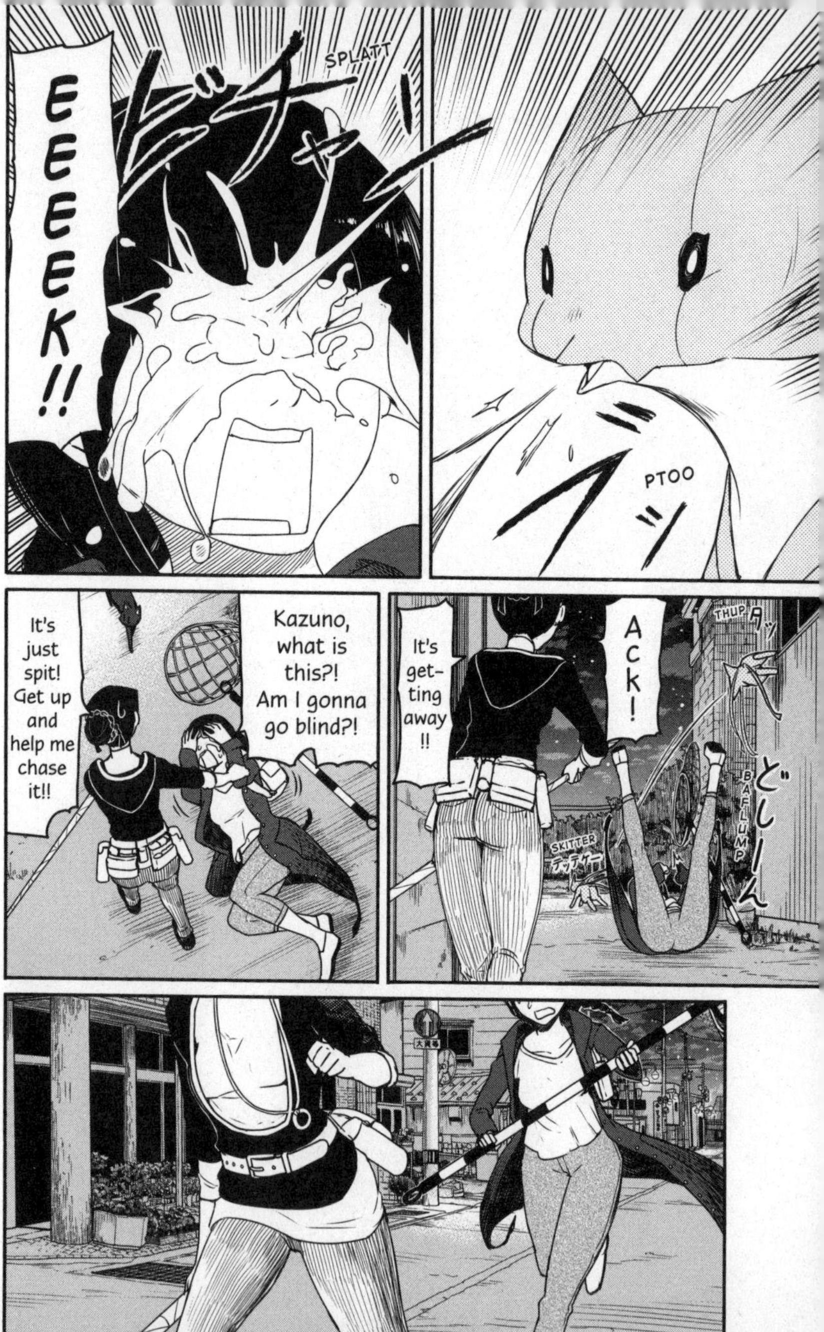
PTOO
SPLATT
EEEEK!!
THUP タッ
Ack!
BAFLUMP
どしーん
It's get-ting away!!
SKITTER
テッテケー
Kazuno, what is this?! Am I gonna go blind?!
It's just spit! Get up and help me chase it!!

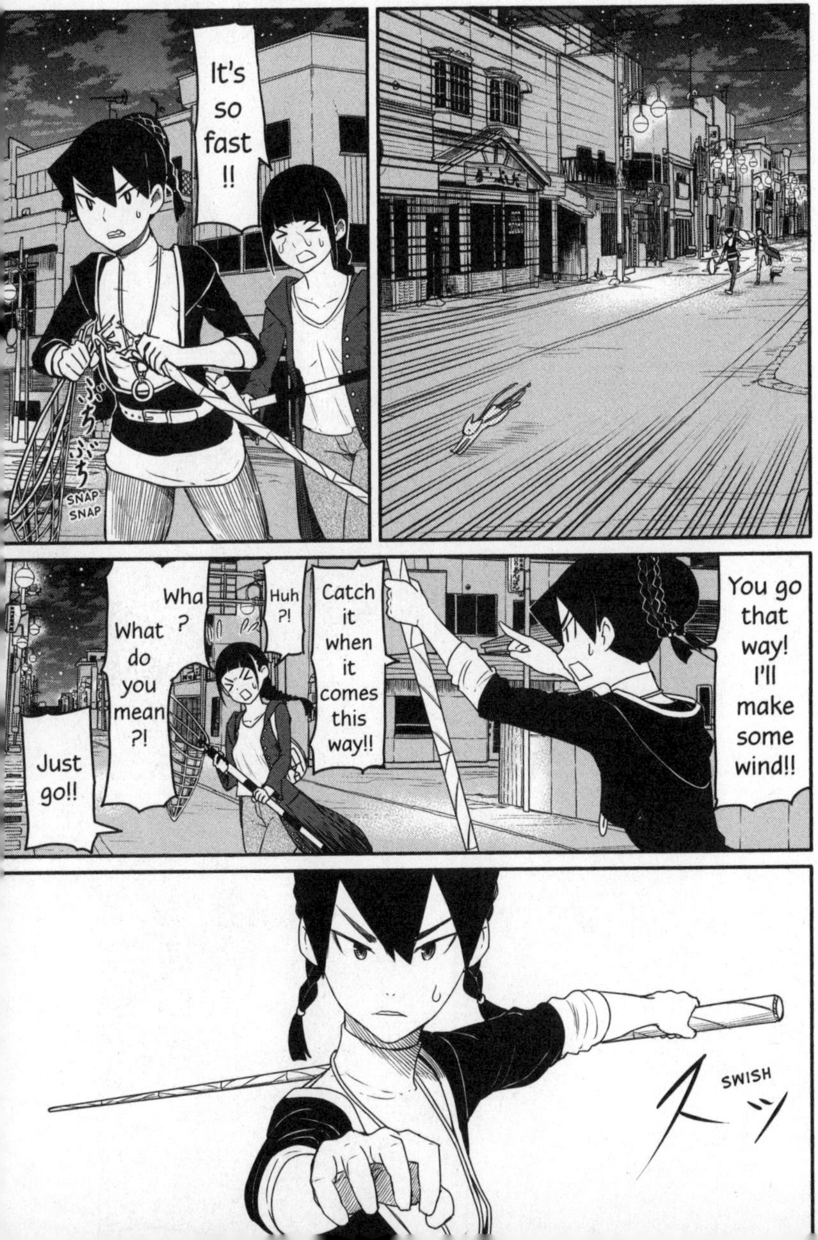
It's so fast!!
ぶちぶち
SNAP SNAP
You go that way! I'll make some wind!!
Catch it when it comes this way!!
Huh?!
Wha?
What do you mean?!
Just go!!
SWISH
スッ

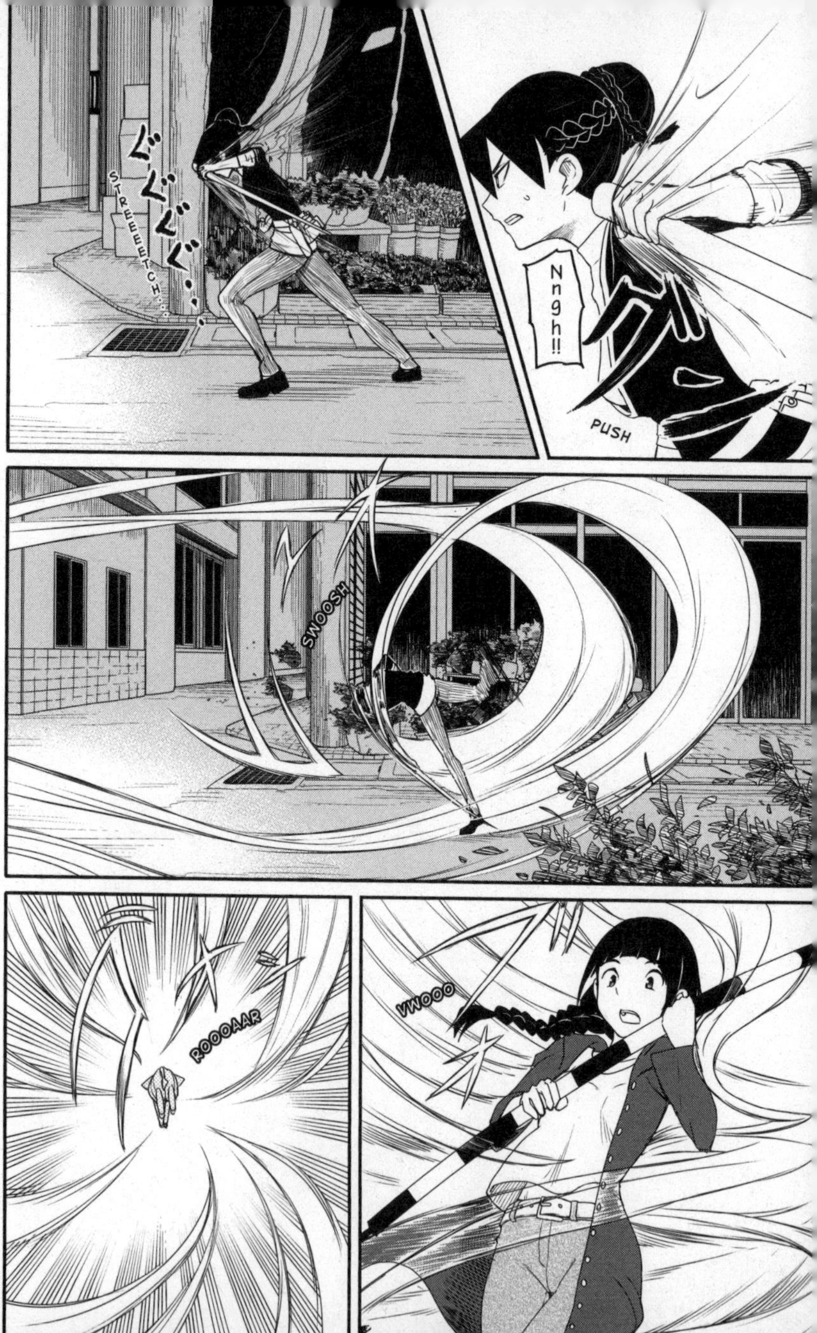
Nngh!!
PUSH
ぐぐぐぐ…
STREEEETCH…
SWOOSH
VWOOO
ROOOAAR

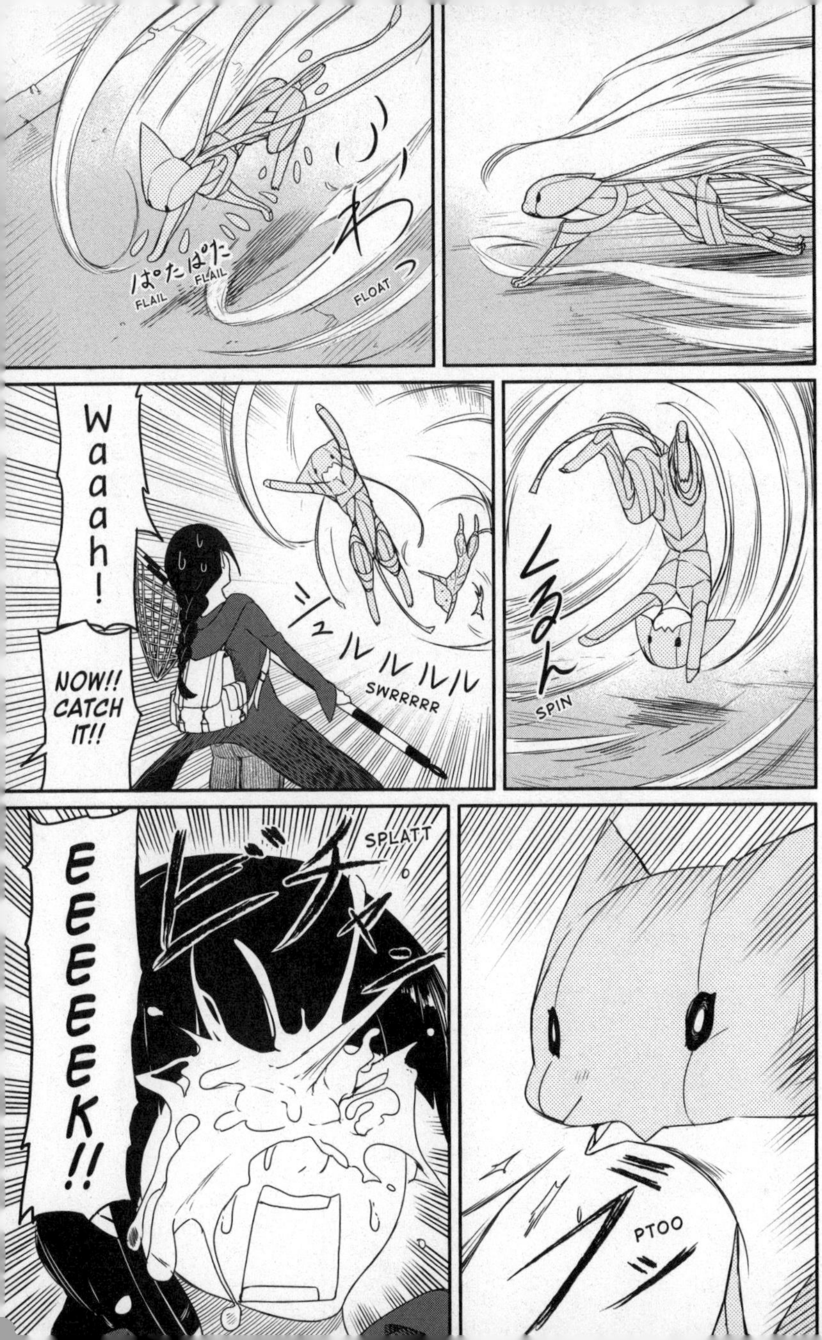
ふわっ
FLOAT
ぱたぱた
FLAIL FLAIL
くるん
SPIN
シュルルルル
SWRRRRR
Waaaah!
NOW!! CATCH IT!!
PTOO
SPLATT
EEEEEEEK!!

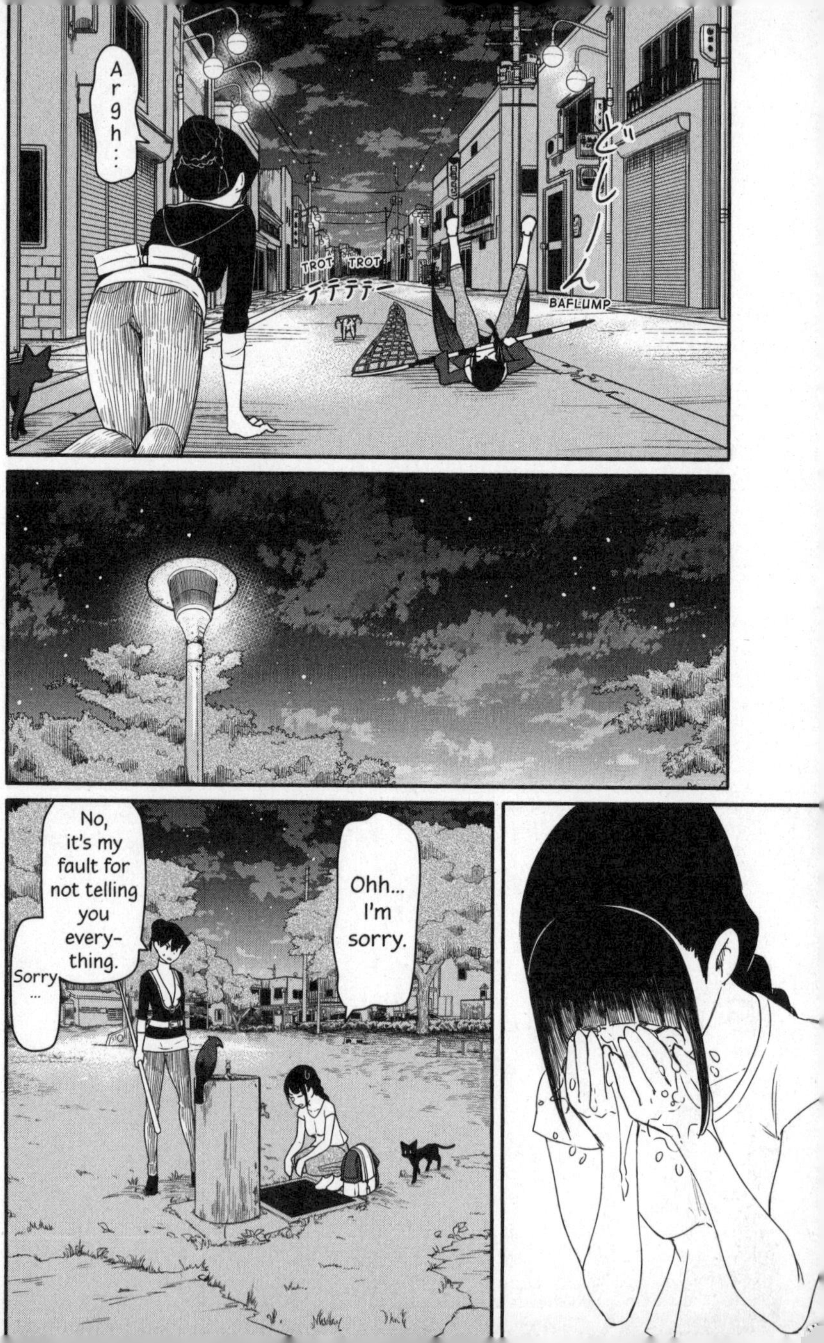
どしーん
BAFLUMP
Argh…
TROT TROT
テテテテー
Ohh… I'm sorry.
No, it's my fault for not telling you every-thing.
Sorry…

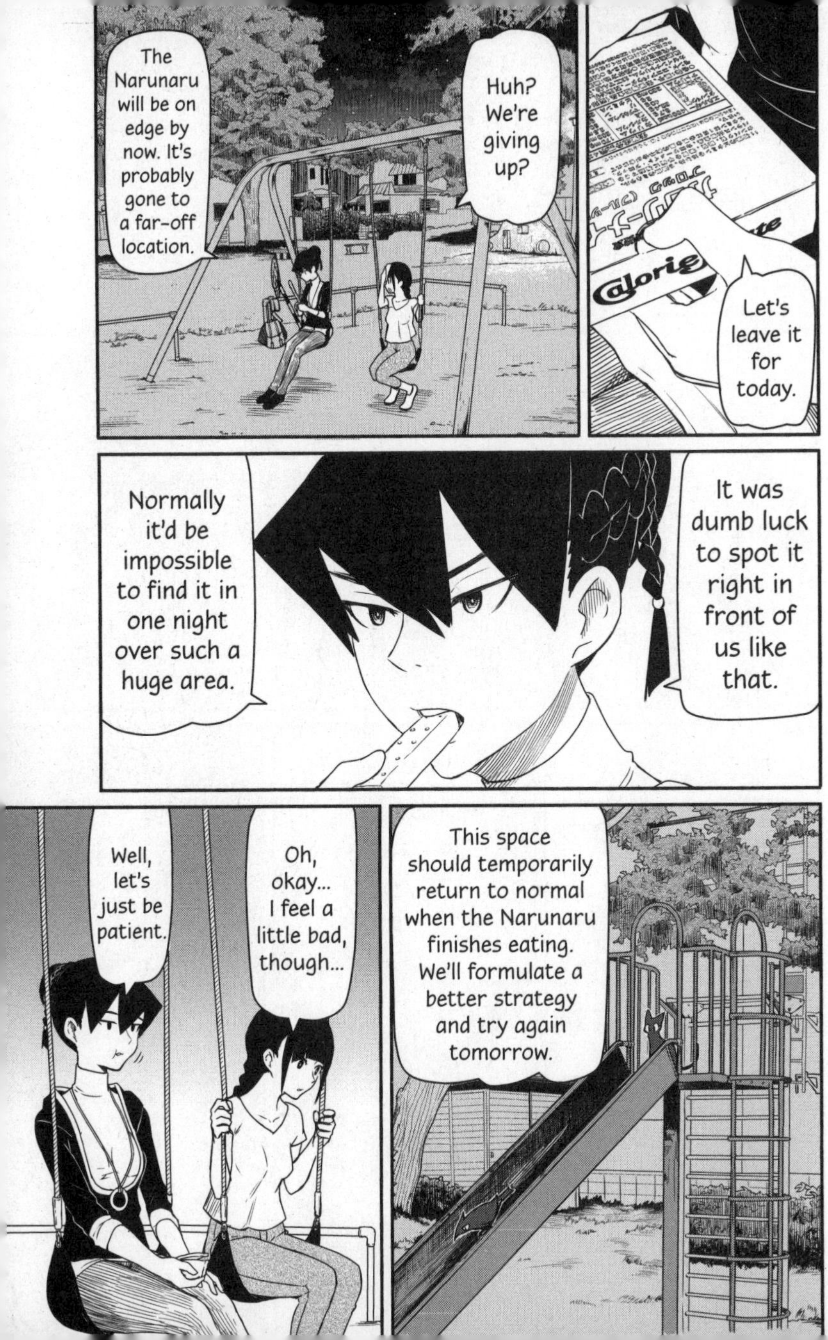
Let's leave it for today.
Huh? We're giving up?
The Narunaru will be on edge by now. It's probably gone to a far-off location.
It was dumb luck to spot it right in front of us like that.
Normally it'd be impossible to find it in one night over such a huge area.
This space should temporarily return to normal when the Narunaru finishes eating. We'll formulate a better strategy and try again tomorrow.
Oh, okay... I feel a little bad, though...
Well, let's just be patient.

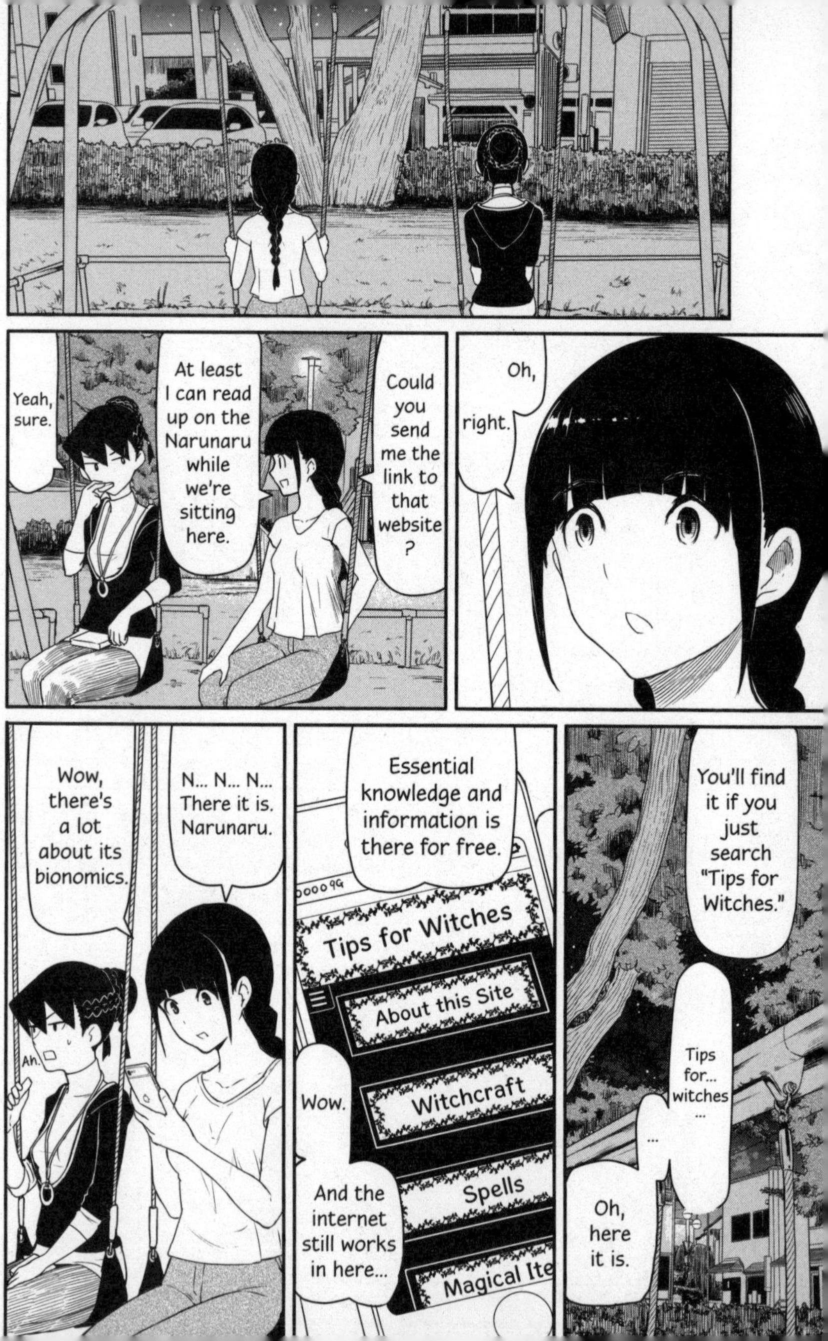
Oh,
right.
Could you send me the link to that website?
At least I can read up on the Narunaru while we're sitting here.
Yeah, sure.
You'll find it if you just search "Tips for Witches."
Tips for... witches ...
...
Oh, here it is.
Essential knowledge and information is there for free.
Tips for Witches
About this Site
Witchcraft
Spells
Magical Ite
Wow.
And the internet still works in here...
N... N... N... There it is. Narunaru.
Wow, there's a lot about its bionomics.
Ah.

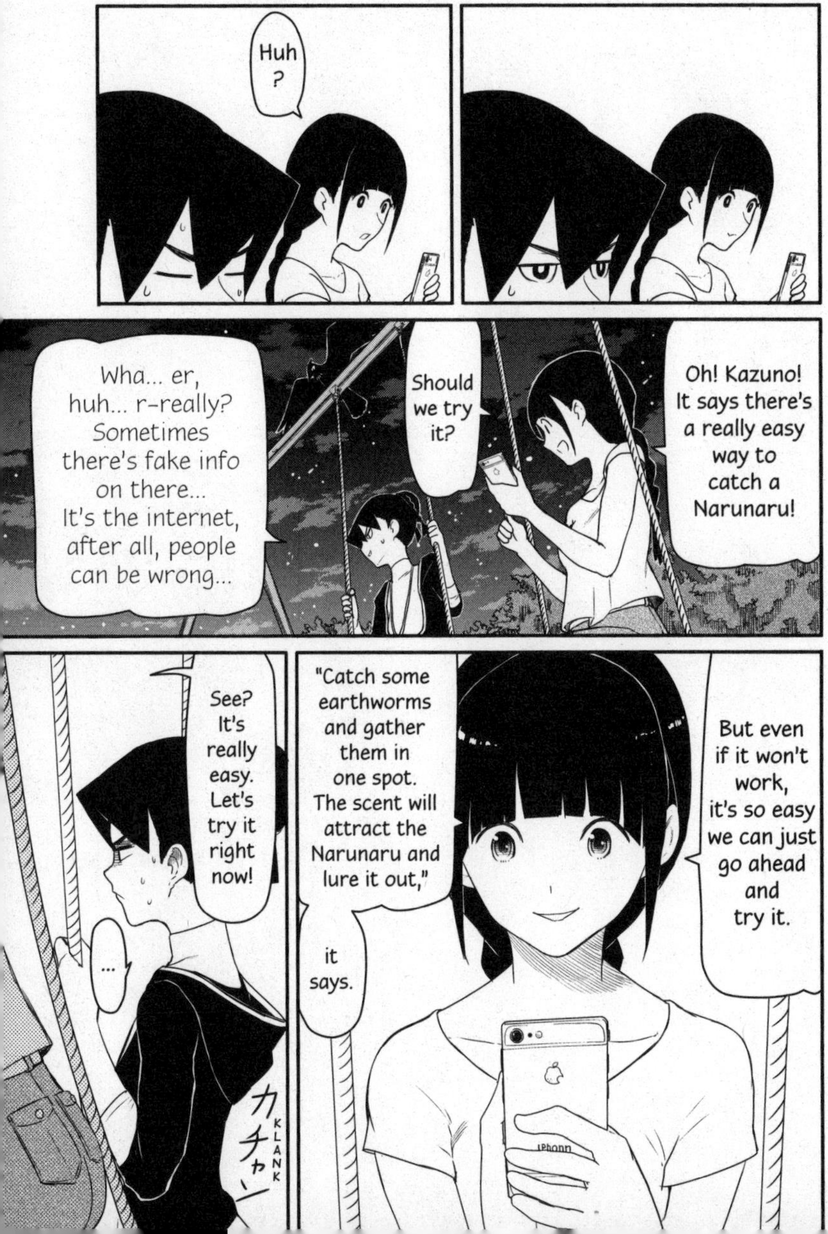
Huh ?
Oh! Kazuno! It says there's a really easy way to catch a Narunaru!
Should we try it?
Wha... er, huh... r-really? Sometimes there's fake info on there... It's the internet, after all, people can be wrong...
But even if it won't work, it's so easy we can just go ahead and try it.
"Catch some earthworms and gather them in one spot. The scent will attract the Narunaru and lure it out,"
it says.
See? It's really easy. Let's try it right now!
...
カチャ
KLANK

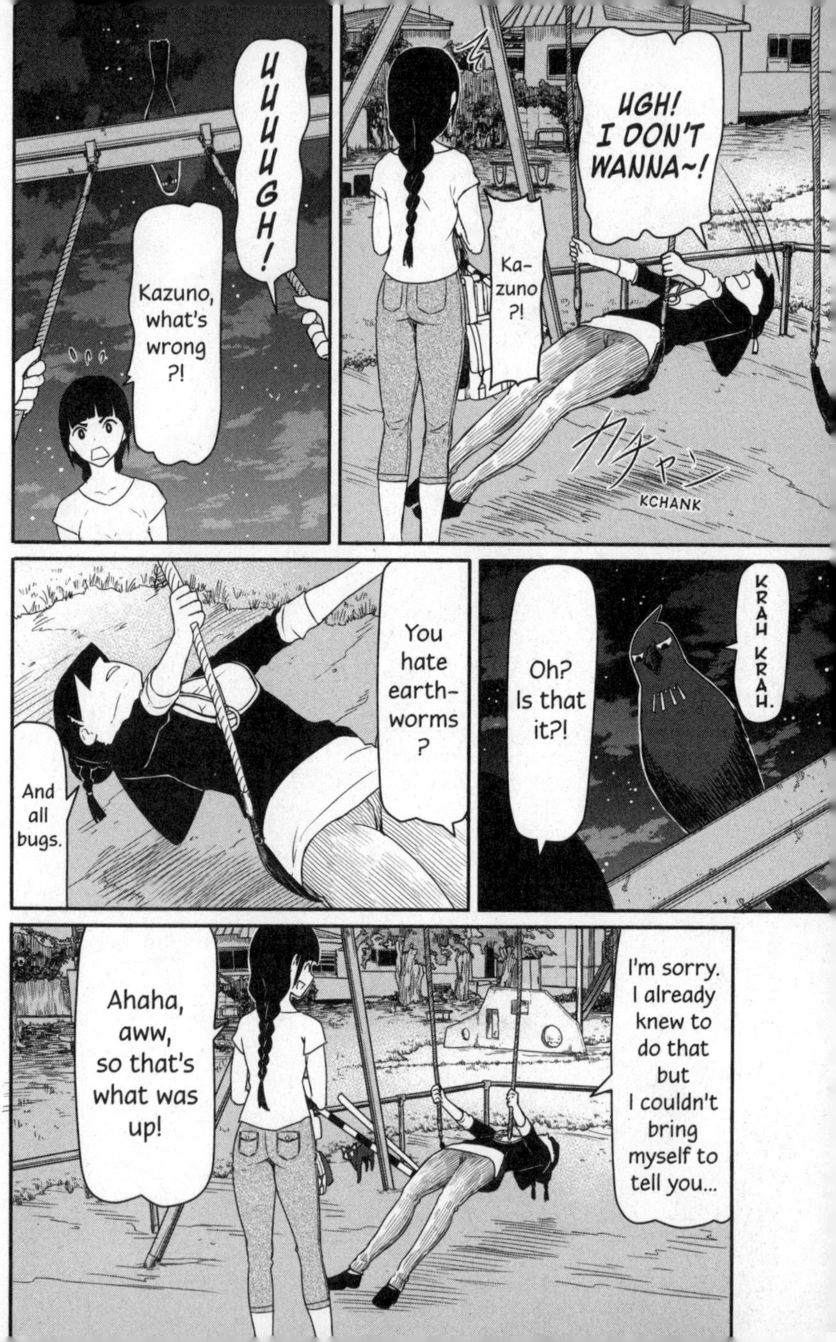
UGH! I DON'T WANNA~!
Ka-zuno?!
カチャン
KCHANK
UUUUGH!
Kazuno, what's wrong?!
KRAH KRAH.
Oh? Is that it?!
You hate earth-worms?
And all bugs.
I'm sorry. I already knew to do that but I couldn't bring myself to tell you...
Ahaha, aww, so that's what was up!

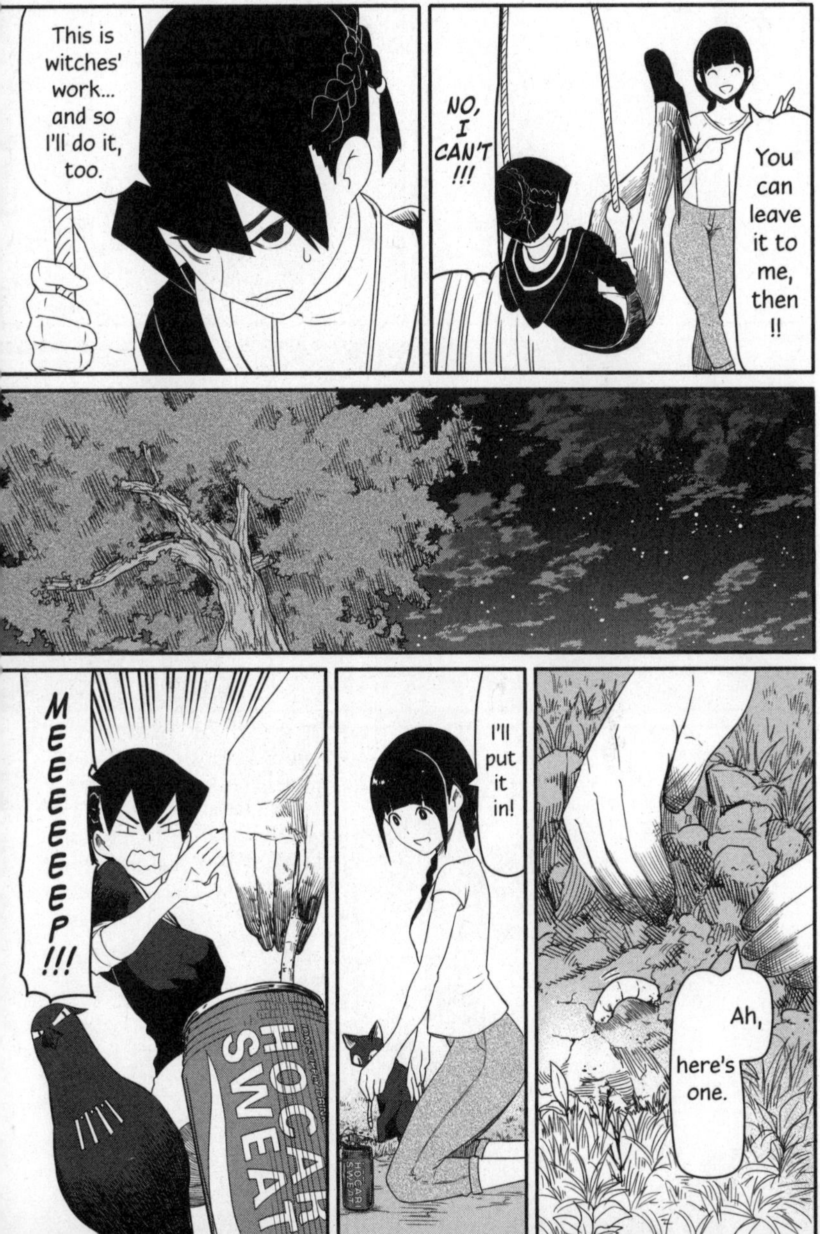
You can leave it to me, then!!
NO, I CAN'T!!!
This is witches' work... and so I'll do it, too.
Ah, here's one.
I'll put it in!
MEEEEEEEP!!!
HOCAR SWEAT
HOCARI SWEAT

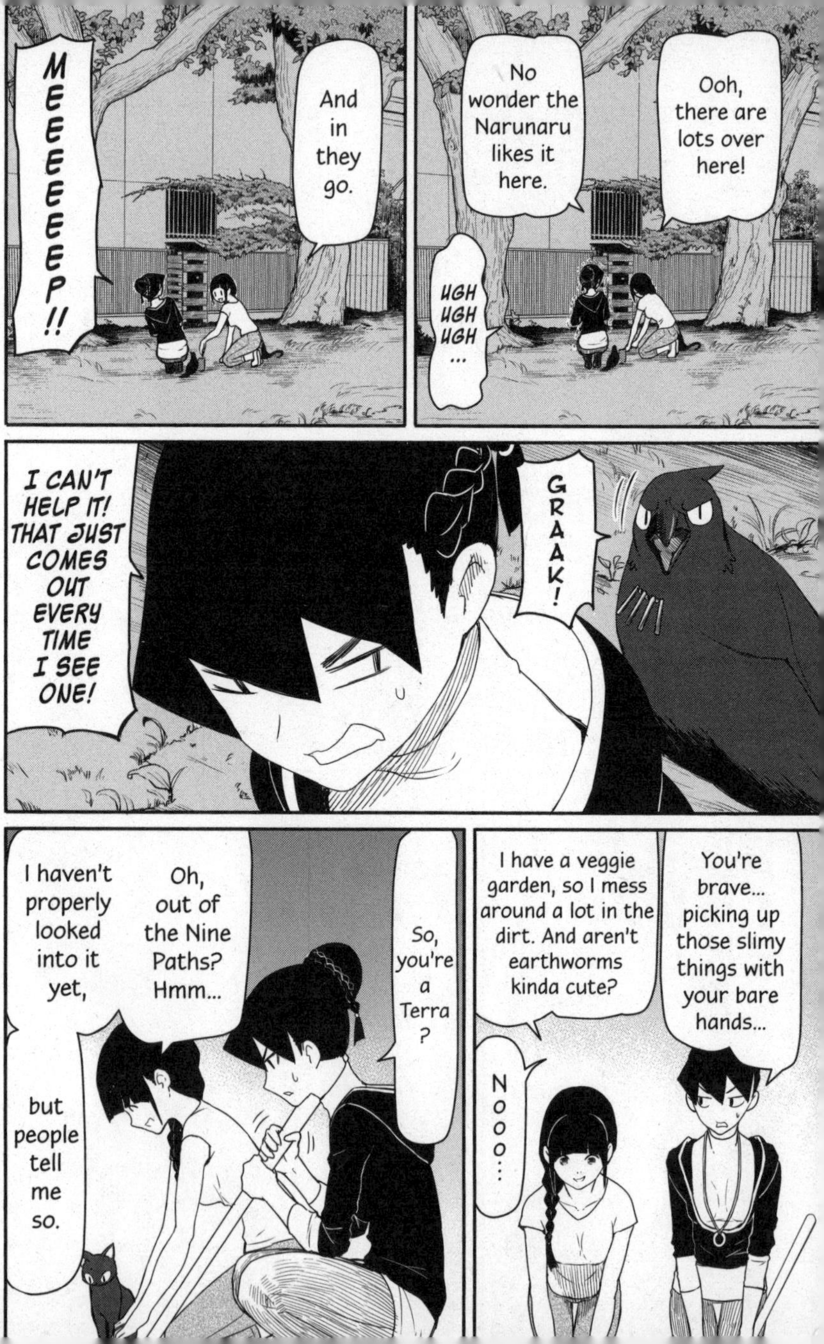
Ooh, there are lots over here!
No wonder the Narunaru likes it here.
UGH UGH UGH ...
And in they go.
MEEEEEEEP!!
GRAAK!
I CAN'T HELP IT! THAT JUST COMES OUT EVERY TIME I SEE ONE!
You're brave... picking up those slimy things with your bare hands...
I have a veggie garden, so I mess around a lot in the dirt. And aren't earthworms kinda cute?
NOOO...
So, you're a Terra?
Oh, out of the Nine Paths? Hmm...
I haven't properly looked into it yet,
but people tell me so.

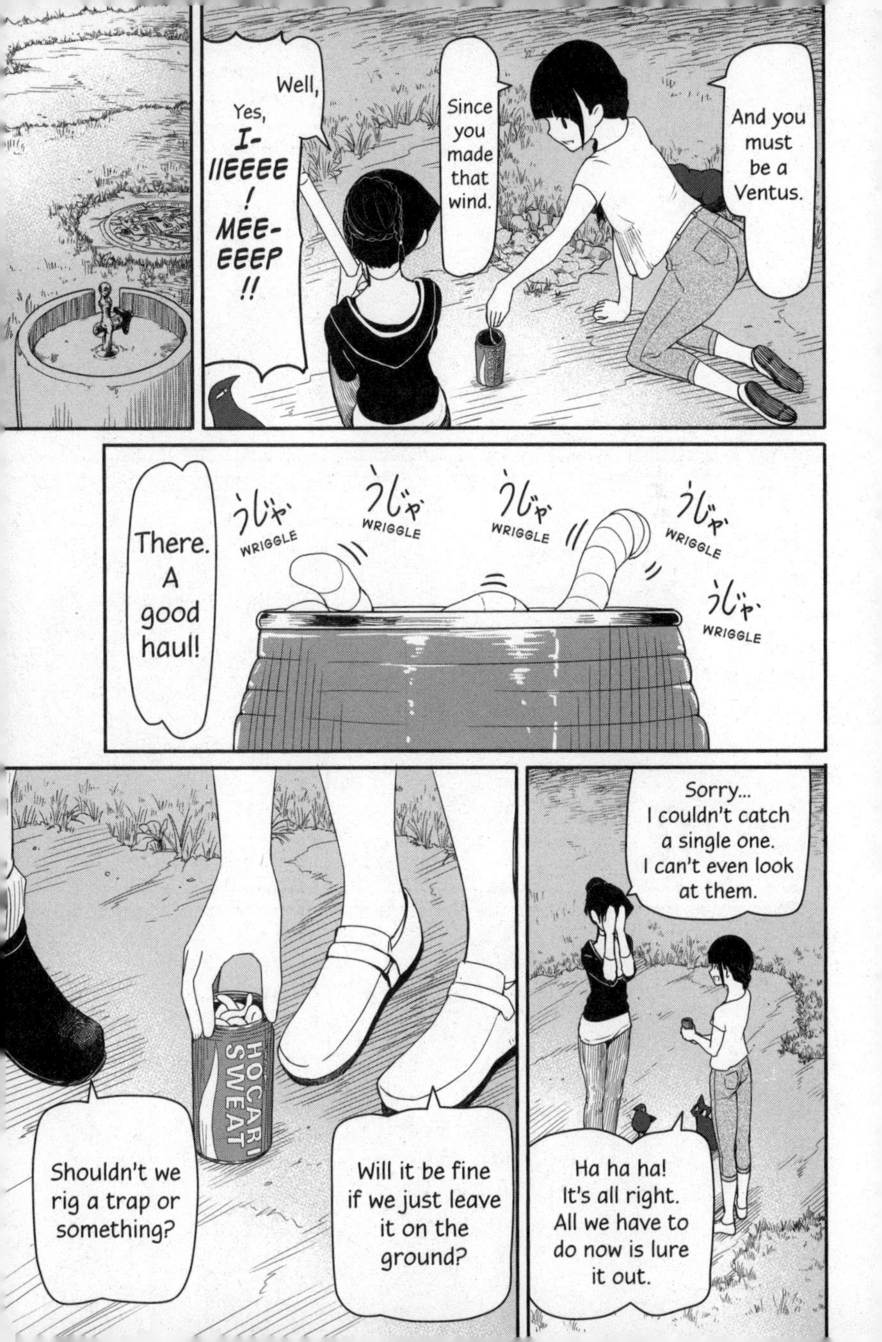

And you must be a Ventus.
Since you made that wind.
Well,
Yes,
I-IIEEEE! MEE-EEEP!!
うじゃ WRIGGLE
うじゃ WRIGGLE
うじゃ WRIGGLE
うじゃ WRIGGLE
うじゃ WRIGGLE
There. A good haul!
Sorry... I couldn't catch a single one. I can't even look at them.
Ha ha ha! It's all right. All we have to do now is lure it out.
Will it be fine if we just leave it on the ground?
HOCARI SWEAT
Shouldn't we rig a trap or something?

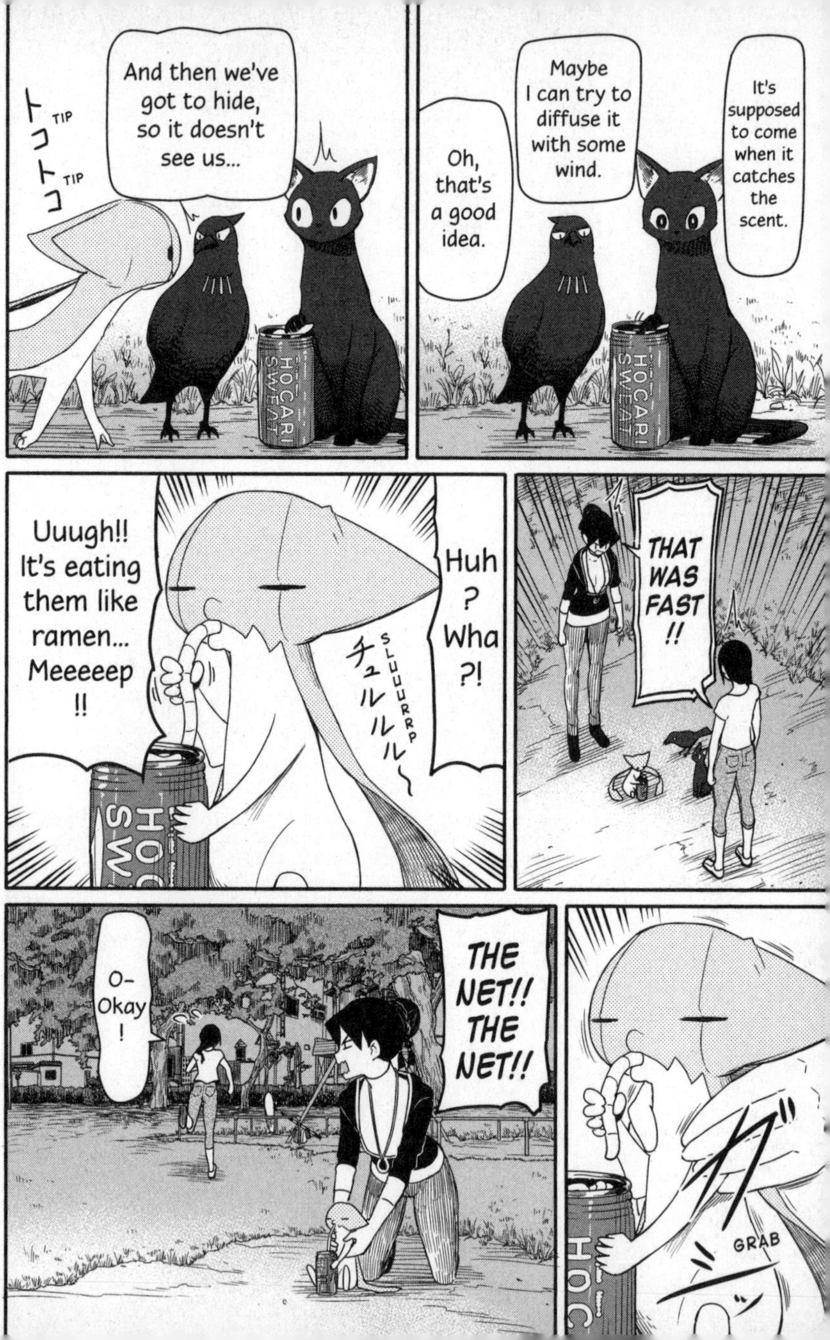
It's supposed to come when it catches the scent.
Maybe I can try to diffuse it with some wind.
Oh, that's a good idea.
HOCARI SWEAT
And then we've got to hide, so it doesn't see us...
トコトコ
TIP TIP
HOCARI SWEAT
THAT WAS FAST!!
Huh? Wha?!
チュルルル～
SLUUURRP
Uuugh!! It's eating them like ramen... Meeeeep!!
HOC SW
ガッ
GRAB
HOC
THE NET!! THE NET!!
O-Okay!

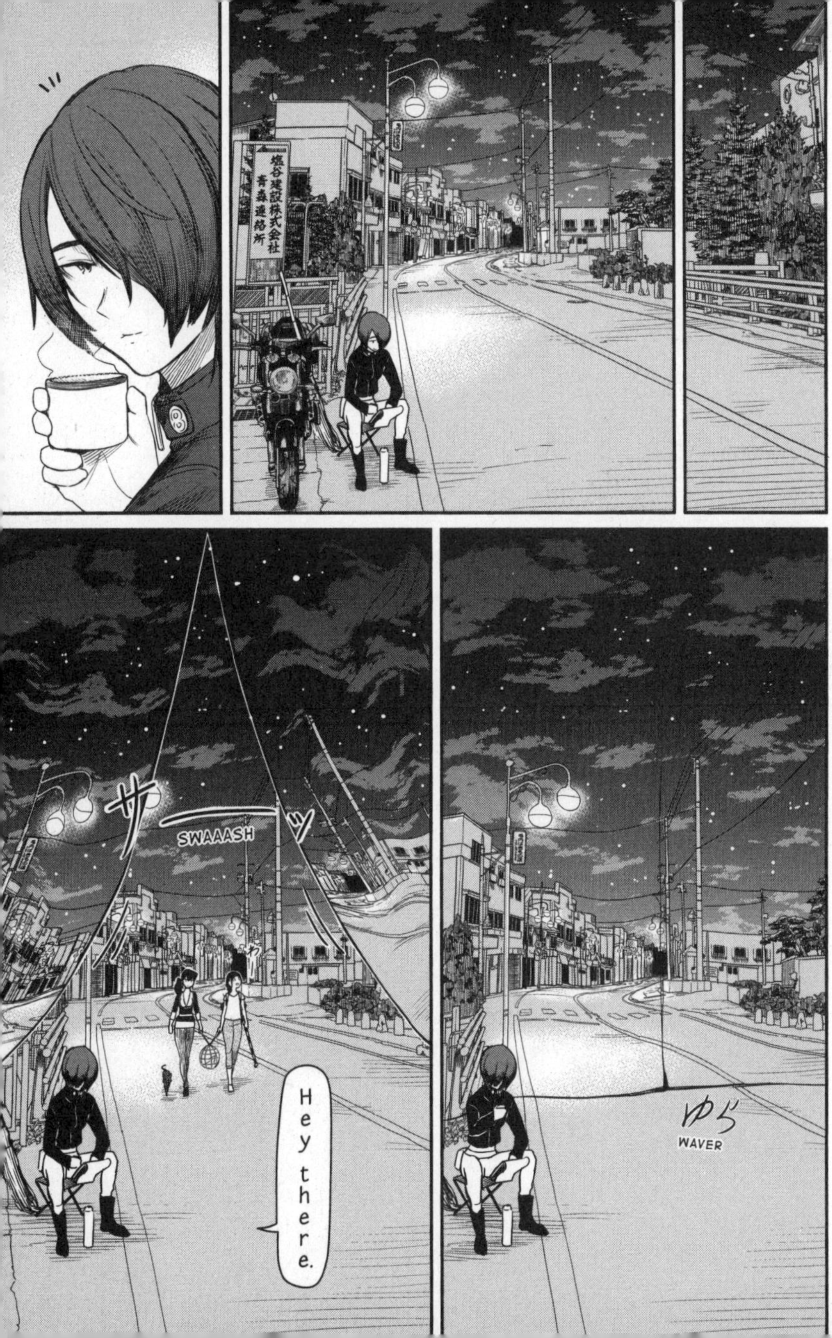
塩谷建設株式会社
青森連絡所
ゆら
WAVER
サーッ
SWAAASH
Hey there.

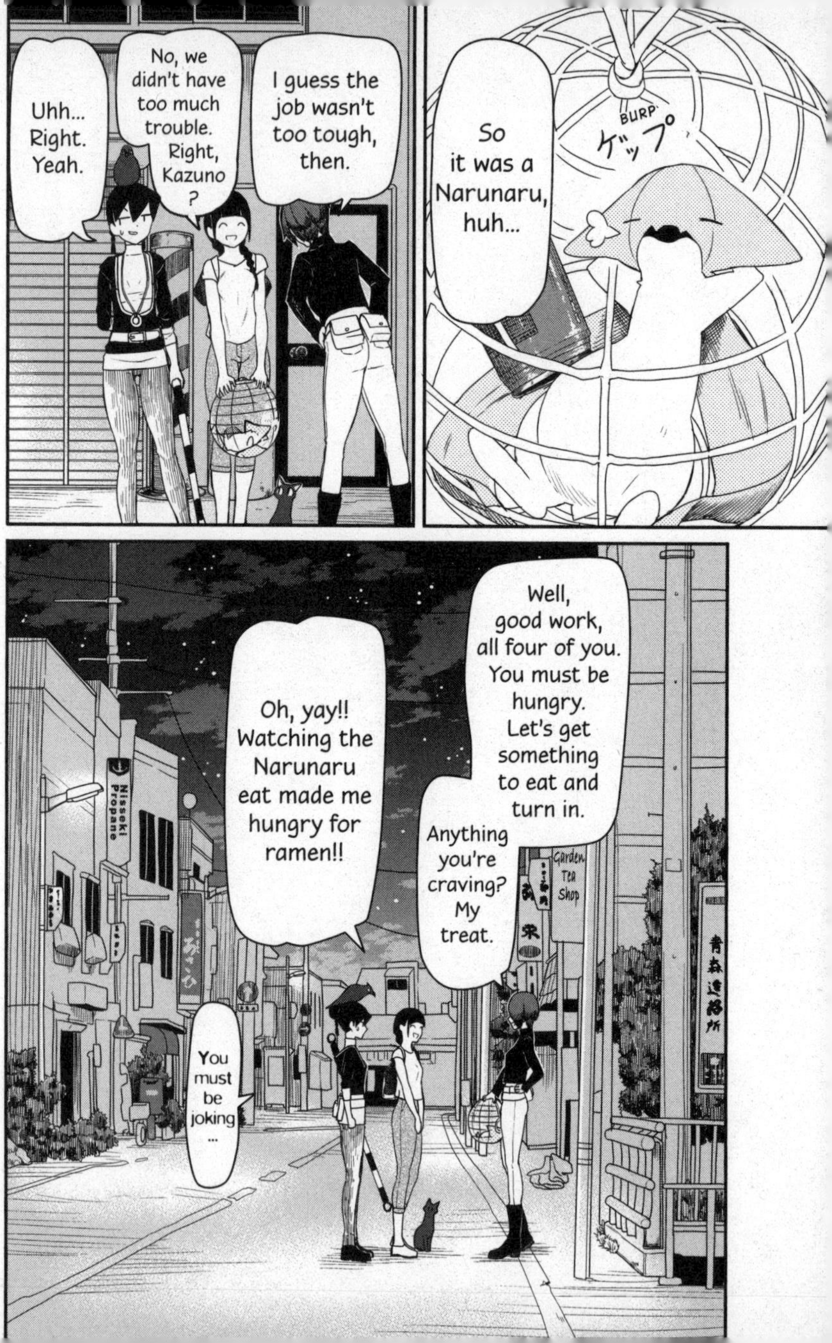
So it was a Narunaru, huh...
BURP
ゲップ
I guess the job wasn't too tough, then.
No, we didn't have too much trouble. Right, Kazuno?
Uhh... Right. Yeah.
Well, good work, all four of you. You must be hungry. Let's get something to eat and turn in.
Anything you're craving? My treat.
Oh, yay!! Watching the Narunaru eat made me hungry for ramen!!
You must be joking...
Nisseki Propane
Garden Tea Shop

Fly again in Volume 7

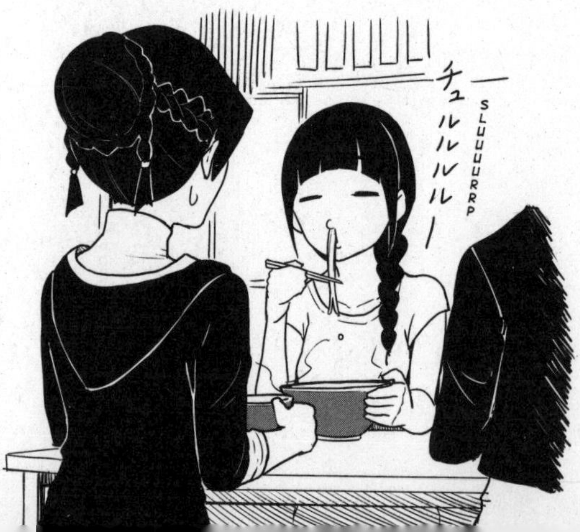
チュルルルルー
SLUUUURRP

Flying
Witch

flying witch ✱ kcm flying witch preview for next volume ✱

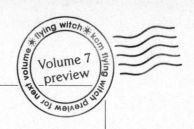

Volume 7 preview

Hi, this is Makoto!
How is everyone?

The dog days of summer have come to Aomori at last!

Kei said it'll be Yomiya season soon. But what is Yomiya?

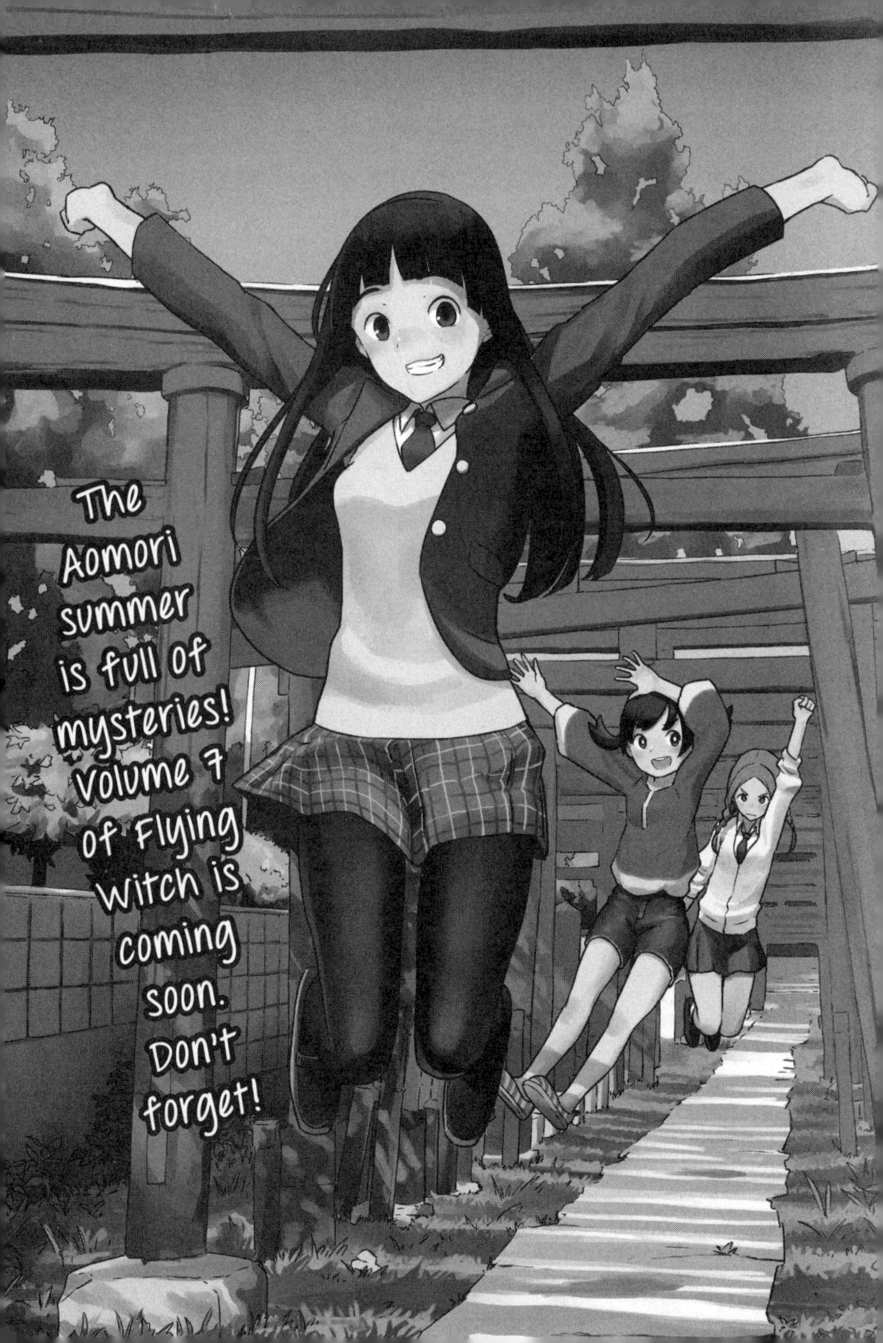
The Aomori summer is full of mysteries! Volume 7 of Flying Witch is coming soon. Don't forget!

Flying Witch 6

Translation - Melissa Tanaka
Production - Grace Lu
Tomoe Tsutsumi

First published in Japan in 2017 by Kodansha, Ltd., Tokyo
Publication for this English edition arranged through Kodansha, Ltd., Tokyo

Translation provided by Vertical Comics, 2018
Published by Vertical Comics, an imprint of Vertical, Inc., New York

Originally published in Japanese as *Flying Witch 6* by Kodansha, Ltd., 2017
Flying Witch first serialized in *Bessatsu Shonen Magazine*, Kodansha, Ltd., 2013-

ISBN: 978-1-947194-04-5

Manufactured in the United States of America

First Edition

Vertical, Inc.
451 Park Avenue South, 7th Floor
New York, NY 10016
www.vertical-comics.com

Vertical books are distributed through Penguin-Random House Publisher Services.